A History of the Religious Life
of
Cedar Grove Community
and
Families Influencing Its
Culture.

I0089769

By J. ANSEL CAUGHMAN

Southern Historical Press, Inc.
Greenville, South Carolina

Please direct all correspondence and book orders to:
SOUTHERN HISTORICAL PRESS, Inc.
PO Box 1267
Greenville, SC   29602-1267

Originally printed: Batesburg, SC 1952
Copyright 1952 by: J. Ansel Caughman
ISBN #978-1-63914-165-4
Printed in the United States of America

TO MY WIFE,
DORA SHIREY CAUGHMAN
AND SON,
ROBERT HOY CAUGHMAN

J. ANSEL CAUGHMAN, Author

AUTHOR'S PREFACE

ON the first day of January 1932 the church council of Cedar Grove Church appointed me as a committee of one, to write a History of Cedar Grove Lutheran Church. This was an obligation that caused me to realize that my ability was far from being equal to the task. Knowing that Cedar Grove sprang from Salem Lutheran Church, I felt that it would be wise to dig up records of the old mother church. In the Clerk of Court's Office, in Lexington County Courthouse I found a record of a deed of or for 16 acres of land conveyed to Salem Church by Christopher and Andrew Kaughman, to be used as a place of worship. This deed was executed on the 8th day of March, 1792. I have been able to find some authentic data from the minutes of the Lutheran Synod of South Carolina. I find no church records of Salem from its organization until it applied for membership in the South Carolina Synod about 1824. In 1852 dissatisfaction arose in Salem Congregation concerning the method of worship. This caused a division in the congregation. At this time Uriah Crout, who was elected Secretary of the new congregation, provided a Secretary's Record, which has been of much value to me in securing authentic data, that substantiates quite a bit of tradition that has been handed down to me.

Later, Secretarial records kept by Lewis Shealy, D. Tillman Hare, Pierce Leaphart, H. M. Caughman, Y. J. Swygert, and Robert Hoy Caughman and others have been valuable.

To all who have contributed in any way whatsoever to make this Salem-Cedar Grove History possible, we in all humility are indeed thankful and most grateful.

In combination with this Salem-Cedar Grove History you will find a History of Old Lexington Baptist Church. We are indebted to Mrs. Susie Langford Taylor, the Langford family, and other living members of that congregation for information.

In connection with these Church Histories, we are including some record of our pioneer settlers on the south side of Saluda River, now Lake Murray.

Special mention is made of W. H. Hare for very valuable assistance in helping me secure information in preparing Biographical Records of some of our Big Hollow Creek settlers, also D. I. Hite and Mrs. J. C. Derrick.

All credit is given W. H. Hare for the Craps, Roberts, Derrick, Fulmer, Blacks, and assistance in others, in preparing these Biographical Records or Sketches.

Quite a number of our people in this area, as well as those who have moved away, have been insisting that I get this material together and have it put in book form. I finally decided I would try it, since my good friend W. H. Hare died before he was able to get his great bulk of material, along this line, which he had been gathering all his active life, in book form.

We know that many mistakes will be found. It is impossible to attain perfection in a matter of this kind.

We trust that this accumulated information might be valuable and interesting to posterity.

Doing this work has been a great task, but I have learned many things about the people and the churches I did not know before.

Since we are living in an age when but little is handed down traditionally, it is a case of necessity to record history.

We hope these records will refresh the dullness of past memories. We are grateful to God Almighty that our Forebears were devout Christians, who sought freedom of worship in this beloved land of ours.

CONTENTS

SECTION I

INDIANS

PRIOR to the coming of the white man, Indians inhabited all this area of our country. In the Saluda Valley and the valleys of all our large creeks we have abundant evidence of Indian inhabitation. Since this history centers around the Cedar Grove area, we wish to make mention of our predecessors.

There were two large Indian Cemeteries in less than one-fourth mile from Cedar Grove Church. Today they are cultivated fields, but I remember well seeing markers to the graves when I was a boy. Indians usually had their burying grounds on low lands, where graves were easily dug. Indians still in their savage state, had some form of religion. When an Indian hunter died, his friends would kill his dogs and bury them with him, along with his bow and arrow, that they might serve him in the Great Happy Hunting Ground beyond this natural life.

In the Hollow Creek Valley we still find Indian utensils, such as stone axes, arrow heads, pottery, etc. They once had practice grounds where they displayed great ability in the use of their war weapons. They also had the knack of knowing how to bring down a buffalo or wild deer with their deadly arrows.

Since the women did all the hard work in cultivating the patches of corn, garden truck, etc., even building the wigwams, providing animal skins for clothing, the men lived an easy, happy-go-lucky life. All in all the women were the providers.

A few years ago I was in the Southwest, in New Mexico, Arizona and California where we still have lots of Indians. I observed then and there that they still maintain to a great degree their original customs.

My great-grandmother, Emily Lybrand, told me when I was a "kid" that she once visited an Indian family near her home on Hollow Creek. The squaw, that is the Indian wife and mother, cooked turnip greens and "corn dodgers" for dinner; as she removed the "corn dodgers" with wooden forks from the pot of greens, she would lick all the "pot licker" from each one. How would you like to take dinner with this cook?

There were numerous large Indian cemeteries on the low lands of Saluda River. In the summer of 1888 there was a terrible freshet on Saluda River. The freshet was so severe that huge branches of trees more than 60 feet high were torn from trees. In this flood, the popular Langford flour mill was washed away.

After the freshet was over and the waters had subsided or receded, numerous Indian skeletons, pottery and relics were observed.

Vacant

N. 30. E. 29.00
80.3.4 Vacant

... April 1847 ...

Stake 3.x.

white oak

511 Acres

Creek

N. 4b. W. 64.00

Red oak 2.

N. 3b. E. 40.00

pine 3.x.

line 2.

whit" 0.2.x.

line 2.

line 3.x.

corner 3.x.

S. 55. W. 30.00

S. 10. W. 36.00

N. 8.0. E.

N. 4b. W. 40.00

South Carolina

HISTORY OF SALEM LUTHERAN CHURCH AND THE EVENTS LEADING UP TO ITS ESTABLISHMENT

A CCORDING to the earliest information available the following transcript is copied from a plat covering all the land where Salem Church once stood, where Cedar Grove now stands and the surrounding territory.

SOUTH CAROLINA

"Pursuant to a warrant from Jno. Wyld Esq. dated 30th of June 1787. I have admeasured and laid out unto Christopher Rofman a tract of land containing of four hundred acres situated in Orangeburgh District on waters of Saluda river South side on Creek called Holle Creek and hath such shapes, marks, Buttings, and Boundings as the above plat Represents.

"Surveyed 10th of July 1787
By Wm. Wright D. S."

This four-hundred acre tract is very odd in shape. The western limit was Joe's Creek, a branch of Big Hollow Creek, all the southern side was known at that time as vacant land, apparently extending from Joe's Creek to Big Horse Creek. The Eastern end and Northeast was land that had been laid out to Andrew Rofman, (now spelled Caughman); also an adjoining tract had been laid out to Martin Rofman. The remainder of the western boundary was known as Thos. Edwards' land, later known as Geiger lands. All remaining lands adjacent to the aforesaid tract was called vacant land.

Tradition hands down to us the fact that Christopher and Martin sold their land possessions to Andrew and acquired land further down Saluda River near Wise's Ferry, not too far from Lexington Courthouse. There they settled, reared families, became civic leaders, left an imprint on civilization, were instrumental in peopleizing a good portion of the territory around Lexington and Columbia. Quite a number of their descendants have been and are now leaders in society. We still find that ambitious desire in this blood to keep themselves out of ignorance and poverty.

After or while in the act of Christopher's conveyance of this real estate to Andrew it seems that a tract of 16 acres was set aside as a place of or for religious worship. This 16 acres to be used for a place of public worship of God.

The following is a reproduction verbatim of the deed executed by Andrew Kaughman and wife, Annie Maria, with all its grammatical errors and all the useless repetitions found in this mixture of German and English:

CONVEYANCE

"November 7, 1881

"CHRISTOPHER CAUGHMAN
"SALEM CHURCH

"This Indenture made on the eight day of March in the year of our Lord one thousand seven hundred and ninety and two and in the sixteenth year of the United Independence States of America: Between Christopher Kaughman and Andrew Kaughman of Lexington County in the State of South Carman and Andrew Kaughman of Lexington county in the State of South Carolina Planter of the one part and Salem Church Congregation of German Protestants on the waters of Hollow Creek of the said State and County aforesaid of the other part. Witnesseth that for and in consideration of the sum of fifty pounds of the State aforesaid to him the said Andrew Kaughman in hand at and before the sealing and delivery of these presents by them the said Salem Church Congregation well and truly paid. The receipt whereof the said Andrew Kaughman and Anna Maria his wife doth hereby acknowledge and thereof and of every part and parcel thereof, doth acquit release exonerate and discharge them the said Salem Church Congregation their heirs executors, and every of them forever by these presents. He the said Andrew Kaughman and Anne Maria his wife hath granted bargained sold aliened released and confirmed and by these presents doth fully freely clearly and sbsolutely grant bargain sell aliene release and confirm unto them the said Salem Church Congregation of true and pure German Protestants into there actual possession now being by virtue of a Bargain and sale to him thereof made by the said Andrew Kaughman and Anne Maria his wife for one whole year for the consideration Money of ten shillings by an indenture of lease bearing date the day next before the day of the date of these presents. To commence from the day next before the day of the date thereof & sealed and delivered before the executing of these presents and also by force of the statute for transfering of uses into possession in that case made and provided and unto their heirs and assigns forever, a certain piece of ground or tract of land containing sixteen acres. It being part of a parcel or tract of land containing four hundred acres, originally granted to the first above named Christopher Kaughman, situated in the County aforesaid on the waters of Saluda River on a branch of a creek called Hollow Creek and hath such shape form and marks buttings and boundings as a plat hereunto annexed represents. It being part of a tract of land that was formerly granted by letters pattents unto Christopher Kaughman and now Andrew Kaughman having obtained lawful rights for the said land. Now grant the said tract of sixteen acres by lease and release as appears by the date of these presents unto the said Salem Church Congregation of German Protestants, Together with all and singular the church now builded thereon upon the said tract of sixteen acres of land and all other buildings in future together the woods underwoods timber and timber trees waters and water courses paths and paths easements profits comodities advantages emoluments hereditsments and appurtenances whatsoever to him the said Andrew Kaughman and Anne Maria his wife belonging or in anywise appertaining and the reversion and reversions remainder and remainders rents issues and profits thereof and of every part and parcel thereof and also all the estate right title intrest possession property profit claim and demand whatsoever either in law or equity which he the said Andrew Kaughman and Anne Maria his wife now hath or ever had or which they or them or there heirs hereafter shall may can or ought to have off into or out of the said tract of sixteen acres of land and other the premises herein before mentioned and intended with their and every of their appurtenances. To have and to hold the said tract of sixteen acres of land an all and singular other the premises hereby granted and released or meant & intended to be granted & released unto them the said Salem Church Congregation and their heirs executors. To and for the only and absolute use and behoof of them the said Salem Church Congregation of the German Protestants their heirs and assigns forever and the said Andrew Kaughman and Anne Maria his wife their heirs executors administrators. The said premises Hereby bargained sold granted and released or meant and intended to be bargained sold granted and released with their and every of their appurtenances unto them the said Salem Church Congregation their heirs executors, against all and all manner of person or persons whatsoever shall and will warrant and forever defend by these presents and the said Andrew Kaughman and Anne Maria his wife and their heirs executors. Doth covenant promise grant and agree to with the said Salem Church Congregation of German Protestants their heirs and assigns in manner and form following that is to say what he the said Andrew Kaughman and Anne Maria his wife their heirs and assigns by these presents in and parteth lawfully and absolutely seized of and in the said tract of sixteen acres of land and all and singular other the premises herein before mentioned and intended to be hereby granted and released and every part and parcel thereof with their and every of their appurtenances of good sure perfect and absolute estate of inheritance in free simple without any manner of condition trust promise power of revocation and limitation of any use or uses or other restraint matter or thing whatsoever to alter change charge defeat or evict the same and also that the said Andrew Kaughman and Anne Maria his wife hath in themselves good right full power and lawful and absolute authority To grant release and confirm the said tract of sixteen acres of land and all and singular other the premises herein before mentioned and intended to be hereby granted and released and every part and parcel thereof with their and every of their appurtenances unto the said Salem Church Congregation as aforesaid of German Protestants their heirs executors forever as aforesaid. And also that it shall and may lawfully to and for the said Salem Church Congregation their heirs and assigns from time to time and at all times forever hereafter peaceably and quietly to enter into have hold occupy possess and enjoy the said tract of sixteen acres of land to enjoy it for a Public Worship of God thereon, and all and singular other the premises herein before mentioned and intended to be hereby granted and released and every part and parcel thereof with their and every of their appurtenances without any of the lawful debt suit trouble molestation eviction or interruption of him the said Andrew Kaughman and Anne Maria his wife their heirs executors, or any other person or persons whatsoever claiming or to lay claim by from or under them And lastly that the said Andrew Kaughman and Anne Maria his wife and all and every other persons lawfully claiming or to claim and estate right title interest possession property profit claim and demand of into or out of the said tract of sixteen acres of land and all and singular other the premises herein before mentioned and intended to be hereby granted and released or any part or parcel thereof shall and will from and at all times forever hereafter at the reasonable request and proper cost and charges in the law of the said Andrew Kaughman and Anne Maria his wife their heirs and assigns make do acknowledge and execute or cause and procure to be made done acknowledged and executed all and every such further and other lawful and reasonable act and acts thing and thing, things conveaynces and assurances in the law. Whatever for the further better and more perfect and absolute granting conveying and assuring this tract of sixteen acres of land and every of their appurtenances. To and for the absolute use and befoof of the said Salem congregation of German protestants their heirs and assigns forevermore as by him or them or by his or their counsel Learned in the law shall be reasonably advised and required. In witness whereof these parties to these presents have hereunto interchangably set their hands and seals the day and year first above written.

"Signed sealed and delivered in the presence of us.

"JOHANES CROUT
"JACOB HAULMAN
"G. B. SHRUM

"ANDREW (his X mark) KAUGHMAN (seal)
"ANNE MARIA (her X mark) KAUGHMAN (seal)

"Recd. the day and year first within written of the within named Congregation the full and just sum of fifty pounds good and lawful money of the state within mentioned. It being the full Congregation money within mentioned I say recd. by us.

"JOHANES CROUT
"JACOB HAULMAN
"G. B. SHRUM
"Witnesses present

ANDREW (his X mark) KAUGHMAN
ANNE MARIA (her X mark) KAUGHMAN

STATE OF SOUTH CAROLINA
ORANGEBURG DISTRICT
MEMORANDUM.

"Before me John Thos. Fairchild Esq. one of the Justices assigned to keep the peace for said Dist. Personally appeared George B. Shrum who made oath on the holy evangelist of Almight God deposeth and sayeth on his oath that he actually was personally present and did see the within named Andrew Kaughman and Anne Maria his wife. Sign seal and as their act and deed deliver the within instrument of writing or deed of lease and release unto the within named Salem Church Congregation near Hollow Creek to and for the full use intents and purpose as within mentioned. And this deponant further sayeth on his oath that he actually also likewise did see the said Andrew Kaughman and Anne Maria his wife sign the receipt hereon indorsed, and that he himself & Johanes Crout and Jacob Haulman subscribed their names as evidences and witnesses to both in the presence of parties of each other.

"Sworn to before me this 10th.
day of March Anno Domini 1792   "G. B. SHRUM

"THOS. FAIRCHILD, J. P.
"Recorded this November 7th, 1881   "WM. J. ASSMANN R.M.C.
"I certify that the foregoing is a true copy of Deed as recorded in Deed Book CC at page 482.   "HENRY E. ADDY, C. C. C. P. & G. S."

A log building was erected as a place for worship by the few German settlers who now inhabited the surrounding territory. Among them were Drafts, Crouts, Van Sants, Jacksons, Addys, Lominacks, and others. We have no records as to whether this church was affiliated with any Synod until the time (1825) of Rev. Godfrey Dreher, who was once its pastor. Up until that time it was known as the Lutheran and German Reformed Congregation. By this time the congregation had grown to be a large body. At this time there was no other church in this part of the state except Old Lexington Baptist Church, which had been organized at Amick's Ferry on Saluda River in 1813.

By this time a more commodious frame building had been erected with a good sized auditorium and a gallery.

ORGANIZATION OF SOUTH CAROLINA SYNOD.

The initial organization of the South Carolina Synod took place in St. Michael's Church (Blue Church) January 14, 1824, and the organizers were John P. Franklow, John Y. Meetze, Godfrey Dreher, Michael Rauch, Jacob Moses and Samuel Herscher. The lay delegates were John Dreher, Sr., St. Michael's Church; George Lindler, St. John's Church; Christopher Wiggers, Bethel Church; Samuel Oswald, Salem Church; and Henry Bookhardt, Santee Church.

These ministers and laymen elected as the officers Rev. Godfrey Dreher, President, and Rev. Samuel Herscher, Secretary.

The (Salem) Lutherans petitioned for incorporation of the church in the South Carolina Synod. The German Reformed members opposed it.

The following is the entire list of both factions just as they spelled their names:

LUTHERANS LISTED IN THE PETITION.

1. Daniel Drafts, Sr., Elder
2. Frederick Seas, Elde.
3. Noah Hallman, Eldei
4. Christian Price, Sec.
5. George Hallman
6. Mary Hallman
7. Saray Price
8. Elizabeth Hallman
9. Mary Hallman
10. Julian Drafts
11. John W. Hallman
12. Lavenia Hallman
13. George Hallman, Jr.
14. Henry Eargle
15. Nancy Eargle
16. John Crout, Sr.
17. John Shumpert
18. Mary Shumpert
19. John Jackson
20. Milly Jackson
21. Patsy Jackson
22. Epsey Jackson
23. Celia Jackson
24. George Oswalt
25. Adam Risinger
26. Miley Risinger
27. Elias Taylor
28. Miley Taylor
29. John Lominack
30. Mittian Lominack
31. Eml. Lominack
32. David Crout
33. Sarah Crout
34. Daniel Oxner
35. Celia Oxner
36. Eml. Taylor
37. Barbara Taylor
38. Parnelia Price
39. Bartley Long
40. Elizabeth Long
41. Uriah Crout
42. Sophia Crout
43. Marian Long
44. G. E. Lominack
45. M. K. Lominack
46. Daniel Lominack, Jr.
47. William Sanford
48. George Long
49. A. E. Long
50. Thomas Taylor
51. Nancy Taylor, Sr.
52. Nancy Taylor, Jr.
53. Henry Oxner
54. Susannah Oxner
55. Mary Magdala Addy
56. Ephraim Sheely
57. C. Jesse Sheely
58. Eml. Z. Swigert
59. Reuben Vansant
60. Mittian Swigert
61. Flora Vansant
62. John Long
63. Joel Taylor
64. Katharine Taylor
65. J. L. Swigert
66. Mittian Swigert, Sr.
67. Lewis Crout
68. Rebeca Crout
69. Jacob Vansant
70. Jacob Drafts, Sr.
71. Elizabeth Drafts
72. Michael Shealy
73. Sarah Shealy
74. Samuel Seas
75. Elias Seas
77. Sally Lights
78. Lewis Shealy
79. Wiley Shealy
80. Jemima Shealy
81. Ahiiah Anderson
82. Katherine Anderson
83. William Plymale
84. Ellender Plymale
76. Mary Lewie
85. Eml. Oswalt
86. Rebena Oswalt
87. Jacob Lominack
88. Philip Alewine
89. B. Alewine
90. Michael Eargle
91. Nancy Eargle
92. Martin Oswalt

93. Celia Oswalt
94. Nancy Vansant
95. Natty Lominack
96. Daniel Alewine
97. John Price
98. Nancy Price
99. Artemas Eargle
100. A. C. Eargle
101. William L. Jackson
102. Nancy Jackson
103. David Crappe
104. Margran Crappe
105. David Oswalt
106. Caroline Oswalt
107. Eml. Hallman
108. A. H. Hallman
109. Jacob Price, Sr.
110. A. K. Price
111. Sally Price
112. Polly Price
113. L. C. Price

GERMAN REFORMED MEMBERS

1. David Risinger, Elder
2. Katherine Risinger
3. Daniel Lominack, Sr.
4. Elizabeth Lominack
5. Rosannah Lominack
6. Lavina Lominack
7. Mary Lominack
8. J. A. Lominack
9. Katherine Lominack
10. M. E. Lomanae
11. Isaiah Vansant
12. John A. Vansant
13. David Fikes
14. Mary Fikes
15. Emaline Crout
16. William Lomanae
17. Barbara Risinger
18. Sally Eargle
19. Morgan Eargle
20. Susannah Lominack
21. Susannah Alewine
22. Christina Lights
23. Jemima Lights
24. Julian Lights
25. Anna Lights
26. Mary Addy
27. Katherine Addy
28. William L. Addy
29. John H. Amick
30. C. K. Amick
31. Andrew Son
32. Solomon Son
33. Henry Son
34. Jacob Son
35. Elizabeth Son, Sr.
36. Elizabeth Son., Jr.
37. Christenia Son
38. William Shealy, Sr.
39. Christian Rall
40. Barbara Shealy
41. Elizabeth Shealy
42. Polly Shealy
43. George Keasler
44. Epsey Heare
45. W. T. Shealy
46. Adam Shealy
47. Miley Shealy
48. Jesse Shealy
49. Sabra Shealy
50. Emanuel Shealy
51. Rebecca Shealy
53. Elizabeth Shealy, Sr.
52. John W. Shealy
54. Marian Shealy
55. Julia Shealy
56. Lueazer Shealy
57. Anna Hallman
58. Jesse Hallman
59. Hepsibah Hallman
60. Elizabeth Hallman
61. Thomas Risinger
62. Polly Taylor
63. Nancy Taylor
64. Pernina Taylor
65. Levinia Taylor
66. J. W. Taylor
67. Katherine Taylor
68. Daniel Taylor

69. J. S. Addy
70. Celia Addy
71. Katherine Long
72. Mary Rice
73. David Taylor, Sr.
74. Adah Taylor
75. Thomas Long

76. Elizabeth Long
77. George Kelley
78. Henry Crappe
79. Adah Crappe
80. Henry Shealy
81. Elizabeth Shealy

DEAD BURIED IN SALEM CEMETERY

Prior to about 1890 the Salem members buried their dead in family plots near their homes.

Sarah Craps
Nancy Craps Howard
James D. Addy
Ora Mamie Addy
Infant
Infant
Ethel Elfeeta Addy
Maggie Pauline Addy
Alice Jumper Derrick
Infant Mr. and Mrs. D. J. S. Derrick
Isabel Huff Long
David Drayton Long
Welton Rhodes
Dunne Mae Rhodes
Rispy Earhart
Benjamin Earhart
Charlotte Black Earhart
Fred G. Caughman
James S. Lewie
Jemima Shealy
Stone Erected to the Memory of Solomon Shealy
Jacob Shealy
Eva Shealy
Infant Twins Shealy
Chicola McCartha

Sumuel Black
Vernon Eugene Kyzer
Alemenia Rhodella Kyzer
Leila Mae Derrick
Infant Mr. and Mrs. Billie Derrick
Mrs. Addy Taylor, German Lady
Agnes Taylor
Sallie Taylor
Fannie Taylor
Ivy Taylor
Elliot V. Taylor
Justus R. Taylor
Eady Ann Oswald Taylor
Vastine Taylor
Dempsey Caughman
Bethany Caughman
Maggie Caughman McElhaney
James A. Caughman, Grandson
Sallie Swygert Caughman
James A. Caughman
Ollie Steele Long Kyzer
Edward F. Long
Two Infants

In the cemetery is a massive monument erected in memory of:
SALEM EVANGELICAL LUTHERAN CHURCH
Burned December 6, 1925.

In Blessed Memory of Our Fathers and Mothers in the True Faith, by whose Prayers and Sacrifices was founded Salem Ev. Lutheran Church 1792.

In grateful Memory of the Worthy Sons and Daughters, whose Contributions Rebuilt and Painted Salem Ev. Lutheran Church 1890-1891.

A. Robert }
I. Caughman } CC.

112 A.
20 chs. p.m.

Nicholas Roof

South Carolina.

Pursuant to the request of
Absalam Robert Jun. I certify for him a
Tract of Land Containing One Hundred
& Twelve Acres, situate in Lexington Dis
trict in the State aforesaid On Branches of
Hollow Creek of Saluda River originally
Granted unto Christopher Caughman, and
have such form and marks as the above
plat represents.
            Surveyed by me the 27th day of June
1823.
                        N. R. Able
                        D. S.

ELIZABETH FINCH

THE earliest land grant that we have been able to find in the Cedar Grove section was to Elizabeth Finch, which reads:
"South Carolina

"King George III, of Great Britian, France and Ireland—King defender of faith and so forth. To all to whom these presents shall come greeting: Know ye that we of our special grace, certain knowledge, and mere motion have granted these presents for us our heirs and assigns, a plantation or tract of land containing 100 acres, located on Big Hollow Creek, waters of Saluda River, bounded on all sides by vacant land, to Elizabeth Finch."

This conveyance was found among the old records of Henry Craps, who conveyed the Cedar Grove Church lot to Cedar Grove Congregation. Mr. Craps was one of our early land owners in the Cedar Grove Community. He once owned a part of the Drayton Long farm; the O. B. Addy farm; the Clarance Addy farm; the E. H. Addy or S. W. Craps farm; and other lands in this community. This Elizabeth Finch farm evidently was some of this land. We have no means of identifying the identical spot, only that it touched Big Hollow Creek, because all boundaries were by vacant land—no individual owned land next to it.

The deed states that it was in Colleton County. That mistake is easily accounted for, for our first surveyor generals were not too familiar with our geographical setup.

The district of Orangeburg, as it was laid out in 1768, included all places between the Savannah, Santee, Congaree and Broad Rivers. This large scope of country was later divided into four counties. In 1804 Lexington was laid off and called the district of Saxe-Gotha. In 1852 it was changed to Lexington District.

This section was originally known as Northern Orangeburgh.

Along from 1740 on for a decade or more came a large number of immigrants from along the Rhine River in Germany and other provinces such as Switzerland.

The Caughman's came directly from the border line of Switzerland. However, the majority of the settlers on the south side of Lake Murray came from the Dutch Fork, being descendants of the colony which came directly from Heidelberg, Germany.

The old Elizabeth Finch deed is now in the possession of Mrs. Alonzo Lown, a granddaughter of the Henry Craps, referred to heretofore. I am grateful to her for revealing this bit of historical information to me, the author of this history.

Just before this sketch was sent to the press, I find that 100 acres of land was deeded to Maria E. Kauffman 1773 in Craven County. I have also found that Christopher Caughman had five grants of land in Orangeburgh. The 1790 census shows that there were Christopher Andrew, Martin and Elizabeth Caughman, all landowners in this section. Our conclusion is that the foregoing Elizabeth Finch was a sister to the Caughman Bros.

Laid down by a scale of 20 chains per inch

South Carolina
Lexington District

Mr. Crapes

Pursuant to the request of Jerome
Mr. Crapes I have returned ... for him a tract of
Lands situate in the State and District aforesaid on
the Wateree Creek waters of Saluda River and on
the Columbia and Charleston Roads And it being
certify the same contains 141 acres with such shape
form marks and bounds as the above Plate represents This survey is made for divisions ...
November the 19th 1851, by

B. Reich...

QP Crapes
Henry Crapes

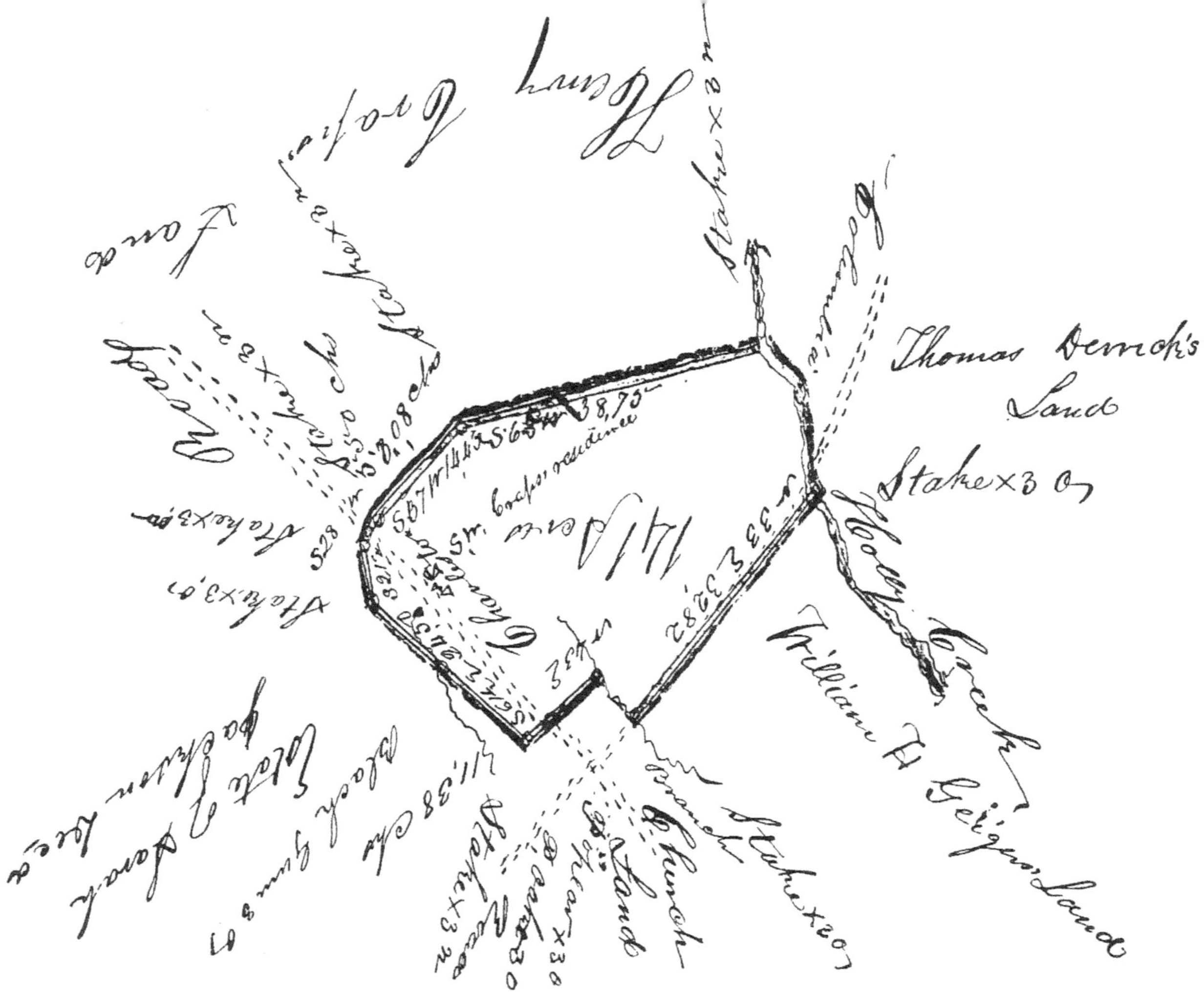
Thomas Derrick's Land
Stake x3 O
Holly Creek
William H Geiger's Land
Columbia
Church Land
branch
Stake x3 n
11.38 chs
Black Gum x3 O
Stake x3.O
528
38,75
141 Acres

HISTORY OF CEDAR GROVE EVANGELICAL

CONGREGATION

A BOUT the year 1850 a great revival wave swept over this area. The method of worship in Salem Congregation was not looked upon with favor by all its members. This caused great dissatisfaction among the members. A division came about, the congregation was divided into two parts, however, both factions continued to use the same church building for worship until the one drawing out could erect a building. This practice continued for about four years.

The first business meeting of the Cedar Grove element was held in January 1852 in Salem Church with the following procedure, which is copied from the original church report.

"According to previous appointment January 1852, a portion of the members of Salem Church met on the 28th day of February, A. D. 1852 for the purpose of transacting certain business pertaining to the church. The following members were present:

Daniel Efird	Emanuel Z. Swigert
Daniel Drafts	David Crout
Adam Risinger	David Craps
Frederic Sease	Noah Risinger
Uriah Crout	Wesley Risinger
Wiley Shealy	Henry Oxner
Lewis Shealy	David Risinger
John Y. Swigert	George Hallman
George Oswalt	David Addy
Wilson Hallman	Ephraim Shealy
George Hallman	

The meeting was duly organized by electing of its officers, which resulted as follows, Daniel Efird, Chairman and Uriah Crout, Secretary.

"The chairman explained the object of the meeting.

"Mr. Levi Boland appeared among us on this occasion, but therefore resolved that he be received as an advisory member among us.

"After which the following preamble and resolution was adopted: 'Whereas the members of Salem Church has hither not kept a church catalogue: Be it therefore resolved, according to our opinion, it is the duty of every member of said church to give in their names to the Secretary of said church, as a matter of church records, that they may be systematically enrolled on the church catalogue.

" 'Whereas as hither to we have not had a church book in which to record the business of the church. But as some of our brethren have procured and arranged a book, be it therefore resolved that said book be received for the above named purpose.

" 'Whereas in the future our secretary is to record the business in Salem Church. Resolved that any person being baptized or having children baptized shall give in the same to the secretary of the church as a matter of church record.

" 'Resolved that each member of said church hand in their names to the Secretary as communicants of the Lord's Table, it being also a matter of church records. Then the meeting adjourned.

" 'URIAH CROUT, Sec.' "

We find recorded on a fly leaf of the aforesaid church ledger, the following statement: "This book was bought by Uriah Crout and presented to the use of the old school Lutheran at Salem Church, Lexington District, S. C., November A. D. 1852, Price $3.00.

"When I am dead and in my grave, this book my name shall ever have, when gredious worms my body have eat, then you can read my name complete. Uriah Crout."

In perusing through his records while he was secretary of the congregation, we find them accurate and very businesslike for the pioneer days of this community. He certainly deserves commendation for his interest, neatness, etc.

Continuing further in getting the new congregation set-up for Synodical business, a meeting was held on the 31st day of July, 1852, with the following members present:

There were quite a number of other members of Salem Church at that time, who were neutral. However, the Lutherans won out and Salem was admitted to the South Carolina Synod about 1824, Rev. Godfry Dreher, pastor. The Rev. Godfry Dreher lived in the Dutch Fork of Lexington County, near where St. Michael's Church now stands. His body is buried in the St. Michael's Cemetery. He was one of our pioneer Lutheran preachers who made great sacrifices in carrying the gospel to our early settlers. While serving Salem as pastor he preached once each month. He had no means of transportation except riding horseback. He would cross Saluda River on horseback. Sometimes it would be necessary for his horse to swim. At the end of the year his members would gather an offering for him. Usually he would give this money to widows and orphans living in the community.

PASTORS 1792-1925.

Hochheimer	J. Wingard
H. Winkhouse	Emanuel Caughman
Godfrey Dreher	J. H. Wertz
J. Y. Meetze	S. R. Sheppard
M. Rauch	A. W. Lindler
David Shealy	D. Kyzer

A. D. F. Mozer
C. P. Boozer
B. Kreps
L. E. Busby
H. P. Counts

J. D. Kinard
D. B. Groseclose
S. C. Ballentine
V. Y. Boozer
W. D. Wise

During the life of Salem Congregation, which was 133 years, three buildings were erected. The first was a log building in 1792. Later a beautiful frame building containing a gallery supported by columns was erected. The gallery was used for slaves, so that they might be able to worship with their masters.

About 1895 a more commodious building was erected under the leadership of Rev. L. E. Busby. This building served the congregation well through the years until the first Sunday morning of December, 1925, when the church burned. Rev. W. D. Wise was pastor. Service had begun. Pastor Wise had just announced his text from First Peter, the fourth chapter and eighteenth verse: "And if the righteous scarcely be saved; where shall the ungodly and the sinner appear?" Immediately the stove flue fell to the floor. Very fortunately no one was hurt. The church building could have been saved if water had been available. The pastor and members present removed all pews, organ, pulpit and other church fixtures.

The congregation was weak, so they finally decided to disband. Later the majority united with Cedar Grove. The real estate was deeded to the South Carolina Synod. The church furnishings were sold and the proceeds used for purchasing an derecting a monument to the memory of her sons and daughters.

Salem was the mother church of Cedar Grove, Union, and St. Mark's.

Rev. Daniel Efird, Chairman
Daniel Drafts, Elder
Frederick Sease, Elder
Adam Risinger, Elder
John S. Addy
George Hallman
David Crout
David Craps
John A. Lominack
William A. Long
Emanuel Lominack
Daniel Oswalt
John Y. Swygert
Daniel Oxner
Jacob Vansant
Joseph Davis

David Addy
Henry Oxner
Noah Risinger
Wesley Risinger
David Risinger
Lewis Shealy
Wiley Shealy
Daniel Lomanack
Henry Eargle
Emanuel Shealy
Jife Shealy
Peter Shealy
Henry Son
William B. Oxner
Hasten Shealy
W. L. Addy

DANIEL DRAFTS

Jacob Lominack	Elias Shealy
Emanuel Taylor	Wilson Hallman
George Souter	Ivy Anderson
Michael Eargle	Michael Shealy
James Sanders	Uriah Crout
Henry Shealy	

Whereas the church council passed a resolution at the regular meeting held at Zion's Church on July 17, 1852 requesting each individual church to petition to the Evangelical Lutheran Tennessee Synod for the connection of our churches to the same and to continue the pastoral services of Rev. Daniel Efird among us, which was unanimously adopted, not a dissenting voice being given.

The members then went in election, whether to send a delegate from Salem Church to Synod or not. Resulted as follows: Yeas 10; Nays, 28."

We find that the next year Daniel Drafts was sent as a delegate to represent the church in Synod which met on Oct. 14, 1853 in Tennessee. We now find the new congregation a full-fledged member of the Tennessee Synod.

This Cedar Grove Congregation continued to function under the Tennessee Synod for about 65 years, then became a member of the North Carolina Synod. There were quite a number of churches in South Carolina that belonged to the Tennessee Synod and then to the North Carolina Synod. But the time had now come when all the congregations in South Carolina were ready to hold membership in one synodical body. Methods of transfer were discussed and plans arranged for the consummation of this transfer at a meeting of the South Carolina Synod held in Grace Church, Prosperity, S. C., Nov. 20-24, 1922.

The applications of the following congregations with their respective representative were presented:

Congregations	Representatives
St. John's	John A. Summers
Mt. Herman	M. N. Kleckley
Zion	C. M. Efird
St. Thomas	J. C. Fulmer
St. Jacobs	R. F. Cumalander
Cedar Grove	J. Ansel Caughman
St. James	R. E. Shealy
St. Paul's	J. L. Sease
Grace	E. C. Davis
Holy Trinity	Fred G. Hartley
St. John's	G. O. Schumpert
Emanuels	Marshall Roof
Pilgrim	D. F. Efird

St. Peter's _____G. B. Wingard
Mt. Tabor _____P. I. Sox
St. Andrew's _____ J. O. Eargle
Bethlehem _____ C. H. Bouknight
Mt. Horeb _____W. A. Ballentine
St. Peter's, Chapin _____ L. B. Frick

By motion the representatives were received as commissioners and given the privilege of the floor. By a unanimous vote of the Synod and their respective commissioners these above named churches were declared members of Synod.

Reverends W. H. Riser, W. D. Wise, R. M. Carpenter, H. A. Kistler, and J. M. Senter, pastors of the congregations just r·-ceived into the Synod, were unanimously received and their names placed on the clerical roll of Synod.

At that time the South Carolina Synod was very unique. Every Lutheran Church in South Carolina at that time was a member of the South Carolina Synod.

The charter members of the new congregation in Salem, 1852, later to be known as Cedar Grove, were as follows:

Frederick Sease, Elder	Barbara Risinger
Daniel Drafts, Elder	Catherine Risinger
Adam Risinger, Elder	Miley Risinger
John S. Addy, Elder	Mary Risinger
Uriah Crout, Sec.	Mittie Risinger
Noah Risinger	Elizabeth Risinger
Wesley Risinger	Julian Drafts
David Risinger	Eliza B. Drafts
Jacob Earhart	Maria A. Drafts
David Crout	Jacob F. Drafts
John Y. Swygert	Rosannah Oxner
Daniel Oxner	Mary Lewie
Henry Oxner	Catherine Addy
George Oswalt	Sarah Crout
Wiley Shealy	Eliza Crout
Lewis Shealy	Eleanor Crout
Wilson Hallman	Celia Oxner
George Hallman	Mitty Ann Swygert
George Hallman, Sr.	Sophia Crout
David Addy	Caroline Crout
Ephraim Shealy	Levina Crout
Henry L. Crout	Mary Hallman
David Addy	Achsa Shealy
William B. Oxner	Eliza Addy
Richard Crout	Sarah Addy
Emanuel Y. Swygert	Emily Crout
Geo. M. Souter	Sarah Crout

Mary Crout
Elizabeth Crout
Celia Crout
Mittie Ann Swygert
Rachel Craps
Mary Lominack

Levina Lominack
Polly Lominack
Elizabeth Lominack
Christena A. Son
Mary E. Son
Miley L. Son

It was first decided to build a new house of worship in front of the old gallery building at Salem for the new congregation. Some lumber and hewed timber was put down there. The leaders assembled for the purpose of beginning the building, their wagons being loaded with building material. After some discussion they arrived at a conclusion that it would be best to move elsewhere. Henry Craps offered the congregation land where Cedar Grove is now located. The group accepted the proposition at once. The teams were driven to this location and work began on the new church building. This building was erected in 1856, and was dedicated November 29, 1857, A. D., by the Reverends Daniel and Adam Efird.

The first Sacramental meeting held in Cedar Grove was in November 1857 by the Reverends Daniel Efird, Adam Efird, and Dr. Eichelberger, 126 communed—51 males and 75 females.

The first officers serving the congregation after the first church was built were Adam Risinger, Daniel Drafts, Capt. E. Z. Swygert, and Henry Craps, Elders; Uriah Crout, Secretary.

The first building was burned by an incendiary fire in 1865.

This calamity did not stop the congregation from holding their regular services. They anchored a bush arbor to a large tree near where the church was and held their services there while a new church was being built in 1866.

The second Cedar Grove Church was a large and commodious building erected principally by its members, with Wesley Hare as foreman. It was a huge structure, built of excellent yellow pine timber. All the sills, sleepers, joist, corner posts and other heavy parts were hand-hewed. Because of its width, it became necessary to tie it together with heavy steel rods.

This building served the needs of the congregation for about sixty years.

In 1924 the congregation began thinking seriously of a new modern church building. Perhaps it would be difficult to name the exact date which marked the beginning of the history of the present Cedar Grove house of worship, as the idea of a new church had been growing in the minds of some of her members for years, but the following gives us dates that were epochal as to historical data and which did produce tangible results. On the 28th day of June, 1924, F. L. Addy, J. Ansel Caughman, D. H. Price, and Rev. W. D. Wise, Pastor of Cedar Grove Congregation, went to North

CEDAR GROVE LUTHERAN CHURCH, BUILT IN 1866

Carolina for the purpose of looking over some of the modern Lutheran churches that had been constructed in the upper Piedmont. The first day of our itinerary permitted us to visit Lutheran Churches at Harden, North Carolina, and Lincolnton, North Carolina. We spent Saturday night in the suburbs of Hickory, North Carolina with Rev. Enoch Hite and family. On Sunday morning bright and early we visited Lenoir-Rhyne College. The writer of this history greatly enjoyed this particular visit, rejoicing over the improvements made by the institution since he was a student there a quarter of a century before this. He passed through the laboratory and was again permitted to look at some of the specimens he put up in alcohol while studying Zoology. One was a snake in the act of swallowing a frog.

We went over the town of Hickory and visited most of the churches there. We left Hickory about 10:00 and went to Statesville, North Carolina, and worshiped with the Lutheran Congregation there. After service we were shown over this plant and were given much data as to cost, etc. We left Stateville and visited other churches in the afternoon, one of which was at Startown, North Carolina. I was very much pleased with this church because I thought it was the building that would come nearer fitting our financial standing than any we had visited. The tower was less expensive than the others. Some of the rooms were eliminated that we found in the Harden, Lincolnton, and Statesville plans.

This scouting party was highly pleased with what it had seen in the way of church plants. Rev. Wise was especially enthused over the Statesville plant as well as the other members of the party. My greatest objection was the enormous amount of brick and labor necessary for the construction of the front part and the tower of this particular plant.

Sunday night was spent at the old home of Rev. W. D. Wise near Lincolnton, North Carolina. His father was a very pleasant old gentleman and we were treated with royalty in his home.

Monday morning, June 30th, we returned to our homes, all in high spirits and hopeful that Cedar Grove may erect in the near future a church building comparing to some extent with those we had visited.

On the 13th of July, 1924, this scouting party (for it was not an appointed committee) reported to the congregation what they had seen in the way of church buildings and made the statement that in their opinion the time was here when Cedar Grove should undertake the erection of a new house of worship. A resolution was then passed by the congregation, fixing the second Sunday in August of this same year as the date for the congregation to vote on this all important matter. The second Sunday was the 10th of the month and at this time the congregation voted to build a new church. There was only one dissenting vote. It was also voted on that the building be of permanent material, either brick or stone. A resolution was also offered that Cedar Grove Congregation, having decided to build a new church, extend an invitation to Salem to join with her in this undertaking. F. L. Addy, D. H. Price, and Rev. W. D. Wise were asked to convey this resolution to Salem.

A building committee was named, the personnel of which was F. L. Addy, J. Ansel Caughman, D. H. Price, Pierce Risinger, J. Rufus Shealy, Geo. W. Swygert, J. J. Seastruck, and Rev. W. D. Wise.

I think we can correctly say that August 10, 1924, marked the real beginning of the new church, for its realtiy was never doubtful after that date. The committee appointed, conveyed the wishes of Cedar Grove Congregation to Salem the first Sunday in September of this year. The congregation seemed to be favorably impressed and set the first Sunday in October for a congregational meeting. At that time it voted to join with Cedar Grove in the erection of a new chuch, there being but one dissenting vote. Salem appointed a committee to work with the Cedar Grove Committee in bringing about a union and setting up a building plan. This committee was Henry Hite, J. E. B. McCartha and Eddie Derrick.

All through the winter months and early spring this joint committee held meetings from time to time endeavoring to determine a location for the new church that would be acceptable for both parties concerned. This joint committee failing to reach a satisfactory agreement, the committee from Cedar Grove felt that they could no longer delay the matter and began to consider seriously a plan for building.

After much discussion it was decided by the leading committee-men to follow the Statesville plan. However, the writer of this history seriously objected to the waste of using these enormous stacks of brick supporting this expensive tower and steeple. We could have saved several thousand dollars right here and to my mind would have looked just as well, as we had no other costly buildings nearby to compete with.

On the 13th of March, 1925, Rev. W. D. Wise gave his personal check to Louis H. Asbury, of Charlotte, North Carolina, for $100.00 and secured the blue prints, which were simply a reprint of the Statesville plan.

The committee, after much time had been expended in getting prices on cutting of stone and buying of brick, came to the conclusion that it would be cheaper to build of brick. The latter part of July, 1925, this committee placed an order with the Georgia-Carolina Brick Company for 300,000 bricks, 230,000 common at $10.50 per M and 70,000 rough texture at $17.00 per M.

The first car of these brick were received at Fredonia August 6, 1925, and two cars every week from that date on until 21 cars had

PRESENT CEDAR GROVE CHURCH, 1926

been received. The people cooperated splendidly in the hauling of these brick. Therefore, we had no difficulty in getting them unloaded in the required time. Our last carload came November 29, the brick all being on the grounds. It was decided next to saw timber on church grounds, that we might have something to cover over brick and also have lumber dry and ready for use the coming summer. F. L. Addy began sawing this timber about December 1, 1925, and would have finished by December 31, but some dissatisfaction arose as to sawing this timber, and until the matter was straightened out January, 1926, had come and was very rainy, so the timber was not finished until February 17, 1926.

After the sawing of timber it was decided to dig the basement of the proposed church. Just to the rear of the old church was the site chosen for the new church. On Monday morning March 15, 1926, the ground was broken for the new building.

I might say right here that I was a member of the building committee, and being very much interested in the erection of our new church building, I accepted the principalship of the Cedar Grove Public School in 1924, with my wife as assistant and continued in that capacity for three years, during the whole period of assembling material and construction of the new church.

When I was a young man in my twenties, I had the privilege and honor of teaching the aforesaid school for four years. I was now teaching the children of those pupils. Therefore, my wife and I had a peculiar feeling of love and interest in the youngsters intrusted to our care and training. They appeared somewhat like our grandchildren. I am giving this bit of history because it is so closely attached to the building of the new church and the boys were so active and energetic in lending a helping hand, I feel that they deserve mention.

On that lovely spring morning of March 14, 1926, a soft balmy breeze was blowing from the west; all of nature was putting on new life; everything seemed to be happy, pleasant and prosperous. The little band of workmen who had assembled for the purpose of excavating the basement seemed anxious to hear the command "Go forward." These men, with the public school pupils and teachers, led by Rev. W. D. Wise and H. M. Caughman, Choir Leader, marched to the rear of the old church, assembled on the naked ground where the new church now stands and engaged in Divine Worship. This number engaged in singing "How Firm a Foundation" and "Work for the Night Is Coming." The sound penetrated the little valley and seemed to re-echo from the Great Spirit "Go Forward, I Am With You."

After the reading of the proper ceremony by Rev. W. D. Wise, he took a shovel and removed the first dirt.

Within several weeks' time, or until the people had to turn their attention to planting a crop, the basement was completed, that is the excavating.

On April 1, 1926, the first car of lime was received from Whaley Bros., Augusta, Georgia. Operations were now at a stand-still, owing to the fact that it was cropping time with our people.

On June 13, 1926, G. T. Whittle and J. J. Swygert began cutting rocks, belt course, window sills, et cetera. On July 12, 1926, the laying of brick began. The following masons worked: Unus Black, Luther Hallman, L. R. Keisler, John Johnston (colored), Bointon Ricard, Murray Ricard and Celee Black working as apprentices. Y. J. Swygert, J. B. Oswald, and perhaps others, laid brick. Before the walls were finished Paul and Rufus Harman laid brick.

Quite a number of the male members pledged themselves to labor one day out of each week until the walls were erected. These responded well at first, and on August 5 the building had been erected up to the main floor of the church auditorium.

The work was now brought to a standstill, owing to the fact that the stone cutters did not have buttress caps and other stone needed as yet cut. The stone cutters also asked to be off for several weeks to get out a job of work which they claimed they had agreed to do before hiring to us.

On July 19 we received all our outside window and door frames. These we bought from the Perkins Mfg. Co., Augusta, Georgia. They cost $672.00. Mr. E. W. Bedenbaugh sized and dressed our lumber which was finished July 21.

The corner stone was laid August 22, with the president of Synod, Dr. H. J. Black, assisting the pastor, Rev. F. G. Morgan, a son of the congregation, preached the sermon. Reverends Enoch Hite and C. I. Morgan brought greetings. These bretheren are also sons of the congregation.

Brick laying was resumed October 11 with the same crew of masons mentioned above.

J. J. Seastrunk, a state-wide known contractor and a member of the building committee, was naturally expected to oversee the erection of the building. This he did up until this time. Now Mr. Seastrunk's contracting business was such that he could not be present regularly enough to carry on the work, without an assistant. The committee was fortunate in securing J. Rufus Shealy, also a member of the building committee to carry on the work in the absence of Mr. Seastrunk. Mr. Shealy was faithful in the performance of his duty and did extremly well with it during this trying period.

I regret very much to make this statement, but now we faced our dark period. It took a long time to build these walls; we had now arrived at the place where it was slow and dangerous. Quite a number of our helpers failed to keep their pledge in helping to construct the walls. Only the faithful few kept their promise and would help at their regular time.

At this time the Lexington Water Power Company was clearing the Saluda Valley and everyone could get a job paying from $2.00 to $5.00 per day. This was a great attraction for a good many of our laborers.

However, our masons were present every day and had to be waited on. It took hundreds of loads of sand, yea, mountains of it. B. W. Asbill and Moses Taylor certainly hauled their share of it.

We couldn't afford to let our masons be idle. A young white man, Raymond Moore, was secured for weeks to draw the mortar up and carry it to the masons while they were working on the high walls and steep gables. Some days we would get help but not every day. The public school boys would handle brick like Egyptian slaves during the recess and noon period. They enjoyed pitching and catching brick and gloried in making fun out of labor.

This young man, Raymond Moore, died from typhoid fever the next summer. While dying he said, "I want to go back to Cedar Grove."

We were not able to get our former stone cutters back on the job, so we employed Geo. Pride and George Washington (colored) from Columbia, S. C., to do stone cutting. Our people would go to the quarry on E. H. Addy's place, burst out and haul to the church grounds, boulder after boulder to be shaped into desirable stones to be placed in the building. This work continued for weeks. Being present nearly all the time, and part of the time helping while the stone work was being done, I kept a pretty close account of what this beautiful and substantial rock work cost. It was about $2,000.00 outside of all the labor expended by the helping members. One certain pilaster cap cost $45.00 till it was permanently placed.

Finally on February 17, 1927, the brick and stone work was completed. Having finished this enormous task or completed this wonderful job we were grateful to God.

Our people again became courageous. The great desire was now to see our beautiful walls covered. An appeal was made again for funds to buy roofing.

Some of our good members responded well and soon metal shingles were in our possession for covering. B. E. Frye was now employed to build trusts and help with covering. I wish to say here that we had a number of carpenters in our congregation who helped with the woodwork in the church. I don't remember all, but I do recall at present Pierce Risinger, J. B. Adams, E. Z. Swygert, A. P. Jumper, F. L. Shealy and J. Rufus Shealy, the foreman. By March 24, 1927, the roof was on. Mr. Frye continued to work on the interior of the building and by September 20, the church auditorium above was all completed.

Guy Hiller and Willie Jeter (colored) began plastering the latter part of July and finished the above auditorium August 18, 1927.

The chancel furniture was bought from J. S. Probst, Hickory, North Carolina, at a cost of $245.00 and presented to the church as a gift.

The first service was held in the new church Sept. 22, 1927. This was a funeral service for Mrs. Sibian Langford.

The first preaching service was on the fourth Sunday in September, the 25th, 1927.

On October 6 the Art Glass Windows, bought from the High Point Glass and Decorative Company, High Point, North Carolina, came and were all installed by October 14. The art glass windows are all memorial windows placed to the memory of the following names: George P. D. and Lillie S. Hite, Allen L. Hite, Mr. and Mrs. Joseph Hite, Rosa and Mary Risinger, Wesley Risinger, Samuel W. and Amanda R. Stockman, Edwin F. and Ellen E. Caughman, Enoch Swygert, Rev. W. D. Wise and family, George Drafts, Pierce Leaphart, Jeremiah Wynn and Grace Eugenia Morgan, David Tillman and Mary Ann Hare, Laura E. Jumper and Daniel A. Jumper, Pierce J. Risinger, Mrs. Pierce J. Risinger, Ervin Risinger and children, Sarah W. and Eufaula M. Risinger, David and wife, Polly, Jemima, Miley and Lemuel Shealy, Sarah Ann Eargle, Irving P. Eargle, Mr. and Mrs. J. L. Hallman, Mr. and Mrs. E. H. Addy, D. H. Price, wife and children, Paul Hite and wife, Mr. and Mrs. J. B. Oswald, Harley Taylor and family, Mr. and Mrs. J. A. Caughman, Hoy and Noah Caughman, The Light Brigade and the Luther League.

From December 3 to December 8 I. G. Smith, Greenville, South Carolina, finished installing the heating plant. This plant cost $1,750 and was bought from the Monbrief Furnace Company, Atlanta, Georgia.

Beginning December 17, Allen Metz (colored) finished plastering the basement. A cement floor was put down in the first part of 1928. Henry Hite was foreman, assisted by a group of faithful laboring members.

January 1, 1928, the pews came and were installed the first two weeks in this month. These pews were bought from the Huntington Seating Company, Huntington, West Virginia, and cost $2,212. The following pews were paid for and labeled as memorial pews to these names: F. P. Shealy and wife; Ervin Risinger, mother and stepmother; J. J. Seastrunk and family; Reed L. Keisler and Mrs. Laura A. Keisler, W. P. Oswald and family, W. F. Taylor and family; Dora E. Caughman; Pierce J. Risinger and Mrs. Bell Risinger; Mr. and Mrs. J. M. Taylor, and Cedar Grove Sunday School.

The installing of pews was done principally by our carpenters. The pews now installed and the cement floor in basement thoroughly dry, work was resumed in the basement, and by the time Synod met with the congregation, which was January 23, the work was about completed.

Soon after Synod the work was all completed with the exception of painting. Sunday School began to be conducted in the basement.

The bell was bought from the C. S. Bell Company, Hillsboro, Ohio, which with fixtures weighs 1,900 pounds, at a cost of $200, and freight. This was presented as a gift to the church.

Noah, Leo, Omar and Rev. Victor Derrick, brothers, gave a very nice communion set to the church in honor of their mother and grandmother.

D. I. Hite gave the pulpit Bible in memory of his parents, Mr. and Mrs. Joseph Hite.

N. H. Hite made and gave to the Sunday School Department a beautiful book and literature case.

The good and faithful women equipped the kitchen and provided for the carpeting of the church.

Richard Roberts bore the expense of providing book racks on the church pews.

J. S. Craps gave the marble slab inclosing the corner stone.

However, on the second Sunday night in May 1928, some thief broke this beautiful marble stone and stole the steel box containing all the records and important facts that a corner stone usually treasures. This box nor material has ever been found. It was duplicated to the best of our memory and replaced, inclosed this time by a marble slab given by Charley Taylor, of Lexington, South Carolina.

George Drafts, son of Daniel and Julian Drafts, left at his death a legacy of $500.00 which was used for the purchase of brick and a memorial window in his memory.

I was not chairman, treasurer or secretary of the building committee, therefore, the keeping of accurate records, dates, fundamental facts, etc., was not binding upon me. However, on the first day of January 1932, the church council, thinking perhaps I was the one best qualified for this work, appointed me as a committee of one to prepare a history of the erection of Cedar Grove Church building. In order to do this I had to resort to my memory for this work, with the exception of a few dates and facts retained by Rev. W. D. Wise, chairman of the building committee. I can't possibly do justice to every one in what they did in this great work, for I have no permanent records. I am writing from memory and facts as I saw and experienced.

This great undertaking by a group of farming people, who can rightly be called small farmers, was a tremendous task. The cost of material plus a reasonable wage allowed for labor, amounted to, according to my knowledge and best judgment, $45,000.00. When finished all was paid for except about 5,000. This amount had been financed by our own members, so there was no indebtedness outside the church family.

Since the erection of the building, one of our dear consecrated and beloved members, Mrs. Grace Morgan, died, leaving a legacy of $500 which was applied on the church debt.

In the erection of this church some were much more active and more liberal than others. I only know of a few of the cash or money contributions in this work. Therefore reference is hereby given to the Treasurer's Register which should contain an itemized list of contributions of how much and by whom. This book was in the possession of H. M. Caughman, who was treasurer of building fund instead of Rev. W. D. Wise who held same while church was being built.

Rev. W. D. Wise, pastor in charge at the time this structure was erected, deserves much praise and credit for the activities he experienced. In addition to the enormous amount of business transacted attached to this work, he did an enormous amount of physical labor.

A good number of our people did well in this work, but some excelled others.

F. L. Addy hauled more brick than anyone else. Bunyan Asbill and Moses Taylor hauled most of the sand.

W. F. and Henry Taylor furnished nearly all scaffolding material, which amounted to thousands of feet.

Sometime in the early part of 1931 Dr. Festus Shealy, of Clinton, South Carolina, provided a beautiful variety of shrubbery and had it planted around our church, which adds much beauty to it. This was done in honor of his parents, Mr. and Mrs. F. P. Shealy.

Any and everything that was done by the membership or friends is highly appreciated.

We are proud of our church building, but we want the world to know by our mode of living that we are worshiping our Creator and not the creature.

In the development of Lake Murray, a certain Lutheran Church named Mt. Pleasant was discontinued because the waters now cover the site. A certain amount of money was paid to the members of the congregation for its possessions. Some of them became members of Cedar Grove Congregation and donated their inheritance to Cedar Grove Church. Among them were Absolom Hendrix and wife and other descendants of them. Quite a number of dead who had been buried in Mt. Pleasant Church yard were removed from that cemetery and re-entered in the Cedar Grove cemetery. Among them were A. I. Shealy, Edwin Shealy, Mrs. Rosa Shealy, Miss Elizabeth Shealy, Mr. and Mrs. Frank Rawl, W. O. Steele and child. The heirs of the estate of A. I. Shealy contributed the sum of $50 to Cedar Grove when these bodies were reentered in its cemetery.

In 1932 the leaders in the congregation realized that it was no

PARSONAGE JOINTLY OWNED BY ST. JAMES, SUMMIT, AND CEDAR GROVE (1906)

longer wise to wait for better times, to remove or cancel the indebtedness hanging over the congregation. The task was great to undertake during this awful depressive period among a farming class of people.

The good people of this congregation put their shoulders to the wheel and by Thanksgiving Day of this good year, 1932, they were ready and did dedicate this church, just 73 years to the very day from the dedication of its first church building.

After Salem Church burned in 1925 the congregation disbanded. The officers executed a deed to the South Carolina Synod for the real estate. This property was held by Synod for about 13 years. A number of our people in Cedar Grove who transferred their membership from Salem had their dead buried in Salem Cemetery. They expressed a desire to buy this property from Synod and deed it to Cedar Grove, so that Cedar Grove would assume the entire responsibility of caring for Salem Cemetery.

Since Caughmans gave the land for Salem, E. F. and J. Ansel assumed the obligation of buying this identical land and conveyed it to Cedar Grove in April 1938. The South Carolina Synod executed a deed and mailed same to J. Ansel Caughman on the same day that the said E. F. Caughman died. I asked him if he thought he could understand any business transaction. He said, "Yes." I made the statement to him, that Cedar Grove had received the deed for the Salem property. His reply was "Thank God." This was the last words he uttered on earth.

In 1947 a toilet system was completed in the church basement. This necessitated a deep well and electric pump to supply adequate water supplies. This well and pump was a gift to the church honoring all our World War Veterans.

PARSONAGES

We have no record of any parsonage ever being provided for a pastor's home until Cedar Grove and St. James, Summit, S. C., became a pastorate. The following is an agreement between the two congregations:

State of South Carolina,
County of Lexington.

To all whom it may concern, it is hereby agreed by the Cedar Grove Charge, composed of Cedar Grove and St. James churches. that the one and one-half acres of land purchased of J. Hite, August 7, 1907 and parsonage now situated thereon, is owned by said churches, according to the proportionate amount each church contributed toward purchasing said land and building said parsonage. Cedar Grove's interest being twenty-two twenty-fifths and St. James three twenty-fifths.

It is also agreed by said charge that when said parsonage shall need repairing or any improvement of whatever kind it may be, then each church shall pay her pro rata of the cost proportioned as the above.

In case of dissolution of said charge, then and in that event each church shall have their pro rata share of said property according to the value at the time, dissolution proportioned as above. When said charge dissolves, the said property shall either be sold at public sale or valued by a committee of at least three disinterested men.

WESLEY RISINGER,
J. B. OSWALD,
E. F. CAUGHMAN,
Elders.

Witnesses:
ENOCH SWYGERT,
J. L. HALLMAN,

LEWIS SHEALY,
H. S. RICARD,
Elders.

Witnesses:
LEVI POOLE,
R. E. SHEALY,

Before a dissolution came about much work had been done on the parsonage and many improvements made about the parsonage. St. James had been paying one-fourth of these costs so it was satisfactorily agreed that she have one-fourth interest in the property.

On July 12, 1948, Rev. Joseph C. Derrick, who was pastor at that time, offered his resignation which reads as follows:

To the Joint Council of the Cedar Grove Lutheran Parish.

Brethren: I hereby submit my resignation as pastor of the Cedar Grove Lutheran Parish in order that the St. James and Cedar Grove Churches may pursue their respective plans for development as individual parishes, the resignation to become effective September 1, 1948. Grace and peace from our Lord Jesus Christ be unto you.

In all sincerity,

JOSEPH C. DERRICK.

So the dissolution of this parish was on September 1, 1948. The property was sold at public auction on the second day of August 1948 to Andrew L. Addy for $4,005.00, he being the highest bidder.

On May 12, 1948, J. Ansel Caughman executed a deed to the officers of Cedar Grove Congregation and their successors in office forever, a lot of land containing five acres more or less adjoining lands of Cedar Grove congregation. This deed is found on record in the Clerk of Court's office in Lexington county, South Carolina,

MODERN CEDAR GROVE PARSONAGE, BUILT IN 1948

in Book 6-1 of Deeds, page 285. This land to be used for a parsonage lot.

On June 13, 1948 the congregation voted to erect a modern parsonage. A Building committee was appointed consisting of Hoy Caughman, Van Eargle, Viera Swygert and Mrs. J. C. Derrick through the preliminaries. After Mrs. Derrick moved, Gordon Oxner served in her place.

Viera Swygert was employed as contractor. The building cost around $17,000. All parsonage indebtedness was cleared up on the fifth Sunday in September 1951 and the parsonage dedicated.

In the fall of 1949 a Hammond Electronic Organ was installed in Cedar Grove Church at a cost of $2,300.

In the fall of 1950 an amplifying set with tower loud speakers were installed at a cost of about $1,000. These were gifts to the congregation in memory of her deceased members and in honor of her living members.

CEDAR GROVE IS INCORPORATED
A Copy

State of South Carolina,
Executive Department
Certificate of Incorporation by the Secretary of State

Whereas, Rev. Joseph C. Derrick and J. Ansel Caughman, both of R. F. D., Leesvile, S. C., two or more of the officers or agents appointed to supervise or manage the affairs of Cedar Grove Evangelical Lutheran Church which has been duly and regularly organized, did on the 6th day of May, A. D. 1947, file with the Secretary of State a written declaration setting forth: That, at a meeting of the aforesaid organization held pursuant to the by laws and regulations of the said organization, they were authorized and directed to apply for incorporation.

That, the said organization, desires to hold, property in common for Religious, Educational, Fraternal, Charitable or other Eleemosynary purpose, or any two or more of said purposes, and is not organized for the purpose of profit or gain to the members, otherwise than is above stated, nor for the insurance of life, health, accident or property: and that three days' notice in the Twin-City News a newspaper published in the county of Lexington, has been given that the aforesaid Declaration would be filed.

And whereas Said Declarants and Petitioners further declared and affirmed:

First: Their names and residences are as above given.

Second: The name of the proposed corporation is Cedar Grove Evangelical Lutheran Church.

Third: The place at which it proposes to have its headquarters or be located is R. F. D. 3, Leesville, S. C.

Fourth: The purpose of the said proposed corporation is for public worship, of the Triune God, and establishing an endowment for the perpetual upkeep of cemetery located by the aforesaid church.

Fifth: The names and residences of all Managers, Trustees, Directors or other officers as follows: Rev. Joseph C. Derrick, R. F. D. 3, Leesville, S. C., Pastor; J. Ansel Caughman, R. F. D. 2, Leesville, S. C., Chairman; R. H. Caughman, R. F. D. 2, Leesville, S. C., Secretary; N. Gordon Oxner, R. F. D. 2, Leesville, S. C., Treasurer.

Sixth: That they desire to be incorporated: in perpetuity.

Now therefore I, W. P. Blackwell, Secretary of State, by virtue of the authority in me vested, by chapter 158, Article III, Code of 1942, and Acts amendatory thereto, do hereby declare the said organization to be a body politic and corporate, with all rights, powers, privileges and immunities, and subject to all the limitations and liabilities, conferred by said Chapter 158, Article III, Sections 8158-8159 and 8168, Code of 1942, and acts amendatory thereto.

Given under my hand and the seal of the State at Columbia this 6th day of May in the year of our Lord, one thousand nine hundred and forty-seven and in the one hundred and seventy-first year of the United States of America.

W. P. BLACKWELL,
Secretary of State.

Department of State, South Carolina

Certificate of Incorporation of the Cedar Grove Evangelical Lutheran Church, R. F. D. 3, Leesville, S. C.

I hereby certify that the within Certificate of Incorporation was filed for record in my office at 11:14 a.m. o'clock on the 6th day of October, 1951 and was immediately entered upon the proper indexes and duly recorded in Book of Charters No. II, page 93.

H. L. HARMAN, Clerk,
Court of Common Pleas and General Sessions,
Lexington County, S. C.

W. P. BLACKWELL,
Secretary of State.

CEDAR GROVE CHURCH COUNCIL (1952)

CHURCH COUNCILMEN OF CEDAR GROVE

We have made an honest effort to get a list of all who have served on the church council. Due to the fact that past records are incomplete, we will not guarantee this list correct.

Adams—Jesse B., Oren B., J. Heyward.

Addy—Andrew L., Clarence V., Evans O., Henry E., H. L., Theo, John S.

Amick—Clarborne H.

Asbill—Bunyan.

Black—C. E.

Caughman—Edwin F., Henry M., J. Ansel, S. Broadus, Robert Hoy.

Crapps—Horace, Henry, Ansel.

Crout—Uriah.

Derrick — Jesse D., Enos, Billia A.

Drafts—Daniel, Franklin.

Eargle—Wesley, Ezelle, Ralph, Vivian, Van.

Epting—Carlos.

Frick—Blandon.

Fulmer—Lamar.

Hallman—Johnnie L., Marrel.

Hendrix—Ray Allen, Ralph.

Hite — Allen, Lomie, Noah, Luther.

Keisler—J. Walter, J. Ralph.

Oswald—Jacob B.

Oxner—Rufus L., Gordon N.

Price—D. Henry, Edgar.

Risinger—Adam, Jacob, Irvin, Pierce, Erie, Charley, Leonard, Monroe, Waldo.

Roberts—Richard.

Sease—Frederick.

Shealy—Lewis, Geor. R., Pressley, J. A. E., Sydney F., J. Fred, F. Pierce, James R., Mark.

Swygert—Zeddo, Enoch, Viera, Carl, Robert, Gurney, Anglo.

Taylor—Cleveland, Harley.

A WORSHIP SERVICE (NOVEMBER, 1951)

CEDAR GROVE CHURCH ROLL

John S. Addy
David Addy
David Addy, Jr.
Robert I. Addy
Daniel M. Addy
James D. Addy
Chesley M. Alewine
Elijah E. Amick
I. D. Alewine
Martin V. Addy
Catharine Addy
Eliza Addy
Sara Addy
Louisa Addy
Martha A. Addy
Jane L. Alewine
Emily U. Alewine
Harriet E. Amick
Elizabeth Anderson
Mary Caroline
    Amick
Laura L. Addy
O. B. Addy
E. H. Addy
Thomas Addy
Nora Addy
Andrew L. Addy
Hassie Addy
Lena Addy
Josie Addy
Brice Addy
Bryan Addy
Evans Addy
Mrs. Eve Addy
Clarence Addy
Mrs. Rose Addy
Mrs. Mary Addy
Alvin Roy Addy
Louise Addy
Evelyn Addy
Carrol E. Addy
Mrs. Carroll Addy
Henry E. Addy
Myrtle S. Addy
F. L. Addy
Lillie Addy

Curtis Addy
Mrs. Curtis Addy
Mrs. Elizabeth Addy
Mrs. Caroline Addy
Dr. W. L. Addy
Bunyan Asbill
Cora Asbill
Pearl Asbill
Jane Amick
Nezzie Amick
Artemus Alewine
Celia Addy
Polly Addy
Martha Addy
Daniel Addy
James D. Addy
Mary Addy
Simeon L. Addy
Elias Addy
Pressley Addy
Walter Addy
Pearl Edna Addy
Henry Adams
Rufus Adams
Leila Adams
Quilla Alewine
Willie Alewine
Jesse B. Adams
Lucy Adams
Edy Adams
James C. Adams
Sadie Adams
Gurney Adams
Heyward Adams
Oren Adams
Ina Adams
Mozelle Addy
Loraine Addy
Freddie Adams
Gwendolyn Addy
A. Roy Asbill
Madge Addy
Maude Asbill
Fay Adams
Frank Addy, Jr.
Kemmel Addy

Leta Amick
Fay Amick
J. P. Amick
Leon Addy
Rhett Addy
Boyd Adams
Merl Ellen Addy
Annie Laura Addy
Wright Evans Addy
H. Lathan Addy
Thomas Curtis Addy
Roxie E. Addy
Grace Addy
Eva M. Amick
T. Harold Amick
Myrtle A. Amick
Edith Adams
Dorris C. Addy
Eddilene Addy
Hubert Clay Amick
Omurl Adams
Robert Addy
Charlie C. Addy
Melvin Adams
Omar H. Adams
Joyce A. Arnold
Rayford L. Arnold
Clyde Lee Adams
Norman R. Adams
Earl O. Addy
Miriam Adams
Annie Mae Adams
Robert Amick
Thomas Amick, Jr.
J. H. Adams, Jr.
Donald Addy
Judith Asbill
Ray Amick
Dalton Addy
Mrs. Dalton Addy
Carroll Addy, Jr.
Mrs. Thom. C. Addy
Nelson Addy
Mrs. Nelson Addy
Lloyd Addy
Mrs. Lloyd Addy

Theo Addy
Mrs. Theo Addy
J. D. Addy
Dixon U. Addy
Mrs. Dixon U. Addy
Corray Addy
Harvelle Addy
Simeon Addy
W. L. Addy
Owen Anderson
Frances Addy
Rae Addy
Roy Asbill
Harry Asbill
Estelle Addy
Elsie Adams
Guy Addy
Robert Amick
H. Clayburn Amick
Mrs. H. Clayburn
  Amick
Frances E. Amick
Herbert C. Amick
Caroline Amick, Sr.
Jane Amick
Laura Amick
Elizabeth Amick
Caroline Amick, Jr.
Ruth Addy
Ethel Addy
Carrie Addy
Louisa Boland
Doscar Boatwright
Lillie Boatwright
Lester Black
Cellee Black
Ressie Black
Etta Black
Elmore Black
Harden Black
Kenneth Black
Oza Black
Estelle Boland
Geraldine Black
Annette P. Black
Dial Black
Leta O. Black
Von L. Black

Theresa Black
Lester Boatwright
Maude Black
Fay Black
E. J. Black
J. F. Black
Leta O. Black
Martha Boozer
Allie Mae Boozer
Efu Black
Retha Black
Ozelle Black
Mrs. A. J. Black
J. T. Black
Leonard Black
Elmore J. Black
Leorane Black
A. O. Banks
Alice Bedenbaugh
Louisa Brison
Jeremiah Crout
Uriah Crout
David Crout
Henry L. Crout
Richard Crout
Simeon Craps
Henry H. Craps
Jacob Crout
Caleb I. Crout
Jacob T. Crout
Samuel Craps
Levi Crout
Lorenza Crout
Edwin Caughman
Henry L. Caughman
Daniel A. Caughman
Thomas Cason
Anne Cason
Sarah Crout
Eliza Crout
Eleanor Crout
Sophia Crout
Caroline Crout
Lavina Crout
Emily Crout
Sarah Crout
Mary Crout
Elizabeth Crout

Celia Crout
Rachel Craps
Mary Ann Craps
Julian Craps
Barbara Craps
Anna M. Craps
Sibian Crout
Caroline Craps
Polly Crout
Lorena Crout
Lucinda Crout
Lanorah Crout
Gracy E. Craps
Elizabeth Chumpiard
Anna Chumpiard
Evilene Crout
Rosy C. Craps
Ann Crout
Ann Caughman
Geo. P. Craps
Evilene Craps
Lonnie E. Craps
John E. Craps
Maude Craps
Butler L. Craps
Mrs. Butler L. Craps
Elon Craps
Lillie Craps
Newton Craps
Truman Craps
Beatrice Craps
Voigt Craps
Mary Jane Craps
Blanche Charles
Horace N. Craps
Mattie Craps
J. Ansel Caughman
Calvin B. Caughman
Mattie Caughman
Raymond Caughman
Rose Caughman
Iva Caughman
Henry M. Caughman
Lessie Caughman
Yancy Caughman
Virgie Caughman
Florence Caughman
Lamar Caughman

Jesse Caughman
Andrew Caughman
Irvin Caughman
Jane Caughman
Geo. E. Caughman
Mae Caughman
Maxcy Craps
Mrs. Maxcy Craps
Hoyt Craps
Loraine Craps
Ansel Craps
Francis Caughman
Monroe Caughman
Frances Caughman
Ruby Caughman
Juanita Craps
Lambert Caughman
Grace Caughman
Birdie Mae Craps
H. Edward Craps
Runnette Craps
Etaline Craps
Katherine Craps
Edsel Caughman
Dial W. Craps
Orel Craps
Nola Craps
Preston N. Craps
Carl W. Craps
Clement Geo. Craps
Geo. Craps, Jr.
Mildred D. Craps
F. Derril Craps
Helen K. Craps
Harold Craps
Etolia Craps
Cline Craps
Edwin F. Caughman
Daniel Ansel
    Caughman
Henry F. Caughman
M. J. Ann
    Caughman
Charley Caughman
Broadus Caughman
Juanita Caughman
Robert F. Caughman

Robert Hoy
    Caughman
Virginia Caughman
J. E. Caughman
Alma Caughman
Fay Cato
Azilea Caughman
Glenn Craps
Gertrude Craps
Seth L. Craps
M. Doris Craps
Mrs. Ethan Cook
Ethan Cook
Hattie Craps
Mary Craps
Willie Craps
John Craps
Jimmie Craps
Jason Craps
Carrie Craps
Lizzie Craps
Lula Craps
Nezzie Craps
Jacob Crim
Mary Crim
Estelle Crim
Amanda Crim
Elizabeth Crim
Shelton Crim
Ella Crim
Elizabeth Davis
Eliza Davis
Amanda Davenport
S. F. Davis
Joseph Davis
Shuford Davis
Daniel Drafts
H. E. Drafts
Geo. M. Drafts
Walter Derrick
Julian Drafts
Eliza B. Drafts
Maria A. Drafts
Jacob F. Drafts
Sarah M. Drafts
Anne Drafts
Jefferson Drafts
S. P. Drafts

John Drafts
Irvin Drafts
Sallie Derrick
Nezzie Davis
Alvin Davis
Minnie Davis
Agnes Davis
Lizzie Drafts
Wendley Drafts
Otis Lee Drafts
George Drafts
Ethel Drafts
Clarendon Drafts
J. Franklin Drafts
Geo. Drafts, Jr.
Marion Derrick
Cecil Drafts
Mrs. Cecil Drafts
Victor Derrick
Otis O. Drafts
Polly Drafts
Daniel Drafts, Jr.
Marjorie Derrick
Maude Lee Davis
Berley Derrick
Martha B. Derrick
Pat Derrick
Nelda Derrick
Patricia Ann Drafts
Leopard Derrick
Eddie Derrick
Jesse Derrick
Nina Derrick
Enos Derrick
Thelma Derrick
Marvis Derrick
Georgia Derrick
Vineta Derrick
Bachman Derrick
Billy Derrick
Willie Derrick
Lillie Belle Davis
Annie Lou Duffie
Myrtle Derrick
Joe Sammy Derrick
J. M. Dowd
Mrs. Berley Derrick

Mrs. Karl Ray
    Derrick
Jacob Earhart
Frederick Eargle
A. L. Eargle
Henry E. Eargle, Sr.
Irvin Eargle
Sarah Ann Eargle
Nancy H. Eargle
Rodella E. Eargle
Henry E. Eargle
Pressley Eargle
Nancy Eargle
Leila Eargle
Ralph M. Eargle
Annie Eargle
Ezelle Eargle
Imo Eargle
Edgar Eargle
Jessie Eargle
Gordon Eargle
Daisy Eargle
Henry A. Eargle
Satcher Eargle
W. P. Eargle, Jr.
Fannie Eargle
Van Eargle
Myrtle Eargle
Wesley Eargle
Maggie Eargle
Catherine Eargle
W. E. Eargle, Jr.
Vivian Eargle
Mabel Eargle
Sedecia Eargle
Victoria Eargle
Jane Eargle
Oscar Eargle
Jason Eargle
Quilla Eargle
Florence Eargle
Jesse Eargle
Minick Eargle
Charlotte Earhart
Tally Earhart
Carrie Epting
Carlos Epting
David Epting

Mrs. David Epting
Edgress Eargle
Azilea Eargle
Marjorie Epting
Margaret F. Eargle
Iris Rose Eargle
Mary Louise Eargle
Delancy Eargle
J. Maxie Eargle
J. Pressley Eargle
Joyce E. Eargle
Violet Epting
Omar Eargle
Eldon R. Eargle
Lois E. Eargle
Mary Nelle Eargle
Janelle Eargle
Walter H. Eargle
Mrs. J. B. Eudy
W. Cline Epting
Andrew Eargle
Laura Eargle
Henry Eargle, Jr.
Bertha Eargle
Charley Eargle
Mary Fikes
Martha Fikes
David Fikes
Beulah Fikes
Ezra Fikes
C. L. Fulmer
Evelyn Fulmer
Gladys Fulmer
Jared A. Fikes
Blandon Frick
Mrs. Blandon Frick
Mrs. Woodrow Frick
Mrs. Ozier Gantt
Mrs. Douglas
    Gedding
James Goff
Martha Goff
Etta Goff
M. C. Goff
Mary Ann Goff
Caroline Goff
Joseph Hite
Martha A. Hite

N. H. Hite
Davis Hite
Sarah Hite
Emma Hite
Allen Hite
Renna Hite
J. C. Hite
Marie Hite
Enoch Hite
D. I. Hite
Dona Hite
Minnie Hite
Lillie Hite
Paul Hite
Mary Hite
Hassie Hite
Luther Hite
Catherine Hare
Amanda Hare
W. H. Hare
Alethia Hite
Elberta Hite
Trannie Hite
Noah Hite
Mrs. Noah Hite
Lomey Hite
Carrie Hite
Elizabeth Hallman
J. L. Hallman
Ophelia Hallman
Marrel Hallman
Lizzie Hallman
Edna Harman
Perry Harman
W. H. Hare
D. T. Hare
Mary Hare
John W. Hare
Wilson Hallman
George Hallman
George Hallman, Sr.
Chesley I. Hallman
Simon Hallman
Patrick Hallman
Martin Hallman
Mary Hallman
Ellen I. Hallman
Simeon Hallman

Samuel Hallman
Aberhart Hallman
Butler Hallman
Jesse Hallman
Christenah Hallman
Levina Hallman
Hepsibah Hallman
Elizabeth Hallman
Eliza Hallman
T. Etta Hallman
Ady Hallman
Luther Hallman
Mrs. Luther
    Hallman
Hinkle Hallman
John Bell Hite
Clayton Hite
D. W. Hite
Amanda Hite
Jane Lybrand Hite
P. W. Hite
Sedecia Hite
Estelle Hite
Wrightman Hite
Ethel Hite
Bertha Hite
Nezzie Hite
Oscar Hite
Joseph Hite, Jr.
D. A. Hendrix
Mattie Hendrix
Ralph A. Hendrix
Lala Hendrix
David Hendrix
Ray Allen Hendrix
Annie Mae Hendrix
Ralph Hendrix, Jr.
Hazelle Hallman
Hartley Hallman
Mrs. Hartley
    Hallman
Miley Hallman
Clarice Hite
Roaslea Hall
Nell Sue Hyler
Hoy Hyler
Price W. Hite
Elmer E. Hendrix

Rebecca O. Hallman
George Hallman
Vivian Hallman
J. T. Hallman
Bettie Hallman
Charles Hendrix
Mary Alma Hite
Von Ray Hite
D. A. Jumper
Billy Hite
Watts Hite
Nelda Hite
Amy Rose Hite
Mrs. Clayton Hite
W. Henry Hare
Amanda Hare
Kellar A. Hallman
Florie Hallman
Nissie Hallman
Sallie Hite
John Hite
Eliza Hite
Sarah Hite
Arrie Hite
Effie Hite
Nora Hite
Virgie Hite
Adelphus Hite
Hassie Hite
Pollie Hite
Vera Hite
Inez Hite
Belle Hite
Alethia Hite
Ruth Estelle
    Howard
Laura Jumper
A. P. Jumper
Mary Jumper
Brady Jumper
Mrs. Brady Jumper
Carrol Jumper
Mrs. Carrol Jumper
Maxcy Jumper
Grace Jumper
Ruby Mae Jumper
D. Ray Jumper
Olin D. Jumper

Helen I. Jumper
Morgan O. Jumper
Russell Jumper
Mrs. Russel Jumper
Evelyn Jumper
Bobby Jumper
Wilford Jumper
Franklin Johns
Tyre Johns
Lillian Jumper
Alice Jumper
Jessie Jumper
Corrie Jumper
Lott Jumper
Irodine Jumper
J. Walter Keisler
Ann Keisler
D. S. Keisler, M. D.
Mrs. D. S. Keisler
D. Edd Keisler
Carrie Keisler
Lewie Keisler
John Keisler
Lillie Keisler
Reed L. Keisler
Laura Keisler
Thelma Keisler
J. Ralph Keisler
Mrs. J. Ralph Keisler
Betty C. Keisler
Julian R. Keisler
Mrs. Julian R.
    Keisler
Mrs. Homer Keisler
J. Mims Keisler
Joan Keisler
G. J. Keisler
Lester Keisler
Thelma Keisler
Legare Keisler
Mrs. Legare Keisler
Mrs. Emmerson
    Keisler
Leo Von Keisler
Ray Keisler
Julia Kaminer
John A. Koon
Robert Fay Kyzer

Irvin Kyzer
Rosalyn Kyzer
Sara Kelley
Wilburn D. Kelley
Mary E. Kelley
Mary Elon Keisler
Irvin S. Keisler
Annie L. Keisler
Lila Koon
Pearl Koon
Joseph I. Kyzer
McCoy Kyzer
Mrs. McCoy Kyzer
S. M. Kyzer
T. M. Kinard
Rama Kinard
Missouri Koon
Brenton Keisler
Frank Leaphart
Pierce Leaphart
Alice Leaphart
Viola Leaphart
Daniel Leaphart
Jacob Long
Elliot Long
John Leaphart
Foster Leaphart
Mary Leaphart
Berley Leaphart
Emanuel Lominack
James Lominack
Wilkes Lominack
Mary Lominack
Polly Lominack
Elizabeth Lominack
Martha Lominack
Martha Ann Long
Laura E. Long
Nancy Lominack
Lilla Langford
W. D. Long
Ridona V. A. Long
Eugenia Long
Abner Long
Alice Long
Belton Long
Mrs. Belton Long
John Long

Enese Long
Drayton J. Long
Eva Mae Long
Rembert Long
Jimmy L. Long
Noah D. Long
Dallie Long
Edward Long
Noah D. E. Long
Jimmie Long
Mary Leaphart
Julia Leaphart
John Leaphart
Berley Leaphart
Alonzo Lown
Harold Long
Mrs. Harold Long
Samuel C. Lybrand
Sedecia Lybrand
J. H. E. Lybrand
Ella Lybrand
Willie Lybrand
Ollie Lybrand
Minnie Lybrand
Zula Lybrand
Annie Lybrand
Elot L. Long
Jacob Lybrand
Daisy Fay Long
Myrtle Long
Eugene Lewis
Mary Lewie
Joe Lindler
Harriet Lindler
Emma Lindler
Girlie Lindler
Henry Lindler
James Lewie
John R. Moore
John A. Moore
Robert C. Moore
July Ann Moore
John T. Moore
Tommy Mack
Mrs. Tommy Mack
J. Wynn Morgan
Henry Morgan
Carrol I. Morgan

Jesse Morgan
Charles Morgan
Etha Metts
Leila Morgan
Ola Mae Mack
Maggie Norris
Wade Oswald
Daniel Oswald
Emanuel Oswald
J. B. Oswald
Samuel Oswald
W. P. Oswald
N. V. Oswald
D. L. Oswald
M. V. Oswald
Bertha Oswald
Rosa Oswald
Vernie Oswald
Viola Oswald
M. Helen Oswald
Ernestine Oswald
Brooks Oswald
Dona Oswald
Stella Oswald
Alethea Oswald
Bessie Oswald
Claudius Oswald
Lester Oswald
Cecil Oswald
Julian Oswald
Estelle Oswald
Odelle A. Oswald
Lewella Oswald
Bessie Lorene
Oswald
Lois Oswald
Ralph Oswald
Mazie Oswald
Bonnie Oswald
Lona Oswald
Rebecca E. Oswald
Mrs. Daniel Oswald
Rudolph Oswald
Grover Oswald
Harold Oswald
Tracis Oswald
Maxcy Oswald
Mertie Oswald

Willie Oswald
Thursey Oswald
Vernon Oswald
Mattie Oswald
Melbourne Oswald
Jurisah Oswald
Nettie Oswald
Cora Oswald
Daniel Oxner
Nathaniel Oxner
Rosannah Oxner
Celia Oxner
Mary L. Oxner
Eliza Oxner
Jane Oxner
Annis Oxner
Henry N. Oxner
Naria Oxner
Amanda Oxner
Myrtle Oswald
M. L. Oxner
Laura Oxner
Gordon Oxner
Rachael Oxner
Leroy Oxner
Alma Oxner
Lula Mae Oxner
Jessie Oxner
Anne Oxner
Corley Oxner
Woodrow Oxner
J. B. Oxner
George Oxner
Willie Oxner
Cletus Oxner
Mrs. Cletus Oxner
Voigt Oxner
Rufus L. Oxner
Blanche Oxner
Ralph Oxner
Ruth Oxner
Catherine Oxner
Bryce Oxner
Martha Price Oxner
Lala Pressley
Lloyd Pressley
D. H. Price
Bertha Price

Aster Price
Carrie Lee Price
Vernon Price
Brady Price
Seth Price
Eulus Price
Guy Price
Ozilee Black Price
Ollie Price
Mrs. Ollie Price
L. Edgar Price
Mrs. L. Edgar Price
Vernon C. Price
Crosson Price
Marvin Price
Everette Price
Melvin Price
Voigt Price
Eleanor Price
Bruce Price
Charley Price
Jeff. Price
Ray Price
Ellen E. Price
Kenneth E. Price
Myrtle Price
Dora Price
James E. Price
J. Ollie Price, Jr.
Duran Price
Hayne A. Price
Hubert E. Price
Norric C. Price
Connie Price
Louise Price
Marvin O. Price
Melvin N. Price
Joyce M. Price
Rillie Mae Price
Betty Ann Price
Lucy Price
Martha Ann Price
Elizabeth Price
Mary Ann Rice
Permelia Rice
Van O. Rice
Noah Rice
Bettie Rice

Eliza Rice
Walter Rice
Cora Rice
Mrs. Walter Rice
Ollie Ricard
Roof Ricard
Jetha Ricard
Mrs. Roof Ricard
Don Riley
Murray Ricard
Delano Ricard
Mrs. Murray Ricard
Algie Ricard
Murray Ricard, Jr.
Perkins Ricard
Chauncey Ricard
Loy Ricard
Gladys N. Ricard
Pascall Ricard
Maude Ricard
John D. Riley
Mrs. John D. Riley
James L. Riley
Edith V. Riley
Geo. I. Riley
Mrs. Geo. I. Riley
Mary K. Riley
Adam Risinger
Miley Risinger
Noah Risinger
Wesley Risinger
David Risinger
Barbara Risinger
Catherine Risinger
Mary Risinger
Mittie Risinger
Elizabeth Risinger
Lottie Risinger
Ira Risinger
Perry Risinger
Jency Risinger
Edy Risinger
Tera Risinger
Elizabeth Risinger
George Risinger
Irvin Risinger
Savilla Risinger
Eufala Risinger

Erastus Risinger
Hattie Risinger
Jacob Risinger
Debbie Risinger
Festus Risinger
Laura Risinger
Ethel I. Risinger
Ola Risinger
Genus Risinger
Mrs. Genus Risinger
Charley Risinger
Edna Risinger
Erie Risinger
Hattie Risinger
Pierce Risinger
Belle Risinger
Gairy Risinger
Mertice Risinger
Virginia Risinger
Mamie L. Risinger
Clara M. Risinger
Thos. C. Risinger
James W. Risinger
Waldo Risinger
Grace Risinger
Ralph Risinger
Leonard F. K.
   Risinger
Mrs. Thomas
   Risinger
Lillie Belle Risinger
Malcom Risinger
Mrs. Ralph Risinger
Lois Risinger
Cleo Risinger
Virginia Risinger
Lewie S. Risinger
Morris Risinger
Nelson Risinger
Rhett Risinger
Mrs. Rhett Risinger
Connie Mae Rice
Van Omar Rice
Mrs. Malcom
   Risinger
Monroe Risinger
Virgil Risinger
Gary Risinger, Jr.

Bessie L. Risinger
Sarah Lou Risinger
James Ricard
Lessie Ricard
Lila Ricard
Robert Rivers
Sibbie Rivers
David Rivers
Mary Rivers
Henry Rivers
Ezra Rivers
Victoria Rivers
Jeremiah Rawl
Achsa Rawl
Franklin Rawl
Lizzie Rawl
Missouri Rawl
Ada Rawl
O. D. Rawl
Patrick Rawl
Lady Rawl
S. Kearney Roof
Lester Oda Roof
Rev. L. O. Roof
Mrs. L. O. Roof
Rev. F. K. Roof
Mrs. F. K. Roof
Naomi Roof
Fay Roof
Gladys Roof
Ruby A. Risinger
Irvin Risinger
Herbert Risinger
Mittie Rose Risinger
Dorothy D. Risinger
Wyman Risinger
Roddey Roberts
Girlie Roberts
Famous C. Roberts
Enos Roberts
Mrs. Enos Roberts
Richard Roberts
Ruby Roberts
Leopard Roberts
Alline Roberts
Lillie Mae Roberts
Vertilla Roberts
Geneva Roberts

Wilma Roberts
Eliza Shealy
Bennet Shealy
Wiley Shealy
Lewis Shealy
Ephraim Shealy
Noah Shealy
Tyre Shealy
M. W. Shealy
Geo. R. Shealy
Presley S. Shealy
Walter R. Shealy
Jeff D. Shealy
Paul Shealy
Gracy Ann Shealy
Elizabeth C. Shealy
Rosy Shealy
Ruthy Ann Shealy
Ava Shealy
Alvin G. Shealy
Sidney L. Shealy
Ralph G. Shealy
Mrs. Ralph G. Shealy
F. L. Shealy
Bessie Shealy
Ernest B. Shealy
Sam T. Shealy
Susie Shealy
Fred Shealy
Arthur R. Shealy
Frederick Sease
Elizabeth Sease
Anna Sease
Samuel Sease
Elias Sease
James Wily Sease
Jacob Sease
Daniel Sease
Permelia Sease
Francis Sease
Rodella Shealy
Laura Shealy
Hasten Shealy
Reuben Shealy
Grady Shealy
Theresa Shealy
Myrtle Shealy
Grace Shealy

Silas A. Shealy
Birdie E. Shealy
Broy Shealy
Lois Shealy
F. G. Shealy
J. R. Shealy
Nettie Shealy
Gussie Shealy
Elmetta Shealy
J. Fred Shealy
Wesley Shealy
Blanche Long
  Shealy
Heber Shealy
Mrs. Heber Shealy
Evetta Shealy
Clyde Shealy
J. D. Shealy
Gillis Shealy
Marion Shealy
Pauline Shealy
G. Ryan Shealy
Mrs. G. Ryan Shealy
Quilla Shealy
Minerva Shealy
Ruthy Shealy
Kate Shealy
Frances Shealy
Pearly Shealy
Eva Shealy
Achsa Shealy
Wendell Shealy
Rhett Shealy
Betty Metts Shealy
Luther C. Shealy
Matthew Shealy
Nezzie Shealy
Lillian Shealy
Kenneth Shealy
Rodella Shealy
Vida Shealy
Thurman Shealy
Omega Shealy
S. L. Shealy, Jr.
Lomey Shealy
David Shealy
Pierce Shealy
Lucinda Shealy

Lemuel Shealy
Eli Shealy
Jemima Shealy
Louisa Shealy
Henry Shealy
Oreta Shealy
Thos. R. Shealy
Addie Shealy
Carrol A. Shealy
Geo. A. Shealy
Annie Lela Shealy
Quilla Shealy
M. Clinton Shealy
Forest L. Shealy
Sallie Sawyer
Etha Swygert
Rene Swygert
Omega Shealy
Thurmond Shealy
Clarence Smith
Mittie C. Swygert
Ruby Lee Swygert
Grover Shealy
Frances G. Shealy
Elma Swygert
Gussie V. Swygert
Mark Shealy
Caroline Shealy
W. K. Shealy
Preston Shealy
Gilman Shealy
D. Brona Shealy
Bessie S. Shealy
Rufus E. Shealy
J. A. E. Shealy
Monroe Shealy
Grover Smith
Sally B. Smith
Luther Smith
Agnes Smith
Minnie Smith
John Z. Swygert
Emanuel Z. Swygert
Enoch Swygert
Mitty Ann Swygert
Edy Swygert
Corrie C. Swygert
E. Z. (Bud) Swygert

Vertie Swygert
John Z. Swygert
Inez Swygert
Anglo Swygert
Lois Swygert
Gurney Swygert
Wakefield Swygert
John D. Swygert
Geo. W. Swygert
Cattie Swygert
Sallie Swygert
Edy Swygert
Margaret Swygert
Viena Swygert
Franklin Swygert
Dorothy Swygert
Francis Swygert
Noma Swygert
Melvin Swygert
Hennis Swygert
Wilson Swygert
Mrs. Wilson
  Swygert
Yoder J. Swygert
Lula Swygert
Viera Swygert
Lovelle Swygert
Robert L. Swygert
Delores Swygert
Marvin Swygert
Jane Swygert
Carl W. Swygert
Sadie Swygert
Verley Swygert
Ezetle Swygert
Lula Ray Swygert
Essie Swygert
Rean Swygert
Elma Swygert
Mittie Swygert
Jacob Swygert
Clara Swygert
Ida Swygert
Louannie Swygert
Lena Swygert
Cornelia Swygert
Deward Swygert
Martha Swygert

Marvin Swygert
Claudia Swygert
Wilford Swygert
Aubrey Swygert
Annie Swygert
M. L. Swygert
Geo. A. Shealy
Grover Shealy
Malinda Shealy
Bud Smith
George Souter
Willie Sanford
Mayme Sanford
Fanny Shirey
L. May Shirey
Callie Shirey
Vera Shirey
Lucinda Son
Lavina Son
Mary Son
Etta Son
Josephine Son
Geo. W. Son
James A. Son
John J. Son
Isaiah J. Son
David M. Son
Christena Son
Mary E. Son
Miley L. Son
Meransa Son
Elizabeth Son
Catherine Son
Cecil Steele
Helen Steele
Faythe Steele
Henry Steele
Ida Steele
Sallie Steele
E. J. Sawyer
Eugene Stockman
Laura Stockman
Edgar Stockman
Lamar Stockman
May Stockman
Gairy Stockman
Samuel Stockman
Amanda Stockman

Elizabeth Shumpard
Anna Shumpard
Jacob Shumpard
Reba Snelgrove
Justus Snelgrove
Marian G. Snelgrove
Betty Snelgrove
Geo. M. Souter
J. J. Seastrunk
Frances Seastrunk
Gordon Seastrunk
Lonnie G. Stowers
Mrs. Lonnie G.
   Stowers
J. J. Summers
Wilbur Summers
Fannie Summers
Lula Summers
Esther Summers
Henry Summers
Alice Strickland
Gersedda S-circle
Frederick Sease
F. M. Sease
W. I. Son
G. F. Son
Permelia Sease
Elizabeth Sease
Mary Ann Sease
Jacob Taylor
Reba Taylor
David Taylor
Aaron Taylor
Wilson Taylor
Joel Taylor
Reuben Taylor
William Taylor
Emsley Taylor
James I. Taylor
Franklin Taylor
Vastine Taylor
Sibby Taylor
Thelitha Taylor
Margaret Taylor
Martha Taylor
Sara Ann Taylor
Catherine Taylor
Artemissa Taylor

Celia Taylor
Jasper Taylor
Henry E. Taylor
A. B. Taylor
Louana Taylor
Ella Taylor
Loderick Taylor
Elvie Taylor
Georgian Taylor
Sidney Taylor
Sallie Taylor
Mertise Taylor
Moses Taylor
Perry Taylor
Pickens Taylor
Nezzie Taylor
Birdie Taylor
Jessie Taylor
Rose Taylor
Addy Taylor
W. F. Taylor
Harley Taylor
Pearl Taylor
Winford Taylor
Henry Taylor
Rose E. Taylor
Martha E. Taylor
Nannie Lou Taylor
Emma Ruth Taylor
Raymond Taylor
Earl Taylor
Lillie R. Taylor
Gladys Taylor
Jefferson Taylor
Elizabeth Taylor
Amanda Taylor
Permelia Taylor
Shelton Taylor
Lloyd Taylor
Eula Taylor
Maxcy Taylor
Cleveland Taylor
Julia Taylor
Rosalie Taylor
Tillman Taylor
Mrs. Tillman Taylor
Vera Taylor
Columbus Taylor

Walter Taylor
Mrs. Walter Taylor
Erskine Taylor
Ann M. Taylor
Virgie L. Taylor
Emanuel Taylor
Barbara Taylor
Marshall Taylor
Jacob Calvin
  Wesinger
Mary Ruth Taylor
Thelma Taylor
Genelle Taylor
J. Wesley Taylor
Gernice Taylor
Wilmer L. Taylor
Herman Taylor
Adam J. Taylor
Verley Taylor
Ruth Taylor

Hazel Taylor
J. W. Taylor
J. Gerstle Taylor
Ella Lou Taylor
Sarah Ruth Taylor
J. P. Taylor
Evelyn R. Taylor
Nola Frances Taylor
Carmise Taylor
Herman Taylor
Virgie L. Taylor
Marie Ann Taylor
Barbara Ann Taylor
Simeon Taylor
Rufus Taylor
Oda Taylor
Essie Taylor
Arrie Taylor
Lilla Taylor
Mariah Taylor

Nutty Vansant
Addison Vansant
Ernest Wheeler
Monroe Wheeler
Evelyn Wheeler
Mattie Lee Wheeler
Geneva Wheeler
Birdie Whiteside
Horace Whiteside
Doris Whiteside
Dorothy S.
  Wessinger
Nevin Whiteside, Jr.
Daisy Watson
Martha Warren
Annie Williamson
Cleveland Taylor,
  Jr.
Nevin Whiteside,
  Sr.

THE DEAD WHO ARE BURIED IN THE CEDAR GROVE CEMETERY

First Row:
  Milie Risinger
  Adam Risinger
  Mittie Risinger
  George Caughman, son of
    Levi
  Edy Risinger Addy Smith
  Gency Risinger Hallman
  Butler Hallman
  Debbie Taylor Risinger
  Jacob D. Risinger
  Jacob G. Risinger, child
  Ira Risinger
  Perry Risinger
  2
  J. W. Stockman, child
  Texana Stockman Hite
  3
  Ernest Wheeler
  Mary Sawyer Crim
  Jacob Crim
  Infant of W. F. Taylor
  1
  Emma Hite Taylor

Clifton Ricard
8
Chester Black's child
Chester Black's child
1
D. U. Addy
Corrie Crout Addy
Second Row:
  Julia Wingard Drafts
  Daniel Drafts
  Jacob Franklin Drafts
  Moses Drafts
  Ruth Drafts
  Infant of Dr. D. R. Kneece
  1
  Henry E. Drafts
  Sara E. Drafts
  Jacob F. Drafts, child
  Sarah Drafts, child
  Ora Drafts, child
  Etau Drafts, child
  Otis O. Drafts
  1
  Infant of Wendley O. Drafts

Robert Olin Shealy, child
Infant of J. W. Shealy
Infant of J. W. Shealy
Infant of J. W. Shealy
Infant of J. W. Shealy
Lizzie Shealy
Infant of B. E. Amick
J. Walter Shealy
Ann Caughman Shealy
Wrightman Taylor, child
Jonah Taylor, child
Infant of Shelton Taylor
Infant of Shelton Taylor
3
Lottie Frazier's child
Lottie Ruth Risinger Frazier
Lou Ellen Lybrand, child of
   J. H. E. L.
Third Row:
   Simeon Addy
   Hartley Hallman
   Mrs. Hartley Hallman
   Miley Hallman Shealy
   Sister of Rev. J. D. Shealy
   Madge Addy, child
   Leon Addy, child
   Lewie Addy, child
   E. H. Addy
   Mary Jane Addy
   Marshall Taylor
   Emanuel Taylor
   Barbara Rice Taylor
   Henry Taylor
   Permelia Rice Hendrix
   Jacob Taylor
   Georgian Price Taylor
   Inez Taylor
   Virgie Taylor, Dau. of Perry
   Rosannah Wise Craps
   Simeon W. Craps
   Jane Taylor Craps
   Sarah E. Jumper Rice
   Daniel Jumper
   Laura Craps Jumper
   Lott Jumper
   3
   Samuel Craps
   Sibbie Taylor Craps

Fourth Row:
   Mary Shealy Snelgrove
   Frederick Eargle
   Infant of Fred Eargle
   Ruth Shealy Eargle
   Tyre Shealy, Sr.
   Infant of Tyre Shealy
   Infant of Tyre Shealy
   Benjamin Snelgrove
   Mary Ann Shealy Snelgrove
   Nancy Eargle Jackson
   Hasten Shealy
   Child of Reuben Shealy
   Frances Lybrand Shealy
   Paul Shealy
   Eva Keisler Shealy
   James Shealy, son of Paul
   Charles Shealy, son of Paul
   Pearl Shealy
   Burtis Derrick, Dau. of
      W. H. D.
   Roy Derric, Son of W. H. D.
   Infant of Mrs. Belle Stephen
   Mildred Swygert
   Pressley Shealy
   Minerva Risinger Shealy
   Horace Abner Shealy
   Lula Craps Shealy
   3
   Sallie Taylor Steele Hite
   Lester Steele
   Mattie Epting Taylor
Fifth Row:
   Infant Crout child
   Henry Crout
   James Craps, son of W. C.
   John Wesley Crout
   Carrie Crout
   Harriet Crout
   Thomas Crout
   Mrs. Thomas Crout
   Nancy Rawl Eargle
   Sarah Rawl Shealy
   Michael Shealy
   Leila Faulkner Morgan
   Julia Lindler Shealy Kami-
      ner
   Enoch Swygert

Cornelia Adams Swygert
Mittie Swygert
Infant of E. Z. Swygert
Louannie Swygert Hagood
Irvin Swygert, child of
  G. W. S.
Grover Swygert, child of
  Y. J. S.
Edith Swygert, child of
  G. W. S.
Essie Swygert, child of
  G. W. S.
Pearle Sease, child of Sam S.
Infant of Henry Adam
  Eargle
Henry E. Eargle
Eliza Shealy Eargle
Eddress Eargle
Sixth Row:
  J. I. Craps, son of S. W. C.
  Martha Craps, Dau of
    S. W. C.
  Henry Craps, son of S. W. C.
  Geo. F. Craps, son of
    S. W. C.
  Ada Morgan, child of W. M.
  J. Wynn Morgan
  Grace Craps Morgan
  Henry Craps (Vault)
  Ada Addy Craps
  Carrie Craps Drafts Adams
  Luther King
  D. Irvin Drafts
  Jesse Morgan's child, Jesse
  Flora Morgan, Dau. of Henry
    M.
  Thomas Hare, child of
    D. T. H.
  Blanche Morgan, Dau. of
    H. M.
  Henry Morgan
  Amanda Hare Morgan
  John Walter Keisler
  Ann Crout Keisler
  Lee Craps, child of W. C.
  Frances Shealy
  Infant of Lomey Shealy
  Vida Derrick Shealy

2
Lucretia Lybrand
A. P. Jumper's child
A. P. Jumper's child
A. P. Jumper's child
A. P. Jumper
Seventh Row:
  Taylor child
  Taylor child
  Bennett Taylor
  Arabella Addy
  Mrs. Bennett Taylor
  Leila Oswald
  Taylor child
  Kara Wingard
  Sedecia Wingard
  D. Brona Shealy
  George Wingard
  Berley Long
  Ridona Craps Long
  Walter D. Long
  Laura Eargle Long
  Achsa Snelgrove Shealy
  George R. Shealy
  Rodella Lybrand Shealy
  Kizzah Oswald Anderson
  Loy Richard Taylor, son of
    T. T.
  Roy Robert Taylor, son of
    T. T.
4
Maxcy Jumper
2
Mary Leona Shirey
Keisler, son of Mrs. Jetha
  Keisler
Eighth Row:
  Della Son
  Infant of Solomon Son
  Infant child of O. B. Addy
  Ernest Addy, child of
    O. B. A.
  O. B. Addy
  Lenora Long Addy
  Luther Hallman's child
  Luther Hallman's child
  Luther Hallman's child
  Luther Hallman's child

Willie Oswalt
Thursay Risinger Oswalt
Lula Moore, child of R. C. M.
Noah Caughman
Child of Horace Craps
Child of Ben Boatwright
Edwin F. Caughman
Ellen Lybrand Taylor
   Caughman
4
Frances Hallman
Daniel Leaphart's child
2
Curtis Addy
Lizzie Ridgell Addy
Thomas Addy
Child of Clinton Oswald
Ninth Row:
   Lamanda Shealy
   Daniel Shealy
   Milie Shealy
   Lemuel Shealy
   Henry Shealy
   Polly Shealy
   Eli Shealy
   Wade Shealy
   David Shealy
   Jemima Shealy
   Louisa Addy Shealy
   Child of Davis Hite
   Child of Davis Hite
   Child of Davis Hite
   Marvin Davis
   Agnes Shealy Davis
   Raymond Davis
   Gladys Davis
   Rebecca Davis
   Lillie Craps
   Newton Craps
   Truman Craps
   Child of Truman Craps
   George P. Craps
   Evelyn Black Craps
   Brady Hite
   William Keisler
   3
Tenth Row:
   Katie Crout Son

Infant Rawl child
Lizzie Rawl
Achsah Crout Rawl
Jeremiah Rawl
Lady Rawl
Ada Rawl
Patrick Rawl
Lorena Crout
Polloy Crout
Polly Black Shealy
Amanda Shealy Hite
Walter Hite
Sedecia Hite
Merrick Hite
Dr. Pope W. Hite
Victoria Eargle Hite
Estelle Hite
Lucinda Shealy
F. Pierce Shealy
2
Mattie Stockman, child of
   S. S.
Samuel Stockman
Amanda Black Stockman
Wilber Stockman
Clinton Oswald
Lena Addy Oswald
Child of Frank Addy
Eleventh Row:
   Maggie Monts
   Henry Monts
   Sidney Summers
   Martha Fikes Goff Shealy
   James Goff
   Emanuel Taylor
   Artemissa Crout Taylor
   Belle Craps Hite
   1
Paul Hite
Mary Taylor Hite
Yoder Hite
Lillie Hite
Martha Ann Oxner Hite
Joseph Hite
Allen L. Hite
Turenna Jumper Hite
Eufala Davis Risinger
Irvin Risinger

Savilla Davis Risinger
James Risinger
Crosson Risinger
Erastus Risinger
Hattie Moore Risinger
3
Infant of Horace Snelgrove
Woodrow Snelgrove

BURIED IN FAMILY PLOTS
Reed L. Keisler
Laura Addy Keisler
Caroline Crout Addy
H. Lloyd Addy
Amanda Snelgrove Oxner
John A. E. Shealy
Louisa P. Shealy
Elizabeth Hallman Eargle
Infant, Mr. and Mrs. J. P.
   Swygert
Patricia Ann Jumper
James Rufus Shealy
John Summers
Infant, Mr. and Mrs. Wilber
   Summers
Infant, Mr. and Mrs. Wilber
   Summers
Infant, Mr. and Mrs. Wilber
   Summers
Geo. S. Drafts
Mary Caughman Swygert
Infant, Mr. and Mrs. William
   Swygert
Infant, Mr. and Mrs. F. Lester
   Shealy
Infant, Mr. and Mrs. F. Lester
   Shealy
Joseph H. E. Lybrand
Catherine Eargle Fulmer
Cora Risinger Asbill
Maude Asbill Price
Infant, Mr. and Mrs. Ray Price
Mildred Gantt
John Long, Jr.
Jefferson Taylor
Mary Jane Ricard Taylor
J. Moses Taylor
Roxie Taylor

Child, Mr. and Mrs. Maxcy
   Taylor
Child, Mr. and Mrs. Maxcy
   Taylor
Martha Oxner
Jacob Wilson Oxner
Infant, Mr. and Mrs. C. V.
   Addy
Luther C. Shealy
Pierce J. Risinger
French Brady Risinger
Mina Nicola Risinger
Daniel Blease Addy
Earl Ralph Addy
Infant, Mr. and Mrs. Sam T.
   Shealy
Johnie L. Hallman
Ophelia Jumper Hallman
Ervin Shuford Keisler
Dr. D. Socrates Keisler
Lula Craps Shealy
Permelia E. Shealy
Rosa Frick Shealy
Elmetta Fulmer Shealy
Andrew I. Shealy
Daniel Edwin Shealy
Jacob Bennet Oxner
Aminee Asbill Oxner
Infant Mr. and Mrs. J. B.
   Oxner
Verley O. Taylor
Adam Taylor
Elvy Taylor
Leila Mae Senn
L. Ruth Senn
Silas Shealy
Infant Mr. and Mrs. C. E.
   Caughman
Floy Aurelia Craps
Twin infants, Mr. and Mrs.
   Hoyt Craps
Infant Calvin C. Caughman
Trannie Bedenbaugh Long
James David Langford
Sibbie Crout Langford
Lucinda Moore Crout Derrick
Pierce Leaphart
Alice Long Leaphart

Cora Price Hite
Eleanor L. Hite
Noland V. Hite
Minnie Hite Ricard
Festus Risinger
Infant, Mr. and Mrs. M.
  Risinger
Jimmie G. Risinger
Sylvia Elizabeth Risinger
R. Rhett Risinger
James Theron Risinger
Gertrude Craps
John W. Black
Voigt Craps
Onelia Roberts
Charles Cody Lybrand
Leon Haskell Lybrand
Myrtle Oswald
Jacob Oswald
Mary Shealy Oswald
Noah Oswald
Charles E. Swygert
Infant Mr. and Mrs. Morgan
  Jumper
Mildred Louise Drafts
Mildred Louise Drafts
William Pressley Eargle
Leila Shealy Eargle
Willie Patrick Oswald
Frank Rawl
Edith Rawl
Willie O. Steele
Infant, Mr. and Mrs. W. O.
  Steele
H. D. Boozer
Ollie O. Boozer
Maximo Gomez Derrick
Leppard Scott Derrick
Sallie Shealy Derrick
Earnest Pickens Derrick
Willard L. Derrick
James Eugene Derrick
Infant. Mr. and Mrs. L. S.
  Derrick
Infant, Mr. and Mrs. Carl
  Craps
Samuel C. Lybrand
Gladys Lybrand

Infant, Mr. and Mrs. M. G.
  Craps
Infant Mr. and Mrs. Von
  Black
Marie Schumpert Black
Noah N. L. Long
Infant, Mr. and Mrs. C. E.
  Black
John Thomas Long
Lonnie Elonzo Craps
Infant, Mr. and Mrs. Henry
  Steele
W. Elmore Black
Etta Goff Black
Harden C. Black
Bessie Black
Mertie Frye Oswald
Tyre Lester Oswald
Infant, Mr. and Mrs. L. T.
  Oswald
E. Z. (Bud) Swygert
Vertie Swygert
Cora Oswald Rice
Myrtle Oswald, child
Emmerson (Bunk) Keisler
John David Craps
Butler Leo Craps
Infant, Mr. and Mrs. F. L.
  Stockman
D. Henry Price
Brady R. Price
Infant, Mr. and Mrs. Walter
  Taylor
Infant, Mr. and Mrs. Ethan
  Cook
Infant. Mr. and Mrs. Earl
  Taylor
Thomas I. Amick
Grandson T. I. Amick
Missouri Epting
D. Abb Hendrix
Mattie Seay Hendrix
Infant, Mr. and Mrs. Ray Allen
  Hendrix
Infant, Mr. and Mrs. Edgar
  Price
Infant. Mr. and Mrs. Clayton
  Hite

THE SUNDAY SCHOOL

CEDAR Grove Congregation organized a Sunday School in 1876 with Edwin Caughman as superintendent. The organized Sunday School in this country, we might say, is a modern institution. The earliest record of any Sunday School was about 1819. This institution did not get world recognition too fast, due to the fact that Sunday School literature was not available and, too, very few people were qualified to interpret the Scriptures.

I received my early Sunday School training in Union Evangelical Lutheran Congregation. This was the nearest church to me, and we had a good straw road to walk practically the entire distance.

My first teacher was Mrs. Susan Derrick Shealy, mother of Rev. Tillman W. Shealy. The study book used was not always religious. Our book was Webster's "blue-back speller" and Scripture verses to be memorized. The service was always begun with reading from the Scriptures, prayer, and gospel hymn singing. This made a lasting impression on the lives of young people, especially those who were spiritually inclined. We had Scripture verses printed on cardboard, called "tickets." We would preserve our tickets, when a number would accumulate, we would turn them in and be rewarded with a beautiful card, containing a favorite Scripture verse. These rewards were highly treasured. Our people around 70 and above still have these cards in their possession, and treasure them as dearly as the old Family Bible.

A lot of this early Sunday School training was done in local school buildings and in Christian homes. One of the delights of young people in that age, was to gather in Christian homes on Sunday afternoons for singing. The older men who were community leaders, would offer prayer after prayer and the young people gloried in Christian hymn singing. This was commonly called prayer meetings and singing.

I don't know who the other Sunday School leaders of Cedar Grove were prior to the nineties. D. Walter Hite was Cedar Grove Superintendent for a long time and his daughter, Estelle, was organist for Sunday School and church services.

Since 1905 Joseph Ansel Caughman served as Sunday School Superintendent for thirty-five years. Among those who have served as superintendents within my recollection have been C. I. Morgan, David Risinger, J. Walter Keisler, George C. Caughman, Yoder J. Swygert, Jacob J. Seastrunk, Henry M. Caughman, Theo Addy, Robert H. Caughman and Ansel Craps who is the present superintendent. There could have been others I can't recall just now. However, I am under the impression that W. H. Hare and O. B. Addy were once Sunday School superintendents. I am sure they were once choir leaders.

WOMEN OF THE CHURCH GROUP

WOMEN'S MISSIONARY SOCIETY OF CEDAR GROVE

THE first organization of the women of Cedar Grove Congregation was about 1906 and was known as the Ladies Aid Society. The only work that I recall of the Ladies Aid Society was the purchasing of the iron fence in front of the old parsonage.

Later this organization became known as the Women's Missionary Society. It continued to function in a way, having short monthly meetings until about 1921 when under the pastorship of Rev. W. D. Wise the organization put on new life and began to accomplish results.

According to the first available minutes, we find that Virgie Caughman was president and Mrs. W. D. Wise, secretary.

This organization continued to function with regular monthly meetings until about 1947. Among the presidents during this period we find the names of Virgie Caughman, Birdie Shealy, Hassie Addy, Mrs. L. O. Roof and Julia Taylor. The secretaries were Mrs. W. D. Wise, Mrs. Cleveland Taylor, Mrs. Birdie Shealy and Mrs. L. O. Roof. Also, Mrs. J. C. Hite, Mrs. Myrtle Addy, Mrs. Pearl Taylor, Mrs. Annie Eargle, Mrs. Enos Derrick, Mrs. Ray Allen Hendrix and Mrs. Edna Risinger.

Under the leadership of Mrs. Henry Addy, the Women's Missionary Society was divided into circles and is known as the Women of the Church. Mrs. J. C. Derrick was the first president, and Mrs. Carl Epting, secretary.

Under this new set-up the society was divided into six organizations known as circles, namely: Cedar Grove, Centerville, Old Field, Caney Branch, Delmar and Ridge Star.

The women now began to work proper, in addition to the missionary work done, they have accomplished quite a number of important projects for the benefit of the modern parsonage and the church.

Among the things furnished by the women as a whole are a refrigerator, electric stove, and venetian blinds for the parsonage.

Each individual circle has some project under consideration at all times. Already each has furnished quite a number of utensils for furnishing the church kitchen, ladies' lounge, etc.

Among some of the outstanding projects, we find the Ridge Star Circle provided shrubbery around the parsonage.

The Caney Branch Circle put two beautiful chairs in the ladies' lounge and a metal cabinet for the church kitchen, with a number of other items.

We note the Cedar Grove Circle has on its list of accomplishments a sink for the church kitchen and a credence table for the chancel.

The other circles have made valuable contributions to parsonage, church and grounds that I do not have at my finger-tips just at this time.

The Women's Council is made up of a general president, which at this time is Mrs. Russell Boggs; a vice-president, who is Mrs. Viera Swygert; a secretary, Mrs. Annie Eargle; and a treasurer, Mrs. Ray Allen Hendrix; and the six leaders, one from each circle.

The ladies of Cedar Grove deserve much commendation for their activity in all branches of church work.

CEDAR GROVE BROTHERHOOD

CEDAR GROVE BROTHERHOOD

THE Brotherhood of Cedar Grove Evangelical Lutheran Church, Leesville, S. C., was organized March 25, 1949. The officers elected at the organizational meeting were: Gurney Adams, president; Samuel Broadus Caughman, vice-president; Robert Hoy Caughman, secretary; Edward Craps, treasurer; Viera L. Swygert, extension secretary, with the Rev. J. Russell Boggs, advisor.

The following men were charter members: Boyd Adams, Gurney Adams, Oren Adams, Evans Addy, Theo Addy, J. Russell Boggs, S. B. Caughman, J. Ansel Caughman, Robert H. Caughman, Monroe Caughman, Ansel Craps, Edward Craps, H. N. Craps, Carl Craps, Seth Craps, Enos Derrick, J. F. Drafts,, Van Eargle, Vivian Eargle, Ralph Eargle, Carlos Epting, Marrel Hallman, Ray Allen Hendrix, C. W. Jumper, J. R. Keisler, Drayton Long, Gordon Oxner, Leroy Oxner, Rufus L. Oxner, Leonard Risinger, Viera Swygert and Yoder Swygert.

The Brotherhood meetings are held monthly. An invited speaker is usually the highlight of the gathering. A business meeting and a recreation period, with light refreshments are also enjoyed.

Finances

In addition to meeting its current expenses, the Brotherhood has secured for the pastor's study a steel filing cabinet; established road signs on Highways No. 1 and 43; secured a lawn mower for clipping lawns; had lawns mowed before buying a mower; bought school house and lot and fitted it for use in holding meetings, by wiring it for electric lights, furnishing a stove, etc.; wired church for lighting yard in front of church; adopted God's Brotherhood Acre Plan in 1951 and raised around $400.00 for Brotherhood work; finished cabinets in kitchen and provided $81.00 worth of material for kitchen use; bought athletic equipment for the young people of the church; also made Franklin Pierce Shealy an Honorary Life Member of the Brotherhood.

The aim and desire of the Cedar Grove Brotherhood is to get every male member of the congregation enlisted for brotherhood work.

At the 1951 Christmas season those in their declining years were remembered throughout the Cedar Grove community, also those handicapped by abnormalties, with baskets of gifts.

Our aim is to be of loving service to all humanity.

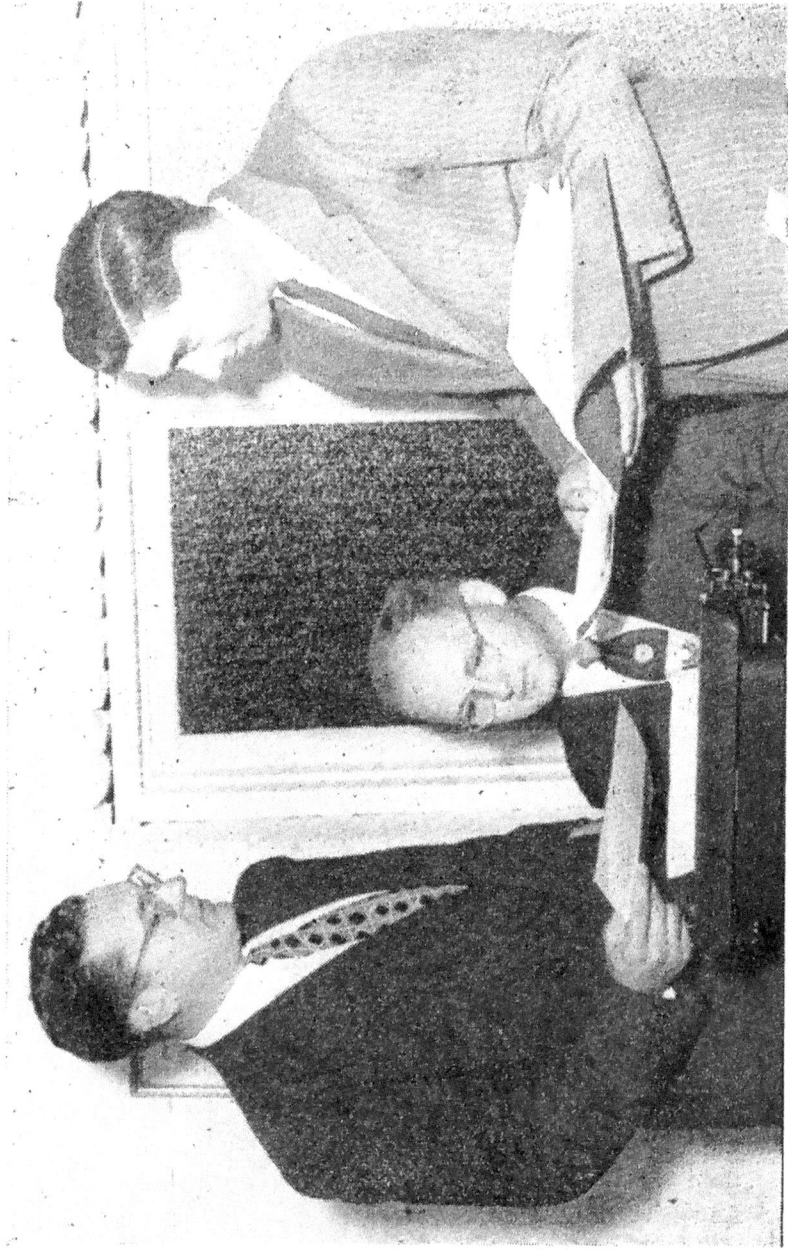

Peter J. Dexnis, evangelist; Hoy Caughman, chairman of local Evangelism Committee; and Pastor Boggs, reviewing evangelism reports.

CHOIR REHEARSAL AFTER PREACHING MISSION SERVICE

PREACHING MISSION STIRS CEDAR GROVE COMMUNITY

DURING the last week in September 1951, being the harvesting season in the rural south, the evangelist or missioner, the Rev. Peter J. Dexnis of the U. L. C. A. Board of Social Missions, preacher and song leader, conducted a wonderful series of meetings for one week.

The intention or design of the mission was to stir up the spiritual life of active church members, to get inactive members back to again hear and live the gospel and to win the lost to repentance and faith in Christ Jesus.

The mission was made thoroughly known to the individual and surrounding communities by news articles, pastoral letters, radio announcements and placards. A Congregational Evangelistic Committee made prayerful and effective plans.

Now let us see what results came from the foregoing preliminaries. A thirty-voice choir was augmented by Electronic Organ, piano and violin, all being expert musicians as leaders. In addition to this soul stirring music were the voices of hundreds in the great audience each night which added great volume to the sweet music.

The entire community for miles around, heard and participated in the singing of old favorite hymns as the amplification system broadcast the service for miles from Cedar Grove. Even the numerous tired negroes, with aching backs from picking cotton, lingered on their door steps and porches listening to their first Lutheran service, from their own homes. They were thrilled with the familiar hymns that were used. They joined in with the great throng of people at the church, in singing, from their own humble homes.

Men came from the Hydrogen Bomb Project seventy miles away, and even from the fields without supper, that they might be present for the entire service, didn't even want to miss the first song in the beginning of the service.

Three ministerial students from Newberry college traveled sixty miles each night, another student came 175 miles from Lenoir Rhyne college in North Carolina to attend the mission. Eight students at the Southern Lutheran Theological Seminary in Columbia, S. C., hearing of the splendid services, attended the last evening service. Visitors from all the towns and cities within a radius of 30 miles were present. Protestants of all faiths were thrilled with the spiritual activity that was displayed in these meetings. A good bunch of Baptists were present every night. They were heard making the statement, "They call it a 'Preaching Mission,' but we call it a 'real good old Baptist revival.'"

Scores of Cedar Grove members, who are real, plain, humble rural folks, never realized that they would ever be able to bear witness for Christ till they were spiritually revived themselves. We have evidence that more than 300 members testified or bore witness for Jesus by talking, calling or visiting.

Some who were physically unable to be moved, remained in their cars on the church grounds to hear the service over the loud speakers. People were carried bodily into the church or on wheel chairs to hear the Gospel preached.

For the six nights the order of worship was carefully planned, beginning with Vespers and ending with a song service in which the entire congregation participated, then an inspirational sermon.

A period of silence after each sermon gave the hearers the opportunity to make their decision.

Daily, Pastor Dexnis would meet with the Evangelism Committee to gather reports and give guidance.

At this season of the year, in the deep rural South where "Cotton is still King," people were not only utterly surprised, but overwhelmed by the results of this wonderful teaching mission.

Quite a number of requests were made to continue the meeting another week. It seemed unbelievable that such a throng of people could be enticed to come out every night after working hard all day, picking cotton, handling hay, and other pressing farm duties this busy season.

Scores in the congregations had never seen an adult baptism in a Lutheran Church, some outsiders had never seen an infant baptism before.

We will venture to say that more good was accomplished in this meeting than any kind of meeting ever held before in this church during its 99 years of existence. Evidently it was the best and most thrilling event that our people have ever experienced.

Our people have put on new life, are more devoted, enjoy sweeter fellowship than ever before. From the faithful attendance, attentive listening, loyal contributing, neighborly serving and Godly living, we are forced to conclude, among our older people especially, that they have realized the fact, greater than ever before that we have a hell to shun and a heaven to win. Therefore, more of our people than ever before are "setting their house in order," seeing that we all are facing the setting sun, and know that we are dropping out one by one.

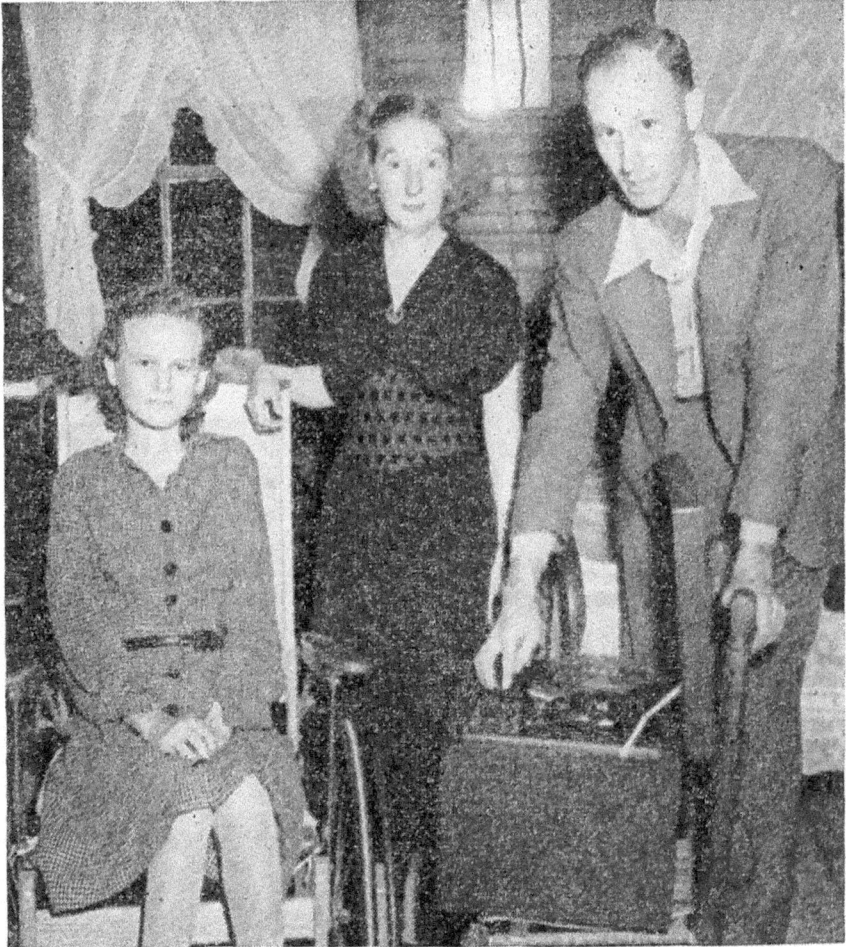

HOME DEPARTMENT

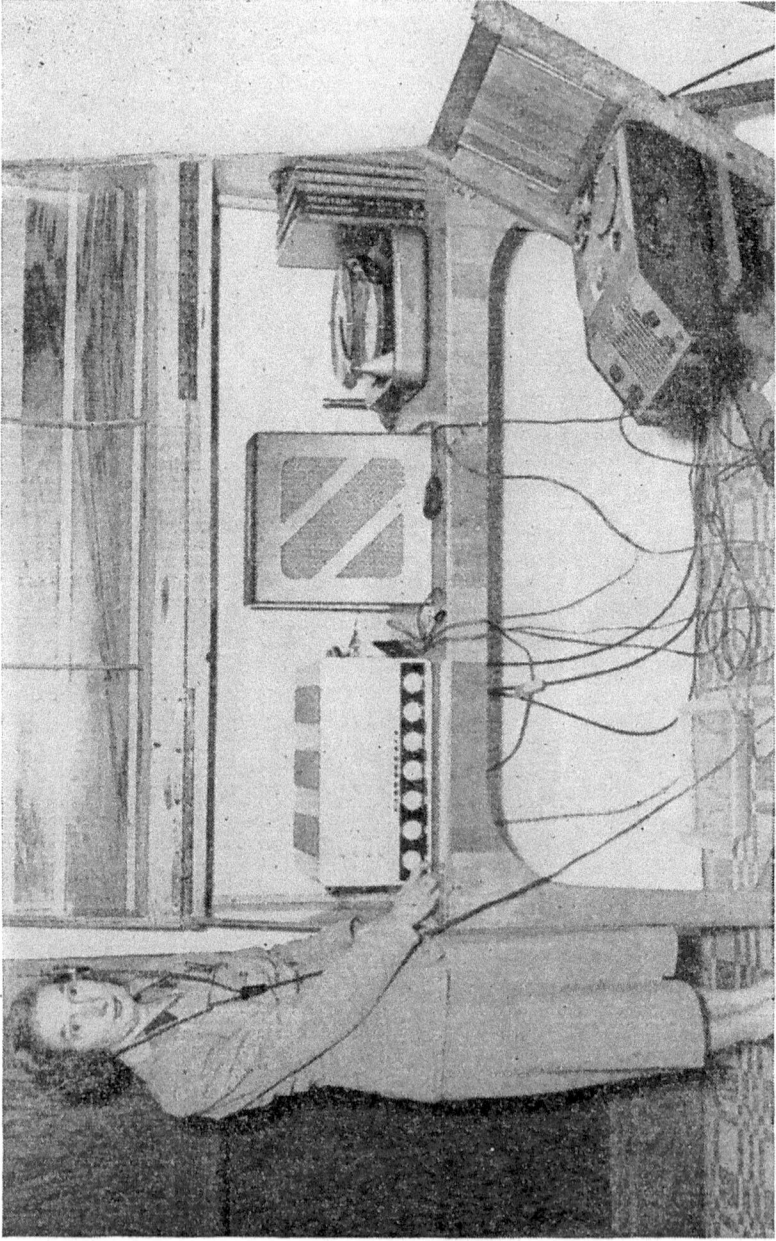

Miss Frances Seastrunk, secretary of the Home Department, controlling the amplification system, sending the Preaching Mission service over the tower speakers to the surrounding community.

CEDAR GROVE PASTORS

REV. D. Efird served as an assistant to Rev. Godfrey Dreher until 1854 when he was succeeded by Rev. Adam Efird, who served until 1870. For two years the congregation was served jointly by Rev. D. Efird and T. Miller. In 1872 Rev. A. L. Crouse began a four-year's service. In 1876 Rev. J. K. Efird, son of Adam Efird, was called as a supply and accepted the work regularly in 1878. He was succeeded by Rev. E. L. Lybrand in 1883. Then followed Rev. E. J. Sox in June 1896, in July 1897 he resigned to accept a professor's chair in Lenoir College. He was succeeded by Rev. W. H. Roof. In September 1904, Rev. Roof resigned to resume his Theological studies in the Seminary. Rev. B. D. Wessinger served as regular pastor from Dec. 1, 1904 to Jan. 1, 1906, then as supply pastor till May 1, 1906. Rev. B. L. Stroup served the Cedar Grove Congregation for three years, 1906-1909. Rev. J. C. Wessinger began his work April 1, 1909 and closed April 1, 1912. Rev. V. L. Fulmer served as supply pastor for six months. While here he revised the parish record assisted by Enoch Swygert and Ansel Caughman. Rev. F. K. Roof served Cedar Grove as pastor for eight years, beginning January 1, 1913, and finishing his work December 6, 1920. Rev. W. D. Wise served the pastorate from August, 1921, until July 1945. Rev. Joseph C. Derrick was pastor from September 24, 1945, until September 1, 1948. Rev. J. Russell Boggs began his work January 1, 1949. He is the present pastor.

SONS IN THE MINISTRY

SALEM gave two of her sons to the ministry, George Kelley and Victor Derrick. Rev. Kelley joined the Baptist Church and served in that capacity his entire life. He organized Pleasant Hill Baptist Church here in our own community. Rev. Victor Derrick is pastor of the Lutheran Church, Memphis, Tennessee.

Cedar Grove has given nine of her sons to the ministry, namely Rev. J. D. Shealy, deceased; Rev. P. D. Risinger, deceased; Rev. C. I. Morgan, deceased; Rev. Enoch Hite, deceased; Rev. F. G. Morgan, deceased; Rev. Kearney Roof, deceased; Rev. L. L. Swygert, Rev. Roy Addy, and Rev. F. L. Frazier, who joined the Methodist Church and is a successful pastor in that denomination.

Three of her sons are now in college preparing for the ministry: Seth Crapps, Robert Swygert and Delano Ricard.

J. D. SHEALY

REV. J. D. SHEALY

THE late Reverend Jefferson David Shealy was the son of Wiley Shealy and wife, Miley Melvina Hallman. He was born February 22, 1862, near Leesville, and died suddenly at his home in Leesville October 9, 1926. He married Catherine Rebecca Green. He has three sons, Fred Leon, Gordon Elbert and Harold Roland.

Rev. Shealy attended the common schools of the community, which at that time were very primitive, then completed his literary education at Newberry College and the Southern Lutheran Seminary. The South Carolina Synod ordained him in 1891. He served the pastorate of the Union charge, for twenty-six years, near Leesville in his own home community. Other charges served were Graniteville Mission, Bethlehem Pastorate of Pomaria, Mayer Memorial and Summer Memorial Mission of Newberry, and St. Andrews Church, Concord, N. C. He spent thirty-five years of his life in the Lutheran Ministry. Being devoted to his ministerial work, he preached with simplicity and power.

He was efficient as a pastor, faithfully serving his people in this capacity.

His funeral was held on October 10, 1926 at Mt. Hebron Church near Leesville. This was one of the last churches he served. Dr. Henry J. Black, president of the South Carolina Synod, conducted the service. His body and that of his wife are buried in the Mt. Hebron Cemetery.

Jefferson Davis Shealy was baptized at Cedar Grove Church on the 23rd day of March, A. D., 1862, by the Reverend Adam Efird. The following class was confirmed on the 23rd day of April A. D., 1876, by the Reverend A. L. Crouse: Walter K. Shealy, Jefferson D. Shealy, N. Davis Hite, Vastine Taylor, Missouri Koon, Eliza C. Shealy, M. J. Ann Caughman, Gracy Ann Shealy.

P. D. RISINGER

REVEREND PAUL DAVID RISINGER

REV. P. D. Risinger was born near Leesville, South Carolina, May 18, 1870, and died at his home in Leesville, November 12, 1950. Funeral services were held in Wittenberg Church, Leesville, South Carolina, November 14, 1950, conducted by Rev. J. M. Frick, assisted by Rev. J. Russell Boggs and Rev. Thos. F. Suber, President of the Western Conference.

In childhood he attended the local school and the Cedar Grove Lutheran Church and Sunday School. There he was baptized and confirmed in the Evangelical Lutheran Faith. As a young man he attended the Leesville Classic and English Institute, Lenoir-Rhyne College and Newberry College, from which he graduated in 1897, and the Southern Lutheran Seminary from which he graduated in 1898. In 1897 he was ordained a minister of the Evangelical Lutheran Church by the Tennessee Synod. For 50 years he served faithfully in the ministry as pastor at Monroe, North Carolina; Lone Star and Elloree, South Carolina; Senoia and Harrelson, Ga.; Dallas, N. C.; Ehrhardt, S. C.; Landis, N. C.; Lexington, S. C.; Johnston, S. C. and Troutman, North Carolina. In 1936 he retired from active service to live at Leesville. During retirement for five years he served as supply for vacant congregations. In 1941, he was recalled to the active ministry by the Silverstreet South Carolina congregation where he served until 1947. Again he retired and was recalled to the active ministry by Corinth· St. Mark Parish in Saluda County. He served them faithfully and efficiently until a tragic automobile accident terminated his active ministry, December 18, 1948. His remaining days were spent in suffering and anguish and faithful waiting on his Lord.

Rev. Risinger served on many boards and committees of the church, including the chairmanship of the Board of Trustees of Summerland College during the presidency of Dr. P. E. Monroe.

He was married twice: first to Miss Ida May Brown, who departed this life in 1940; later to Miss Grace Caughman, who survives.

Other survivors include three sisters: Mrs. Annie Williamson, Pomaria, South Carolina, Mrs. Jesse Taylor, Columbia, South Carolina, Mrs. Birdie Taylor, Leesville, South Carolina, and a number of nieces and nephews.

He was a man of firm and steadfast conviction, energetic and eager to promote the work of the Kingdom.

C. I. MORGAN

REV. CARROL IRVING MORGAN

REV. Carrol Irving Morgan was born September 8, 1873, in the Cedar Grove section of Lexington County, S. C. He died January 28, 1948 at the Columbia Hospital, Columbia, S. C., at the age of seventy-four years.

The Rev. Mr. Morgan attended Cedar Grove Public School. He was graduated from Lenoir Rhyne College, Hickory, N. C., and the Southern Seminary, then located at Mt. Pleasant, S. C. He also did Post Graduate Work at Northwestern Seminary, Chicago, Ill. Rev. Mr. Morgan was ordained to the Gospel Ministry in 1902 by the Tennessee Synod.

He served the following parishes: Gastonia, N. C.; Salisbury, N. C.; Burlington, N. C.; St. James Church, Catawba County, N. C.; Landis, N. C.; Luray, Va.; The Union Parish and the St. Mark's Church, Leesville, S. C.

In 1925 he came to Summerland College, Leesville, S. C., as Instructor in Bible and as Business Manager. Here he served for three years. Rev. Morgan was devoted to his work at the college. He made great sacrifices for it. In addition to his Bible Classes and Business Management, he did much of the actual farm work.

At the last commencement, Dr. Derrick said, "There has been a miracle performed here, and Uncle Callie has done it." The college had come through the year free of debt.

Uncle Callie was good natured; yes, too good for his own good. Often at the close of the church year, when all church bills, including salary, should have been paid but was not paid, he would say, "Let's knock off even and begin a new year, hoping to do better."

He would never cherish a grudge, no matter how great the provocation. He had a hard struggle, securing an education, but he was always willing to pull for himself.

After his retirement, he served various parishes as supply pastor.

Pastor Morgan became a Charter Member of Faith Church, Batesburg, S. C., where he taught the Men's Bible Class until his death.

On December 26, 1911 he was married to Miss Elizabeth Russell Tyson, of Saulsbury, N. C., to which union two children were born: Margaret Russell, who died in infancy, and Grace Carrol. He is survived by his widow, Mrs. C. I. Morgan, of Batesburg, S. C., and his daughter, Mrs. Rudolph Ludwig, of Konnarock, Va.

Funeral services were conducted at Faith Lutheran Church, Batesburg, S. C., by his pastor, the Rev. R. R. Ellsworth, assisted by the President of Synod. Interment followed in the Leesville Cemetery.

Pastor Morgan was a faithful and conscientious minister of his Lord. It can be truly said that a good man is gone to his reward.

THE REV. ENOCH HITE

REV. ENOCH HITE

REV. Enoch Hite was born near Leesville, S. C., April 27, 1873, son of Joseph and Martha Oxner Hite. He was catechised and confirmed in Cedar Grove Church at the age of 13.

He was educated in the Public Schools of Lexington County, attended High School at Summit Academy 1893, taught by Rev. E. L. Lybrand, from which he received a Certificate of Proficiency.

In 1894 he began teaching in the public schools of his county, continuing for five years. He entered Lenoir Rhyne College in 1898 in Hickory, N. C., from which he graduated in 1903. He then entered the Southern Seminary, Mt. Pleasant, S. C., graduating in 1906.

He was ordained to the gospel ministry in St. Thomas Lutheran Church, Lexington County, S. C., in 1906 by the Tennessee Lutheran Synod. He served the following parishes: St. Jacobs, Chapin, S. C., (1906-1909); Emmanuels, New Market, Va. (1909-1911); Emmanuels, Lincolnton, N. C. (1911-1918); Bethlehem and St. Matthews, Pomaria, S. C. (1918-1920); St. Stephens and Mt. Olive, East Hickory, N. C. (1920-1925); Silver Street and Corinth, Silver Street, S. C. (1925-1928); Mt. Moriah and St. Mark's, China Grove, N. C. (1928-1931); Friedens, Peace and Sharon, Gibsonville, N. C. (1931-1935).

He was President of the North Carolina Conference of the Tennessee Synod, and later served as President of the Western Conference of the United Synod of North Carolina. He filled a number of important positions on boards and was always found true to the trust committed to him. He was instrumental as a pastor in building new churches at Mt. Olive, Hickory, N. C.; Corinth, Silver Street, S. C.; Mt. Moriah, China Grove, N. C.; and was laying plans for a new church at Sharon, Gibsonville, N. C., at the time of his death. This church was built to his memory a few years later.

Rev. Enoch Hite married Miss Annie Roof of New Brookland, S. C., on Nov. 20, 1906. To this union were born three children, Thesta, Wilbert and Jayne.

Rev. Enoch Hite died at his home in Gibsonville, N. C., on Saturday, August 31, 1935 of a heart attack. Funeral services were held at Friedens Lutheran Church, Gibsonville, of his parish, on Monday, September 2, 1935 by the President of N. C. Synod, Dr. J. L. Morgan, and his body was laid to rest in the Friedens Cemetery.

Mrs. Enoch Hite died of a heart attack on Feb. 20, 1948 at her home in Gibsonville, after an illness of one year, and is also buried beside Rev. Hite in Friedens Cemetery.

—Written by Jayne Hite Bryson,
Dec. 5, 1951, Gibsonville, N. C.

THE REV. AND MRS. FRANCIS GROVER MORGAN

DR. FRANCIS GROVER MORGAN

THE following is a clipping from the "Hickory Daily Record" of Friday, June 18, 1948:

"Francis Grover Morgan, 58, B. D., Ph. D., Professor of Bible and Philosophy at Lenoir Rhyne College, Hickory, since 1934, was claimed by death at his home at 1223 Third Street at 10:44 o'clock Thursday night. He had been in declining health for five years and critically ill for the last week.

"Dr. Morgan, born near Leesville, in Lexington County, South Carolina, Nov. 19, 1889, a son of the late Henry S. Morgan and Amanda Hare Morgan, received his A. B. Degree at Lenoir Rhyne College 1909, did graduate work at the Lutheran Theological Southern Seminary in 1913, and received his B. D. Degree in 1925. He was a graduate student at the University of North Carolina in the summers of 1917 and 1924.

Doctor's Degree

"He received his Ph.D. Degree at the University of South Carolina in 1928, and was Professor of Latin and Education at Lenoir Rhyne College from 1913 until 1918, then served as pastor and teacher at the U. S. Marine Barracks, Parris Island, S. C., and Madison, Va., until 1922. From 1922-1924, he was engaged in work in the field of education and psychology and was director of extension work at Lenoir Rhyne College. He served as President and Dean of Summerland College from 1924-1928, and as Professor of Biblical Literature at Converse College from 1928 until 1934.

"Dr. Morgan, who was a member of the National Association of Biblical Instructors and the Phi Beta Kappa Fraternity, returned to Lenoir Rhyne in 1934 as Professor of Bible and Philosophy, a position in which he remained active through the present year.

"He was married to Miss Letitia Doak, of Rural Retreat, Virginia, in August of 1912, who survives with the following sons and daughters:

Survivors

"William D. E. and James H. Morgan, of Hickory; Mrs. Joe E. Turpin, of Hickory; Mrs. V. L. Solace, of Long Beach, Calif.; Mrs. Earl Townsend, of Columbia, S. C.; and Miss Joana Morgan, of Hickory.

"He is also survived by one sister, Mrs. John Trudell, of Miami, Florida, and four grandchildren.

"Funeral services will be conducted at St. Andrews Lutheran Church on the Lenoir Rhyne Campus at three o'clock Saturday afternoon, with the pastor, Dr. F. P. Cauble, officiating. The body will be taken to the church from the Shuford Funeral Home at two o'clock Saturday afternoon to lie in state until the funeral hour. Burial will be made in the St. Stephen's Lutheran Church Cemetery near Hickory.

"Dr. Morgan was baptized and confirmed in Cedar Grove Lutheran Church near Leesville, S. C.

THE REV. KEARNEY ROOF

FRANCIS KEARNEY ROOF

FRANCIS Kearney Roof, son of Rev. Francis Keitt Roof and Mary Etta Campbell Roof, was born November 23, 1904 in Catawba County, North Carolina, Route 3, Hickory, in the temporary parsonage of St. Timothy's pastorate where his father was pastor from May 1900-December 1912. He was the third child and only son. His two older sisters are Naomi A. Roof and Mrs. V. D. (Lela Fay Roof) Derrick, and his youngest sister is Mrs. J. G. (Gladys Evelyn Roof) Carter.

Kearney was baptized by Rev. J. A. Yount in early infancy. He was thus a baptized member of St. Timothy E. L. Church of the then Tennessee Synod, Route 3, Hickory, N. C. He began school at St. Timothy Graded School, which was located on grounds adjoining church property.

The family moved to Cedar Grove Lutheran Church, Route 3, Leesville, S. C., January 1913. Kearney then attended Cedar Grove School and later Leesville High School. He was confirmed in Cedar Grove Church by his father on October 27, 1917 with the following class: Henry Edwin Addy, Gilman Harold Shealy, Cecil J. C. Hite. Kearney finished his high school work in the sub-fresh class at Lenoir Rhyne College in 1921. He graduated with an A. B. degree from Lenoir Rhyne College, Hickory, N. C., in 1925. The following is copied from the "Hacawa," published by the 1925 Senior Class of Lenoir Rhyne College, Hickory, N. C.

"Francis Kearney Roof, A. B., New Brookland, S. C., President of Class of '25; President of Chrestonian Society, '25; Assisting Advertising Manager of the Lenoir Rhynean, '25; Manager of Class Play, '24."

The family moved to Morganton (Burke County), N. C., in the Fall of 1920 where his father was pastor of the Burke Parish. Kearney then became a member of Mt. Calvary E. L. Church, Morganton, N. C. His mother died there July 27, 1923. When the family moved to New Brookland, now West Columbia, S. C., in May 1924, Kearney became a member of Mt. Herman E. L. Church.

After graduation from Lenoir Rhyne College in 1925, Kearney worked for one year with the New York Life Insurance Company, Columbia, S. C. The next year he was principal of the Holly Grove School in the St. Andrews section of Richland County. In 1927 he entered the Lutheran Theological Seminary, Columbia, S. C., from which institution he graduated with the B. D. Degree in May 1930. He was ordained at Mt. Herman, his church where his father was pastor, on May 25, 1930. Those ordained at this time were: Rev. C. Ernest Seastrunk, Rev. Joseph C. Derrick, Rev. Lewis Koon, Rev. William H. Stender, Rev. Daniel M. Shull, Rev. F. Kearney Roof.

Rev. Charles J. Shealy was then President of the S. C. Synod and Rev. Thomas Suber, secretary.

Kearney was pastor of the Swansea-Sandy Run Parish, composed of the three churches, Good Shepherd, Swansea, S. C.; Sandy Run,

Route, Swansea, S. C., in Calhoun County; and Orange Chapel, Springfield, S. C. He served this pastorate from June 1, 1930 to his death June 30, 1931. In the summer of 1929, before his last year at the Seminary, he supplied the St. Luke's Church, Summerville, S. C. While Kearney was in the Seminary, he was very active in the State Luther League and served as a state and district officer in the League.

The following is an account of the death and funeral of Kearney, copied from "The State":

"Funeral services for the Rev. F. K. Roof, Jr., 26-year-old Lutheran minister of Swansea, who was drowned early Tuesday night at Boyden Arbor, will be held at 11 o'clock this morning at Mt. Herman Lutheran Church in Lexington County. The Rev. C. J. Shealy, of Cameron, President of the Lutheran Synod of South Carolina, will officiate. He will be assisted by Dr. A. G. Voigt, Dean of the Lutheran Theological Seminary, of which Mr. Roof was a graduate.

"Two sisters, Misses Fay and Naomi Roof and his fiancee, Miss Marion Roof, 1634 Taylor Street, looked on as the young minister sank in the lake, 15 feet from a raft. He was swimming beside his fiancee when he went down. His two sisters were on shore. The party had been in the lake about two hours when the tragedy occured.

"His body was pulled from the lake on the raft where efforts were made at resucitation. Later a lung motor was used, but in vain. Dr. N. B. Heyward, who was swimming at the time and examined the body, said that he could not feel the pulse beat when the body was pulled on the raft. There were a dozen or more people in swimming at the time and there was no difficulty in rescuing the body. Where he sank, about 150 feet from shore, the water was about 15 feet deep.

"Mr. Roof was a graduate of Lenoir Rhyne College. He was in the insurance business for one year and taught school another year before entering the Lutheran Seminary here from which he graduated in 1930. At the time of his death he was serving three churches, the Sandy Run Lutheran Church, the Church of the Good Shepherd at Swansea and Orange Chapel at Springfield. He lived at Swansea.

"Six friends and ministers will be active pallbearers. They are the Rev. Samuel L. Sox, of Newton, N. C., the Rev. L. O. Roof, of Leesville. S. C., the Rev. J. C. Derrick, of Blythewood, S. C., the Rev. D. M. Shull, of Pelion, S. C., and the Rev. Voigt R. Cromer, of Lincolnton, N. C.

"Members of the councils of the three churches will be honorary pallbearers.

"Mr. Roof is survived by his father and stepmother, the Rev. F. K. Roof, Sr., and Mrs. Roof, and by three sisters, Misses Naomi and Fay Roof and Gladys Roof, all of New Brookland.

THE REV. LEGARE L. SWYGERT

REV. LUTHER LEGARE SWYGERT

LUTHER Legare Swygert, son of Yoder J. and Lula Oxner Swygert, was born near Leesville, S. C., on August 31, 1905. He grew up in the Cedar Grove community, attended the local country schools, completed the elementary grades. He received his high school education at the Batesburg-Leesville High, graduating with State High School Diploma in the class of 1927. That Fall he entered Newberry College, graduating with the A. B. Degree on June 9, 1931. In the Fall of 1931 he entered the Southern Lutheran Thealogical Seminary, Columbia, S. C., finishing from that institution with the B. D. Degree May 17, 1934.

On May 24, 1934, he was married to Louise Addy, of the Cedar Grove Community. The marriage took place in Ebenezer Lutheran Church, Columbia, S. C., the ceremony being performed by the Rev. P. D. Brown, D. D., pastor of Ebenezer and president of the South Carolina Lutheran Synod.

May 27, 1934 he was ordained into the ministry of the Gospel of the Synod of South Carolina at Mt. Horeb Church, Chapin, S. C.

On June 1st. he entered upon the duties as pastor of the Lexington Lutheran Parish, consisting of the Congregations of Nazareth, Pisgah, Providence and St. John's. He served this parish until September 29, 1941, on which date he entered the U. S. Army as chaplain. For more than four years he served as chaplain of the 63rd Infantry, Sixth Infantry Division. He saw combat service in New Guinea and Luzon (P. I.). He was awarded the Bronze Star Medal for "Meritorious Achievement" during combat in the early days of the Luzon Campaign in 1945. Besides this he wears the American Defense Ribbon with one bronze arrowhead and two campaign stars; the Victory Medal; the Philippine Liberation Ribbon with one bronze star and perhaps eligible for others.

After V-J Day he served for three weeks with occupational forces in Korea, returning to the U. S. Dec. 3 and received his separation papers at Camp Gordon, Ga., Dec. 13, 1945, though not officially discharged until April 8, 1946. In all, he served his country more than four and one half years. Twenty-nine months of that service was overseas.

Three wartime poems of his have received some publicity and were well received by the public. "The Christian Soldier's Hymn," "The Chaplain's Duty," and "In Memoriam."

February 15, 1946 he entered upon the duties as pastor of the Bethlehem Lutheran Parish, Irmo, S. C., where he is still serving This parish consists of the congregations of Bethlehem and St. John's. As pastor and chairman of the building committee, he recently completed the building of a beautiful new church edifice at Bethelehem, two miles east of Ballentine on National Highway 76.

Legare and Louise have an adopted daughter, Mary Louise, now about 15 years old. She is in the ninth grade at Irmo High School. She is also taking music and voice in Columbia, S. C.

Legare grew up a member of Cedar Grove Lutheran Church, was confirmed in the "old church" by Rev. F. K. Roof. He taught in the Sunday Daily Vacation Bible Schools while attending college and seminary.

Opportunity Missed!

Text: "But Thomas, one of the twelve, called Didymus, was not with them when Jesus came." John 20: 24.

On the first Lord's Day Thomas missed church: What else did he miss? It was the first Easter evening. St. Thomas was absent from the assembly of the disciples. Into the presence of that group Jesus, the Risen Lord, came. He does not stay away from His Church though His people might! St. Thomas missed the fellowship with his "Lord and God." What an opportunity—missed!

That evening Thomas also missed the fellowship with the other disciples. There is a peculiar joy and blessing—we are lifted up in spirit and morale—when we join others in the service and all worship as one people with one faith in One God. But Thomas missed that.

That evening Jesus breathed upon that assembly and there was a new outpouring of the Holy Spirit—as there is at every service on every Lord's Day when the Word is proclaimed or the sacraments administered—when one's faith is begotten or strengthened. Oh! How Thomas needed that, but he missed it. This is too often true, the ones who need the service the most, are most often absent. Yet, they wonder why their spiritual progress is so slow and the fruits of faith so few.

That evening Jesus blessed that little congregation with a benediction of peace—but Thomas missed that blessing. He had to live another week as "the Doubter," confused and ill at ease. But isn't it something to glory in—to attend Church and at the end of the service to feel in one's heart the Peace of God which passeth understanding?

Did you ever miss Church? What else did you miss?

Chaplain Luther L. Swygert, Easter 1943.

(The above sermonette was published in the Camp paper at Camp San Luis Obispo, California, and also printed in the "News Letter" of the National Council Service Commission.)

The Christian Soldier's Hymn
(Tune: "Rock of Ages")

Jesus, Captain of my Soul,
Let me take a soldier's role,
I would join Thy host for life;

In Thy ranks I'll ever fight,
Till life's battle all is done,
And the field for Thee is won.
Supply Thou my every need;
Thy commands I will all heed.
While Thy orders I obey,
Hear me as I fight and pray;
When into the fight I go,
Give me grace to meet the foe.
Dress me in Thine armor, Lord,
It shall be my rich reward.
Arm me with Thy mighty sword,
Conquer with Thy Holy Word.
Issue me faith for a shield,
Lest to Satan's darts I yield.
Thy helmet of salvation
Will assure the victory won;
Righteousness to clothe my breast,
Girded with Thy truthfulness,
Swift I'll bring the news of peace,
With Thy sandals on my feet.
Jesus, Captain of my Soul,
When the battle all is done
And the glorious victory's won,
May I hear Thee say, "Well done,
Thou hast fought the goodly fight,
Enter to Eternal life." Amen.

—Chaplain Luther L. Swygert.

THE CHAPLAIN'S DUTY

I sat beside a soldier's bed
In an army hospital ward;
I had not spoken of Christ the Lord,
Waiting till he should turn his head.
And as I waited in the silent now
I saw his wounded side,
His bandaged hands and feet,
The bloody scar upon his brow.
I pondered deep his sacrifice;
It made me think of the suffering Christ.
At last he awoke and looked my way
With a kind of greeting smile and nod;
And this I thought I heard him say,
"Thanks, Sir, you've made me think of God."

—Luther L. Swygert, Chaplain, 63rd Infantry,
July 1944.

IN MEMORIAM

Lest we forget:
The tears, the blood, the sweat—
The place, the ground upon which they bled,
The hallowed spot where they lie dead—
The cause and reason why
It was theirs to do and die.
They fought and bled at Alacan,
Sison, Munoz, Montalban, Mataba, Kiangan and Bataan;
Had they not died, we had not won,
So nobler still's the task they've done.
They died to set men free,
They bled for democracy.
Lest we forget—today,
Beside their graves we take our stand,
To proclaim liberty throughout the land.

—Luther L. Swygert, Chaplain, 63rd Infantry.
Written day after J-V Day, 1945.

(Dedicated sacred to the memory and honor of the men of the 63rd Infantry who gave the last full measure of devotion in the liberation of Luzon and for the freedom of men everywhere.—January 9-August 16, 1945).

THE REV. ROY ADDY

REV. ROY ALVIN ADDY

REV. Roy Alvin Addy, son of H. E. and Mary Addy attended the Cedar Grove public school. He entered the high school at Lexington, S. C., September 1918. He graduated with an A. B. Degree from Newberry College in 1924. Rev. Addy taught for two years in the Batesburg-Leesville High School. In 1929 he was graduated with a B. D. Degree from Chicago Lutheran Theological Seminary.

Rev. Addy organized the Acacia Park Evangelical Lutheran Church, Oriole and Cullom Avenues, Chicago, Oct. 28, 1928; served as Student Pastor during senior year at the Seminary. He was called as the first pastor of Acacia Park, May 1929, and served this congregation for fifteen years until January 1943, at which time he received appointment as chaplain in the U. S. Navy.

He was indoctrinated at Norfolk, Va. His first assignment was Corpus Christi, Texas, as assistant chaplain. He was later ordered to the U. S. Naval Air Station, Beeville, Texas, as senior chaplain. He helped build this station from scratch, erected a chapel, library and recreational building.

In May 1944 he received orders for oversea duty in the Southwest Pacific as senior chaplain of his unit. While there the attendance grew from 98 on the first Sunday to an attendance of 4,416. A native type chapel was built with a seating capacity of 1,100 which was later enlarged on two occasions. The monthly attendance at the Holy Communion Service was well over 1,000. He published the first newspaper in the Southwest Pacific. In addition to regular duties as chaplain, which often called for six or seven services on Sundays, he was appointed War Bond Officer. He sold $58,000 War Bonds over a period of thirty days, and on another drive sold $104,000 during a period of fifty days. Commodore Boak personally awarded him a medal and letter of commendation for notable accomplishment.

March 1945 he reecived orders to report as senior chaplain to the U. S. Naval Air Station, Olathe, Kansas, near Kansas City, Mo. He served there until discharged from the service June 1946. He received a letter of appreciation from Captain W. M. Drane on accomplishments while at Olathe, Kansas.

June 1947 Rev. Addy received a call as pastor of the Epiphany Evangelical Lutheran Church, Spring Road and Vallette Street, Elmhurst, Illinois, which is 18 miles directly west of Chicago, Illinois. In four years the membership of the congregation had trebled; the benevolence has increased fourfold. During 1951, more than 100 new members have been received into the church. Two services are conducted each Sunday and three sections for Sunday School each Sunday.

Pastor Addy married Miss Violet A. Pyles. A son, Paul Luther, is a student in the University of Illinois.

THE REV. VICTOR D. DERRICK

REV. VICTOR DEWEY DERRICK

R EV. Victor Dewey Derrick, son of Leppard Scott Derrick and Sally Medora Ann Shealy Derrick, was born October 25, 1898 near Leesville, S. C. He was baptized in infancy in Salem Lutheran Church by Rev. J. D. Kinard, pastor. He was confirmed in Salem Lutheran Church by Rev. S. C. Ballentine, pastor. He played the organ in Salem Church for Sunday School and church services for several years, attended church at Salem regularly from birth until the church burned. He then became a member at Cedar Grove.

He attended Cedar Grove School, receiving his elementary grades there. He received his high school education at Leesville High School. He attended Newberry College, graduating with an A. B. Degree in 1923. For college activities see the 1923 Newberrian, page 34. He attended the Southern Lutheran Seminary, Columbia, S. C., 1923 and 1924. During 1923 and 1924 he also attended the University of S. C. with post graduate work in Sociology. He attended Chicago Lutheran Seminary 1926-1928, graduating in 1928 with a B. D. degree.

While attending Chicago Seminary he was a student pastor with Dr. F. W. Otterbein of North Austin Lutheran Church, a membership of over 5,000 at that time. He was ordained in Illinois Synod in May 1928. He became pastor of First United Lutheran Church, Memphis, Tennessee, of the Indiana Synod in June 1928 and is still there.

First United Church, during the time he has been pastor, has grown from less than ten members to over 450 at the present time; from a Mission Church with an indebtedness of $20,000 to its presents self-supported basis with all mortgages liquidated and a beautiful Gothic type, brick church building (built in 1949-1950 and dedicated, completely furnished on October 15, 1950.

He married the former Miss Lila Fay Roof, second daughter of the late Rev. and Mrs. F. K. Roof. She was educated at St. Timothy Graded School, Hickory, N. C.; Cedar Grove School; Lexington High School and Lenoir Rhyne College, graduating in 1921, and at the University of South Carolina with an M. A. Degree in 1926.

She was a teacher of English for nine and a half years in North and South Carolina High Schools prior to marriage December 30, 1941. They have two daughters, Ann Mary Derrick, born Nov. 9, 1932, now a sophomore at Southwestern, at Memphis; Fay Ruth Derrick, born June 6, 1936, is now in the tenth grade at Central High School, Memphis.

Pastor Derrick, now a member of the Kentucky-Tennessee Synod which was formed in 1936, is at present Chairman of the Synodical Social Missions Committee.

He was a teacher in Kentucky-Tennesee Leadership Training School in 1947 and 1951.

OLD LEXINGTON BAPTIST CHURCH (1852)

OLD LEXINGTON BAPTIST CHURCH

SALUDA Church was constituted March 20, 1813 by the Rev. Brother Joseph King and Chesley Davis. The church called Brother King for pastor.

The church agreed to the following covenant: The solenm covenant of the Saluda Baptist Church of Jesus Christ:

"Whereas it is the incumbent duty of those who are favored with the dispensation of gospel grace, to embrace God's Covenants, acknowledge his government, profess his name and unite together in the faith and fellowship of the gospel.

"We whose names are hereto annexed, do in the presence of the great eternal God, Who knows the secrets of all hearts, and in the presence of angels and men acknowledge ourselves under the most solemn obligations to be the Lords, and we do solmenly covenant and agree,

"First, that we will take the only living and true God, one God in three persons—the Father, the Son and the Holy Ghost, to be our God;

"Second, we unreservedly and solemnly give up ourselves and what we possess to Almighty God, to be ordered by, directed by and disposed of by Him, according to His Holy Will. This we do in an humble dependence on the grace of the Holy Spirit to aid and support us in these sacred engagements, hoping for acceptance and salvation through the merits and meditations of our Lord and Saviour Jesus Christ;

"Third, we take the Scriptures of the Old and New Testaments to be our rule of faith and practice in the great concerns of religion and for a directory in the general affairs of life and particularly for transacting the affairs of the church;

"Fourth, we promise to maintain communion and fellowship with each other in the public worship of God according to the various ordinances of the Gospel—not forsaking the assembling of ourselves as the manner of some, but embracing all regular and convenient seasons for this purpose if Providence or God permit, and that we will exercise Christian forbearance and love one toward another, praying for and sympathizing with each other in the various circumstances of life and using every laudable endeavor to provoke to love and good works;

"Fifth, we promise individually to pay a respectful regard to the minority of the gospel and their advice and the admonitions of the church, and be subject to its discipline as directed by the Word of God, and as conducted in the spirit of the Gospel;

Sixth, we promise to endeavor to encourage and to contribute in a reasonable manner according to our ability for the support of the ministry and other charges of the church and to use our influence in the settlement to promote the great cause of religion —that we will be careful to conduct ourselves with uprightness, integrity and in a peacful and friendly manner toward mankind in general and toward serious Christians of other denominations and that we will pay a conscientious regard to civil government and give it its dues as an ordinance of God."

Old Lexington Baptist Church is located in the midst of Lutheranism. It is surrounded by Lutheran Churches. Since the development of Lake Murray the church is about the center of a peninsula containing 3,000 acres of land, bounded on the north by Saluda River proper; on the east by Big Hollow Creek; on the south by Highway 43, and on the west by Big Rocky Creek. Only one way to go in and come out. The church has always had a small membership, and the probability is that it may continue that way for some time to come, however, it is about as strong now as it ever has been in membership, but I presume about ten times as strong financially. It doesn't have much chance to grow numerically, due to the fact that if her daughters get any man at all, they have to take a Lutheran.

This community was settled before the Revolutionary War, principally by the British. Some of them came from England, scouted in Virginia for awhile, came to Charleston and found their way up the rivers to the interior of Carolina, found a desirable place on Saluda River and settled there. They settled near the river for the purpose of navigation, for they had to sell their produce at Charleston. They also had to buy the necessities of life at Charleston. At that time on streams was the only mode or method of conveyance. A little later all roads led to Charleston, and of course all

Around 1800 there was a Camp Meeting site located about one-streams flowed toward Charleston.

Around 1800 there was a Camp Meeting site located about one-fourth mile southeast of the George Dreher old home on the Langford lands. These camp meetings were held under bush arbors near a good spring.

Tradition says that they were held during the "lay by" season and would continue for at least three weeks on a stretch. The families participating would even bring their milk cows with them and keep them 'til the meeting closed. These camp meetings evidently were held for a number of years before the church was organized.

A log building was erected about one-half mile south of Lewie's Ferry, later known as Amick's Ferry. The church was near the Calk road.

A few of the Charter Members were Asa Langford, George Lewie and a Mr. Taylor, who moved to Arkansas. Asa Langford was born June 8, 1773 and died June 23, 1857. His monument stands in the church cemetery, but his body is resting in an island jutting up out of Lake Murray. This Asa Langford was the first Clerk of this Saluda Church. Rev. Joseph King was the first pastor, then Rev. Pilly Williams, then Rev. Baker, M. M. Abney 1839 and William Watkins 1841. Rev. Arthur Fort preached there about 1850; Rev.

Simeon Spruell about 1860. There could have been others but we find no record of any.

About 1852, the congregation decided to locate further from the river. Therefore, the present building was erected about that time, at the location where it now stands. ·

On the 9th of March, 1855, a terrible forest fire, beginning in Edgefield County, swept this entire section, devastating practically everything that lay in its pathway, especially rail fencing. At that time there was no stock law; all stock was allowed to run at large, therefore all fields had to be fenced. At that time people owned droves of geese, principally to produce feathers for bedding. They also owned large herds of sheep and cattle. At that season most of the geese were setting, mostly in fence corners. The geese were burned to death. The sheep had heavy coats of wool; many of them caught fire and were burned to death. There was no means of stopping this destructive fire. It travelled faster than a horse could gallop. The heavy forests had lots of dead trees; fire would run to the tops, and the severe wind would blow chunks of burning sap for hundreds of yards.

In the construction of this frame building, many chips and shavings fell to the ground and were left there. This fire swept through under the church and burned this refuse, but a Kind Providence spared the building.

Since then that has always been spoken of in this country as the "Great March Fire."

People were left in bad shape. They had to go in the woods and split rails to fence their fields before they could plant a crop.

When the present building was erected, a number of its leading members owned slaves. Provision was made for the slaves to be seated separate from the whites. Slaves held their membership here. Several are buried on the south side of the road from the church.

Just after the Civil War, slaves being set free, Daniel Drafts gave the Negroes land on which to build a church of their own. They erected a building and named it St. Mark's. This church sprang from Old Lexington. However, one good slave "Mammy," Charity Langford, continued to worship here as long as she lived.

When this church was built, where it now stands, it was called Lexington and was built on James Langford's land. Later the land passed to John Langford, then to his son, Lewis J. Langford (familiar to all us older ones), who on the 31st day of August, 1907, executed a deed for three acres to the deacons of this church as a place to worship and burial, but contained a clause with a reverter that if it was not so used, deed was to be null and void.

However, pursuant to the request of Frank W. Shealy, deceased, and J. Ansel Caughman, the said Lewis J. Langford and J. Boyce Langford, who had become owner of the surrounding lands, jointly executed a deed for four acres of land to the deacons of Old

Lexington Baptist Church and their successors in office forever, as a place of worship and burial forever, without any "strings" whatsoever.

When the Baptist Church at Lexington Court House was organized, it was called Lexington, then this church was afterwards known as Old Lexington.

In 1907 this church building was renovated, the building was pulled around at the angle it now stands, a vestibule and recess were built to it. New weatherboarding was put on it, it was painted inside and out. Luther S. Shealy was pastor at that time. The organ and pulpit stand were given to the church at that time by George C. Shirey.

Heretofore, we have named a number of pastors who served before the Civil War. Since that time we have had quite a number of pastors. We are not able to name them altogether in order as they served. The following is a list as best we can remember: Rev. Spruell, Rev. Harris, Rev. Melton Norris, 11 successive years; Rev. Nathan Burton, Rev. Jewell, Rev. Joab Edwards, several periods; Rev. Nick Cooner, several periods; Rev. Henry Bell White, 1910-1911; Rev. James Steele, Rev. Wood Corder, Rev. L. S. Shealy, 1907-1910; Rev. Andrew Hartley, Rev. J. M. Culbertson, Rev. Myers, Rev. Bragg, Rev. Monroe Kneece, 1918; Rev. O. W. Crowder, Rev. J. L. Hiers, two periods; Rev. Funderburke, Rev. G. W. Gurley, Rev. Sheppard, Rev. J. W. Bradley, 1929-1930; Rev. Dr. Young, Rev. Ernest G. Ross, Rev. R. N. Thompson, Rev. Cary L. Steele, Rev. N. D. Roland and Rev. Carey L. Steele, present pastor.

We do not know how many men have gone out from this church as ministers of the Gospel. We have the record of one, Elsie Daniel Taylor, born 1812, who became a minister and preached 65 years in Arkansas. He was the grandfather of our Dan J. Taylor, who was once church clerk. Church clerks since organization were Asa Langford, Charley Harris, John Langford, Lewis J. Langford, G. Clarence Shirey, Dan J. Taylor and Mrs. Alice Koon Craps, who is the present Clerk.

Since a Sunday School was organized the following have served as superintendents: Henry Dickert, Addison Vansant (a Lutheran), for 30 successive years; J. Ansel Caughman (a Lutheran), a Mr. Rogers and Frank Langford, who is the present Superintendent.

Since an organ was placed in the church about 1907, the following have served as organist or pianist: Lilla Shirey, Agnes Shirey, Quilla Shealy, Sedecia Kelley, Mrs. Tart, Florence Seigler, Gladys Shealy, Jessie Shealy and Jennie Bruce Koon.

To my recollection, before the church owned an organ, choir leaders were Lewis J. Langford and Stanmore Shealy.

About 1945 the church was recovered with metal, cement steps were erected and memorial windows placed in the recess, an extra-good-toned piano purchased and new carpet on the aisles.

A beautiful and substantial pulpit set was placed in the church

OLD LEXINGTON BAPTIST MISSIONARY SOCIETY

by the Women's Missionary Society, also flags, both religious and national, were presented to the church. About the same time a new Bible was placed on the pulpit.

In 1947 a deep well was punched and an electric pump was installed to the Glory of God and in honor of our World War veterans. This well affords a bountiful supply of good free stone water. The church has electric lights. In 1949 Sunday School rooms and a baptistry were erected and provided.

With all these progressive steps, the little congregation is far from being satisfied. Twelve months ago they started a fund for a new building of permanent material and, so far, have raised around $2,000.00.

The membership of this congregation is to be highly commended, since its organization, for their lovely attitude toward other denominations. They have always given others a cordial invitation to worship with them and to take an active part in the work of the church. In proof of this fact, they have always had good Lutheran and Methodist leaders worshiping with them. Today in their services, a good percentage of their audience are Lutherans.

The present deacons of this church are Frank Langford, Quincy Lybrand, Carl Koon and Charles Shealy.

This church was legally incorporated on the 20th day of July, 1948, A. D. and was entered upon the proper indexes and duly recorded in Book of Charters No. II, page 94, by the Clerk of Court in Lexington County, S. C.

LIST OF OLD LEXINGTON BAPTIST CHURCH MEMBERS

Montagu Asbill
Pansy Smith Amick
Carrie E. Adams
Bessie Boles
John Boles
Glenda Boles
Annie Bedenbaugh
Evie Boatwright
W. O. Boatwright
Dora Shirey Caughman
Mertie Crout Caughman
Ruth Caughman
Ellis Caughman
Alice Koon Craps
Lula Smith Derrick
Elizabeth Fulmer
Maude Langford George
Alvin Ray Gillian
Laconia Gillian
Alvin Ray Gillian, Jr.

Eunice Norris Gemole
Sidney Goff
Rama Goff
Elmer Goff
J. S. Goff
Barbara Gantt
Mary Eva Gantt
Elizabeth Lybrand Gunter
Mary Lee Koon Hallman
Lilla Shirey Holley
J. D. Hyler
Rose Ann Shirey Hyler
Mattie Wooley Harman
Pearle Wooley Harman
Frances Boatwright Henderson
Ernest Jones
Mary Dickert Jones
Ernestine Jones
Jasper Johns
Charley T. Koon

Rebecca Shirey Koon
George W. Koon
Charles A. Koon
Carl B. Koon
Jennie Bruce Porth Koon
Almenia Lybrand
Quincy Lybrand
Julia Koon Lybrand
Charles Lybrand
Paul Lybrand
Wendell Lybrand
Frank Langford
Eva Langford
Boyce W. Langford
Viola W. Langford
Sallie Mack
Grace Amick Mack
James Mack
Shirley Mack
Maggie Snelgrove Norris
Betty Norris
Edna Ruth Norris
Carl Norris
Ola Norris
Jesse Norris
Grace Norris
Odell Norris
Dorris Smith Price
Ray W. Shealy
J. C. Shealy
Gladys J. Shealy
Francis W. Shealy

William "Bill" Shealy
Charles Shealy
Wilson Shealy
Monroe Shealy
Jessie Shealy
J. Monroe Shealy, Jr.
Ray Shealy
Edward Shealy
Carrol Shealy
Willie E. Seigler
Marvin W. Seigler
Harold Seigler
Sara Koon Swygert
Blanche Gillian Smith
Perry Smith
Beulah Seay
Alice Smith
Julia Smith
Herman Smith
Theodore Smith
Gladys Norris Shealy
Lewis Smith
Berdie Gillian Smith
Jewell Taylor
Susie Langford Taylor
Winfred Walker
Wayne Walker
Lucille Shirey Wood
Ravenel Wingard
Sam Wingard
Clara Wingard

WORSHIP SERVICE—OLD LEXINGTON BAPTIST CHURCH (1951)

SECTION II

PERSONALITIES FROM THE COMMUNITY

WILLIAM HENRY HARE

WILLIAM HENRY HARE

WILLIAM Henry Hare (1866-1936), son of John Wesley Hare (1840-1910) and wife, Catherine Fulmer (1833-1918), was born on the western border of Lexington County, S. C., among the head waters of Hollow Creek, August 4, 1866. The family moved across into Edgefield (now Saluda) County in 1868, and to the present Hare homestead in the winter of 1869-'70. He was educated in the "Old Field" schools of that period, with only one term in high school, The Leesville English and Classical Institute 1887-'88. He studied land surveying and took a course in Commercial Law and Bookkeeping under Professor D. P. Busby in the summer of 1888. He was a partner and manager of General Merchandise Business of Hare, Eargle and Company, Delmar, 1888-1897. Postmaster of Caughmans (later Delmar) January 1889 to October 1897, inclusive. He taught school intermittently 1884-1904; practiced surveying 1895-1905; studied telegraphy and railroad station agency and did work for the Southern Railway 1897-1900 at Ward, Batesburg, Leesville, Gilbert, Lexington, Blythewood, Pomaria, Honea Path, Belton and Seivern; appointed rural letter carrier and began work on Route 1, Delmar, August 1, 1905; attached as Route 7, Leesville, April 1909; carrier for Consolidated Route 2 and 7, Leesville June 1930 and retired September 30, 1931. He was married to Mary Isabel Craps, November 3, 1889. They reared two daughters and three sons. He joined R. C. L. Association soon after entering service and is still a member. He was treasurer of the county association 1908-1909; president 1910-1911 and 1925-1926; Secretary 1912-1922; Financial Secretary-Treasuruer 1929-1932. He attended all state meetings since 1910, except two, was a delegate to National Convention, Nashville, Tennessee, 1912, and Cleveland, Ohio, 1925, when S. C. broke the record of states and went 100 percent membership. Visitor to National Convention, Philadelphia, 1926, and Savannah, 1929. Member of I. O. O. F. and W. O. W. and filled all chairs in former and clerk of latter for six or seven years. Member of Lutheran Church; Superintendent of Sunday School in younger days and has been Superintendent of Mt. Hebron Sunday School since 1917 and a member of its church council for more than 30 years. Editor of Rural Carriers Association Department in the State for one year and is now Historian of the State Association. Has served 35 years in the United States Postal Service.

The foregoing was copied from A History of South Carolina

Rural Letter Carriers Association with the said William Henry Hare as Historian.

Wlliam Henry Hare was baptized in Cedar Grove Lutheran Church by the Rev. Adam Efird. He was confirmed on May 25, 1879 in the following class: Johnie L. B. Hallman, W. H. Hare, Henry Hite, Henry Morgan, Simeon Addy, Shuford Davis, Mary Craps and M. C. Goff.

Henry Hare was a very active churchman in Cedar Grove during his younger days: He was Sunday School Superintendent, Choir Leader, Sunday School teacher, etc. When Mt. Hebron church was built, near his home in the Delmar section, he was a charter member.

At the time of his youth, schools in this part of South Carolina were still in a very primitive condition. Young Hare was an ambitious young man and from his early youth was of a studious nature. Due to the fact that he was physically handicapped in his feet, by being scalded with a kettle of boiling water when a baby, he realized when a boy that it would be best for him to prepare himself for mental work instead of physical work.

We find from his life's study that he applied himself in every undertaking. His all important principle was to be accurate in his work.

As a teacher, he was successful, because he was firm in his expression, thorough and accurate in his principles of teaching.

As a surveyor, he stood for what was right, was neat and accurate with his work, was firm to express his convictions in settling disputes.

No better Mail Carrier ever served the patrons on his route. He was always interested in discharging his duties as required by postal regulations.

We quote from Shealy Family History:

Adam Shealy, Sr.

"Adam Shealy and wife, Mary Seittenberg, had a large family. A sektch of his children was prepared by the late Mr. W. H. Hare, of Leesville. His records were published in the county papers several years ago. Mr. Hare was a gifted writer. Being much interested in tracing out the pioneer settlers of his section. He wrote for our local papers and ran these interesting accounts and sketches of families, for news items. These sketches were so interesting, that practically every home in Lexington and Saluda Counties have clippings of his writings from these papers."

We think so much of them that we are using some of his own family sketches in this edition, rightly giving him credit for his work.

I have often wished his whole life's work of news gathering, records, files, data of every description, that he was interested in preserving, could have been compiled and put in book form.

Mr. and Mrs. Hare were the parents of five children, three sons and two daughters. William Everette married Eloise Hite, daughter of Dr. P. W. Hite and wife, Victoria Eargle; Edgar Allen (1894-1942) married Anna Ruth Hare (1895-1950), daughter of Mr. and Mrs. Allen Hare; Leonard Murray married Juliette Fulmer, daughter of Tyre Fulmer and wife, Ione Mitchell; Rosannah Catherine married M. Gairy Crout; Elvira married Callie Moore. All his living children are living in the home community and are loyal citizens and good church people. Mr. Hare, with his wife, mother, and son, Edgar, also Edgar's wife and two children sleep in the Hare family plot in Mt. Hebron cemetery.

DAVID S. KEISLER, M. D.

DR. DAVID SOCRATES KEISLER

DR. DAVID Socrates Keisler was born September 13, 1878, the oldest son of Jasocb Walter and Ann Crout Keisler. He was born and reared in the Cedar Grove section near Leesville, was a lifetime member of Cedar Grove Lutheran Church, having served as Superintendent of the Sunday School at one time.

He graduated from Lenoir Rhyne College and received his M. D. degree from the Medical College of South Carolina, Charleston, in 1911.

In 1910 he married the former Miss Frances Pauline Hutto. They have seven children, four daughters: Mrs. Hugh C. Lucas, of Orlando, Fla., Mrs. A. L. Buck, of Sumter, Mrs. Homer M. Aull, of Leesville, Mrs. Paul W. Kamman, of Chicago, Ill., and three sons, Lt. Col. David S. Keisler, now serving with the armed forces in Alaska, Walter P. Keisler and William G. Keisler, both of Leesville.

Dr. Keisler began his profession in New Holland, later moved to Ward, then to Inman, S. C. and in 1920 moved to Leesville, S. C. He practiced for 35 years. He served as President of the Lexington County Medical Association for several years.

Dr. Keisler was like the good Samaritan—always doing good for others. His quiet manner, friendly personality, and willingness to help all who were in trouble, made him near and dear to the hearts of all who knew him.

Dr. Keisler was stricken early Sunday morning on March 24, 1946, after making a call in the country. Although ill, he continued to serve others until within a few minutes of his death.

Funeral services were conducted March 26, 1946 at Cedar Grove Lutheran Church, the officiating minister was the Rev. Joseph C. Derrick. Interment followed in the cemetery.

DR. J. GORDON SEASTRUNK

DR. J. GORDON SEASTRUNK

DR. J. GORDON Seastrunk, son of Jacob J. Seastrunk and Dona Hite Seastrunk, was born December 7, 1908. Gordon received his literary education from the Cedar Grove Public School, Batesburg-Leesville High School, finishing there in 1928. He completed his college course at Newberry College in 1932. He finished at the Medical College of the State of South Carolina in 1937. He served his internship at Columbia Hospital 1937-1938. Dr. Seastrunk was Resident Physician of S. C. Sanitorium, State Park, S. C., 1938-'39. He was Superintendent of Ridgewood Sanitarium 1940-'42, U. S. Air Force Flight Surgeon 1942-1945, serving in the European Theater for 18 months. He is a Fellow of American College of Chest Physicians and is a Columbia physician.

Doctor Seastrunk married Miss Elizabeth Allen Parrott of John's Island, South Carolina, on July 9, 1940. They have two children, John and Ellen.

Doctor Seastrunk and family reside at 1707 Maplewood Drive, Columbia, South Carolina.

MYRTLE ADDY

MYRTLE SEASTRUNK ADDY

MYRTLE Seastrunk Addy was born September 14, 1905, daughter of J. J. Seastrunk and wife, Dona Hite Seastrunk. She attended the Cedar Grove Public Schools until she completed the elementary grades. She received her high school training at the Batesburg-Leesville High School, then took a four-year course at Summerland College. Being musically talented and inclined, she studied music for eight years, graduating in music at Summerland College. She studied piano for eight years and violin for three years.

After completing her musical education she taught piano for twenty-five years.

She organized the Light Brigade in Cedar Grove Congregation about 1921 and was head of this organization for 15 years. In 1940 she organized the Primary Department of the Sunday School. She was elected organist of Cedar Grove in February 1941 and served in that capacity for about ten years. (Miss Mary Alma Hite succeeded her and is now the present organist.)

In the year of 1947, with the assistance of Mrs. J. C. Derrick, she was instrumental in organizing the Women's Missionary Society in circles, which is known as the Women of the Church.

Mrs. Addy is now employed at the Columbia hospital, Columbia, S. C.

She was married to Henry Edward Addy June 15, 1926. They have one daughter, Doris (Mrs. Lewis Shealy) of West Columbia, S. C.

DR. F. K. SHEALY, FATHER AND SISTER

FESTUS KILLIAN SHEALY, M. D.
Clinton, S. C.

DR. FESTUS Killian Shealy was born in the Cedar Grove Community of Lexington County, South Carolina. The only son of Franklin Pierce Shealy and wife, Lucinda Shealy. Dr. Shealy received his elementary training in the public schools of his home of 1905, completing his A. B. Degree in 1909. His medical course community. He entered Lenoir College, Hickory, N. C., in the fall was taken in the South Carolina Medical College of Charleston, finishing in 1912. His first practice was in the city of Newberry, S. C.

For more than 25 years he has been a very successful practitioner in the city of Clinton, S. C., besides doing considerable work in the hospital.

Dr. Shealy has taken graduate courses in children's diseases and medicine in New York. He served as assistant surgeon in Roper Hospital, Charleston, S. C., and for a short while, was connected with a hospital in New York.

Dr. Shealy is a specialist in diseases of children and in anesthetics. Other medical men value his opinion and often call him in consultation.

Dr. Shealy is a member of the County, State and American Medical Association. He has been active in the Rotary Club and the Methodist Church.

O. C. HOLLEY, M. D.

DR. HOLLEY

DR. OLIVER Cromwell Holley was born Nov. 1, 1883, son of William B. and Debbie Nichols Holley. Being born of Lutheran parents, he was baptized in infancy and in young manhood became a confirmed member of Union Evangelical Lutheran Church, one of its founders being his grandfather, Luke Nichols.

He received his literary education in the schools of Edgefield County, later becoming Saluda County. His preliminary medical education was under Dr. P. W. Hite. He read medicine for some time under Dr. Hite, as was required at that time. Therefore, Dr. P. W. Hite served Dr. O. C. Holley as a preceptor when he read medicine.

He received the first two years of his medical education at the University of Georgia. He completed his medical course at Maryland Medical College located at Baltimore, Maryland, graduating there in June, 1905. He took his internship at Franklin Square Hospital, Baltimore, Maryland. He specialized in Gynecology, the diseases of women and their hygeine.

In 1907, he married Lilla G. Shirey, daughter of George C. and Eliza Eargle Shirey. They were the parents of one child, a son, George Ray Holley, who married Mildred Chadwick, of Saluda, S. C.

Dr. and Mrs. Holley have two grandchildren, William Chadwick, having graduated at the University of South Carolina at the age of 19, and who is now a foreman of the Celanese Corporation of America, located at Rock Hill, S. C. The other grandchild is a girl, named Betty Rae, who is now a freshman at Converse College, Spartanburg, S. C.

These grandchildren are much devoted to "Grand-Doc," as they commonly call him.

Dr. Holley has been president of the Lexington Medical Association several times.

He is now a member of the Board of Delegates to the State Medical Association.

Dr. Holley did the greater part of his early practice in the state of Georgia until 1915. Due to the fact that his aged parents needed regular attention from him, it became necessary for him to locate near them. Since then he has regularly covered a radius of 15 miles or more until now, since age is creeping up on him, he is losing some of his physical activity. This necessitates his slowing down, his office practice has increased, so he doesn't have a chance to do a great deal of traveling practice.

Dr. Holley, being intensely devoted to his profession, soon won the confidence and respect of the people he served. Dr. Holley would respond to the call of one poverty-stricken even though he be of the colored race, as quickly as he would to the wealthy and influential.

Since Dr. Holley began praticing medicine, he has delivered more than 3,000 babies.

During the terrible Influenza Epidemic that invaded this country in 1918, Dr. Holley states that he passed through some very trying ordeals. In the early part of 1919, this epidemic became a deadly foe over a good portion of his practice. He employed a chauffeur to do his driving, for eight weeks on a stretch and he seldom had time to change clothes or shoes. Sometimes it would be necessary for him or his assistant to bring a corpse out of the house for the undertaker. On one occasion it was necessary to stop at a cemetery and help lower dead bodies in the graves. So many people were sick, all activities ceased. Dr. Holley reports that in all his travels for six weeks in succession, he never saw anyone traveling except the R. F. D. Mail Carrier.

I can verify this statement. I was principal of the Holley School in Saluda County at that time—a three-teacher school with 128 pupils. The majority of the pupils and teachers were stricken with the disease in less than 48 hours. Some becoming deathly sick at school, unable to walk home. About this time a business man from the northeastern section of the U. S. contacted me on a certain business deal and reported that in his city deaths were so numerous that it was impossible to give people decent burials. The city authorities would provide trenches made by bulldozers to bury thousands of dead bodies at the time.

I firmly recall the fact that at Camp Jackson, Columbia, S. C., soldiers of World War I died so rapidly that caskets could not be provided. It was no uncommon thing to see dead bodies stacked in baggage cars as trains passed stations.

Dr. Holley is recognized by the surrounding hospitals as a good diagnostician. He seldom fails on a diagnosis.

Dr. Holley is much loved and highly respected by the great multitude of people he has had opportunity to serve. He has always been very lenient in charges for his service. He has always been very accommodating in his practice in that he carries his medicine with him and diligently looks after his patients. All said, he talks in the language of us common country folks.

His father, W. B. Holley, died at the age of 78 and his mother died at the age of 91. Mother Holley attributed her long life to the fact that she always obeyed her father and mother.

The first child Dr. Holley delivered was Nancy Catherine Eargle Fulmer (1905-1930).

IN PUBLIC OFFICE

GOOD INFLUENCE SPREADS AFAR FROM CEDAR GROVE

(A clipping from "The State," Oct. 27, 1947, written by
Mrs. J. C. Derrick).

CEDAR Grove? "Why, there's no such post office"! you exclaim. You're right. There isn't. And it's not incorporated. But there is such a place. It's a populous section between Leesville and Lexington, enclosed by highways No. 1, 43, 391 and 113.

It is the home of Lexington County's Auditor, C. E. Leaphart, and his predecessor, the late Clyde Addy, who served in that capacity for many years.

It is the home of the County Clerk of Court, Henry E. Addy, brother of the late auditor.

It is the home of the County Sheriff, Henry M. Caughman.

Within two miles of Cedar Grove Church is the birth place of the late P. C. Price, affectionately known as "Mr. Columbus Price," who was well known as a business man and church man in Columbia.

Two of the state's physicians, Dr. J. Gordon Seastrunk, of Columbia, and Dr. Festus K. Shealy, of Clinton, who heads the widespread Shealy clan as president, hail from the Cedar Grove section.

The Rev. Victor D. Derrick, pastor of the first United Lutheran Church of Memphis, Tennessee, and the Rev. Clyde G. Steele, pastor of Holy Trinity Lutheran Church of Chicago, Illinois, which numbers more than 1,100 members, are sons of the community, as are the Rev. P. D. Risinger of Silver Street and the Rev. L. L. Swygert of Irmo. The Rev. Roy Addy, now pastor of a large Lutheran church in Chicago, the Rev. C. I. Morgan, retired Lutheran Minister of Leesville, and the late Rev. Enoch Hite, who served Lutheran pastorates in North Carolina, also were reared in the community and were members of Cedar Grove Lutheran Church. Dr. F. Grover Morgan, of Hickory, N. C., and all his noted ancestors were Cedar Grove people.

N. E. Derrick, well known business man of Columbia, a C. P. A., is a brother of the Rev. Victor Derrick. Their mother and sister, Mrs. Blake Kelley and her family are residents of the community.

The lates Dr. D. S. Keisler, past president of the Lexington County Medical Association, was a native of the Cedar Grove section.

His father, J. Walter Keisler still lives in the community. A former school teacher, Mr. Keisler keeps well informed through the daily newspapers which he is able to read without the aid of glasses, although he is 93 years old. He enjoys comparatively good health.

The governor of the state awarded the five star trophy to Mrs. Andrew L. Addy of this section, whose five sons served in the late war, two of them are still serving as officers, one with the army of occupation in Stuttgart, Germany.

This same family of Addys are the producers of the fancy peaches known to Columbians as "Addy's Specials" and so featured in some of the chain groceries in the capitol.

Miss Grace Addy, in the Music Department of Bishopville High School, Miss Ruth Oxner, at Greeleyville High School, Eddie Derrick, principal of the school at Cape Hatteras, N. C., E. Leo Derrick, principal of Chadbourne, N. C., High School, Miss Catherine Oxner at Monetta, Omar Derrick, at Edgefield, and Mrs. Virgie C. Hite, Superintendent of the schools at Chapin, are a few of the native sons and daughters given to the teaching profession. Others serve in California, Georgia and North Carolina and in the local schools.

Cedar Grove Lutheran Church, a large red brick structure with white trim and tall spire, which can be seen from the surrounding territory, numbers more than 700 in its membership and dominates the life of the community.

Its pastor, the Rev. Joseph C. Derrick, is a graduate of Newberry College and the Lutheran Seminary at Columbia. Its Sunday School Superintendent, R. Hoy Caughman, is a Clemson College graduate. Its treasurer, N. Gordon Oxner, a former University of South Carolina student, is a local farmer.

CedarGrove Church rose to its present size largely through the misfortune of a sister congregation, old Salem Church, which lost its church building through fire. The members, many of them, brought their names, property, their loyalty and devotion into Cedar Grove Church. Many members of another sister congregation, Macedonia Church, Little Mountain, likewise came into Cedar Grove Church when the back waters of Lake Murray forced them to move into other farming sections. Another Lutheran Congregation, Mt. Pleasant, was forced to disband on account of the development of Lake Murray. A number of members came from that church to Cedar Grove. The church service flag during the late war was not large enough to contain its eighty stars—not one of which was gold.

Cedar Grove has no business section, though numbers of small stores dot its cross roads. There are the Ridge Road, C. Covington's and A. Bedenbaugh's stores on the Ridge Road; A. J. Snelgrove's and Paul Ray Snelgrove's on Highway 43; C. V. Addy's and Quincy Lybrand's near Rawl's Mill, and several other stores at Murray, the neighboring community; Rawl's Flour Mill, now operated by Qincy Lybrand, attracts people from distant sections.

No account of Cedar Grove life would be complete without mention of J. Ansel Caughman, who is Lexington County's Chairman of the P. M. A. Mr. Caughman's extensive acreage is kept clean and ordered. Hunters and fishermen are given free access to his lands. For many years he was a school teacher, but now Mr. Caughman's time is given entirely to his business and farm interest and to his community service. He is sometimes affectionately called Cedar Grove's "preacher," perhaps because he has for years taught the adult Bible Class at Cedar Grove Church, and served the church in nearly every other official capacity, for many years as superintendent of the Sunday School.

But Mr. Caughman has earned the title in other ways—through his friendship of the poor, his council and guidance so freely given in family and personal matters, his expenditure of effort and time in humane and civic affairs, his love and care in preserving the best in the community.

In Mr. Caughman's fine meadow, so reminiscent of some of those in the Shenandoah Valley and grazed by a splendid herd of white faced Herefords, stands the living hull of an enormous walnut tree, the haunt of willowy white cranes and the vantage ground of fussy, greedy crows. Everything else is so well ordered and clean, you wonder why it is left standing.

It stands on the skirmish grounds where a bunch of Tories were defeated, captured and hanged during the Revolutionary War. The huge walnut tree marks the identical spot where the Tories were buried.

SCENE ON BIG HOLLOW CREEK

SECTION III

ORIGINAL FAMILIES
WHO HAVE CONTRIBUTED
to the
RELIGIOUS LIFE OF CEDAR GROVE
and
SURROUNDING COMMUNITY

CAUGHMAN

THE Caughmans are of German extraction, according to dates on land grants to them, Andrew, Martin and Christopher, they came to this country about 1787. A grant was made to Christopher Caughman for 400 acres of land which covered the identical lots on which Cedar Grove now stands and where the abandoned Salem stood and the entire surrounding lands.

Christopher and Martin decided to establish homes on Saluda River near where the Wyse Ferry was, now under waters of Lake Murray. Therefore, they conveyed their interest in the aforesaid grant to Andrew Caughman who had already settled on these premises, near where Roddy Roberts now lives.

We find that on the eighth day of March, 1792 Andrew Caughman set aside 16 acres of land to be used for religious purposes and conveyed same by deed to Salem Congregation, a true copy of which is found in this edition.

The children of Andrew Caughman and wife, Anne Maria, were John (1789), Barbara, Jemima, Emanuel (1802-1881), Daniel (1800), Jacob (1796-1860), Catherine and Elizabeth. Andrew died after 1830. He and his wife are buried east of Salem about one-half mile, between two enormous boulders of stone.

John Caughman married Catherine Risinger and the following children are recorded: Andrew (1816) whose wife was named Elizabeth, and among whose children were James (commonly called "Crosseyed Jim") who married Sallie Swygert, and Laura, who married first Ensley Taylor and second, Henry Hite; Thomas (1818) whose wife was named Polly, were the parents of Levi Caughman, who married Tera Risinger and lived for many years near Salem Church, then moved into Saluda County and is buried in Good Hope Cemetery.

Bethany (1819), Dempsey (1825), Julia (1830), three maids who lived with their nephew, Levi, for a long time and then with their nephew, James, until they died. Noah died when a young man.

Barbara married Absalom Roberts, of Lexington county; Jemima Caughman married John Black of Edgefield county, now Saluda County.

Emanuel Caughman, who became a prominent Lutheran minister of his day, married first Susannah Black, who was the mother of all his children. Second, Nancy Derrick, sister of Emanuel Derrick and Mary Derrick, who married John William Ballentine. Emanuel Caughman's third wife was Mrs. Anna Gates.

The children of Emanuel Caughman were Ellen (1825-1911), who married Jesse Derrick (1813-1884); James married Mary Ann Wise and died in the Civila War in Mississippi; Allen died while attending the Theological Seminary at Lexington, S. C.; Martin Luther (1836-1861) died in the Civil War; Martha married Captain A. P.

West, of Edgefield County; Elizabeth (1840-1938) married John S. Derrick, a brother of her step-mother; Kate married Joseph Hiller, of Georgia and was the mother of Rev. W. H. Hiller; and John C. married Laura Derrick, daughter of Emanuel Derrick. He spent his whole life at the Caughman homestead near Delmar. He, with his family, was a charter member of Mt. Hebron Lutheran Church. He was the first treasurer of Saluda County. He, his wife and several children are buried in Mt. Hebron cemetery. There was a son, Berley, who died young.

Daniel Caughman married Mary Shealy, a sister of Jacob J. and David C. Shealy, of Leesville. The following children are recorded: William married Elizabeth Swygert, a sister of Zeddo Swygert and daughter of Christian Swygert. They left no children; Josiah married Mary M. Swygert. They moved to Mississippi. Rev. Carl Caughman, D. D., of Orangeburg, S. C., is a direct descendant of this couple; George E. (1829-1862) married Maria Drafts (1834-1897). Their children were Edwin F., Henry, Ansel, Irvin and Ann. George died of typhoid fever in the Civil War. His brother, William, went after his body, brought it home and buried it in a family plot at home one Sunday. His brother, William, took sick, died and was buried in Union Cemetery the next Sunday. Martha Caughman married Forest Derrick and moved to Mississippi.

Jacob Caughman married first a Shealy, then Katie Kinard and lastly Elizabeth Wise Derrick, the widow of John Derrick and the mother of Jesse Derrick. We can note the following children of Jacob Caughman: Juriah married Adam Kinard; Noah married Elizabeth Matthews; George D. married Sarah Rinehart.

Kate Caughman married a Bickley and Elizabeth, the last named of the children of the first Andrew Caughman, married Acel Roberts.

All the Caughmans of the Andrew line moved away from the ancestral home or died out except one family of the Daniel line, the family of George. All the Caughmans of the George line have moved away except the descendants of Edwin F. (1853-1938). This family and one son of Irvin, Charley, are the only remaining Caughmans in Big Hollow Creek Valley.

LEWIS J. LANGFORD

LANGFORD

THE Langfords came from England in Colonial days; some settled along the Potomac River in Virginia, and thence emigrated into the southern colonies; some probably landed at Charleston and gradually worked their way to the interior of South Carolina. The Langfords who were the progenitors of the Lexington County families, came from one John Langford, according to the traditions handed down through the generations. This John Langford was killed by the Indians in Alabama, and there are two brothers mentioned in the traditions: Tom, who was a slave trader and was killed and robbed of his money in Alabama; and Sam, who fought in the Revolution under William Washington's command and was killed on Rocky Creek in what is now Saluda County. After the war his gold watch was found by John Faulkner while clearing land.

The first John Langford had a son named John, who was the ancestor of all our Lexington County Langfords. He died from wounds received early in the Revolution and was buried somewhere about the location of the Sibley Cotton Mills in Graniteville, S. C. His wife, whom he left with two small sons, Asa and James, was Nancy Presnall, a French woman. After the war she married William Calk.

Asa Langford (1773-1857), son of John and Nancy Presnall Langford, settled in Lexington District on the south side of Saluda River at the place now known as the George Dreher Place. His first wife was a Snelgrove, who bore him the following children, John Ray, who went to Alabama; Dorothy, who married Joshua Miller; Elizabeth, who married George Roberts; and Anne, who first married a Matthews and then Carey Snelgrove. His second wife was Susannah Bell (1781-1845), and she bore him William Stanmore, ancestor of Newberry Langfords, who married Sarah Sawyer; Susan, who married Hezekiah Dreher and was the mother of George L. Dreher; and Almenia, who married George Haltiwanger. One of the Haltiwanger children (Kate) married Jimmie Hendrix, of Lexington, and celebrated her 96th birthday on October 18, 1935. Asa Langford's monument, with that of his second wife, are in the cemetery of Old Lexington Baptist Church in the home community, having been moved from the Lake Murray area.

Asa Langford was the first secretary of Old Lexington Baptist Church which was organized in 1813, near Amick's Ferry, now covered by waters of Lake Murray. About 1852 the church was moved to where it now stands. In those days great care was taken in the construction of buildings by morticing and pegging together the structure, which made quite a bit of refuse, such as chips, shavings, etc. A terrible fire, always known afterwards as the Great March Fire, swept through this country, burning all the chips, shavings, etc., under this church, but a kind Providence spared this building which is still in use today (1951).

James Langford, the other named son of John and Nancy Presnall Langford, married Nancy Bell, a sister of the second wife of his brother, Asa, and their home was about two miles up the river from that of his brother, and near the mouth of Rocky Creek, where his son, John J., lived within the memory of our older people now living. They reared the following children: James (1810-1875), who married Ascenith Davis (1808-1897); William, who married a Waites and moved to Alabama; John, who married first Rosannah Holley, a sister of Daniel D. Holley, and then Sarah Ann Langford; Nancy, who married Tyre Snelgrove; Martha, who married John Harman; and Susie, who married Julius Snelgrove. Besides these children, Asa, Joab and Elizabeth died young.

A third John Langford (1797-1862), son of Asa Langford, married Milberry Matthews, a sister of the wife of Garrett Matthews. They settled a little farther up the river on Rocky Creek near the old spring known as the Langford Spring which is now covered by the waters of Lake Murray. This property is now owned by the writer, J. Ansel Caughman, and I would like to inform all readers that is was one of the most beautiful springs I ever saw, a beautiful stream of ice cold water continually flowed from its veins, which came from under huge flint beds of rock. People living in this community for a great distance around used this spring. The writer used this plantation for a pasture from 1914 to 1925.

The children of this John Milberry Matthews were as follows: John, who died in infancy; Dr. Asa (1828-1904), who married Susie Rinehart; Sarah Ann (1839-1881), who was the second wife of John J. Langford, son of her great uncle, James Langford; Dorcas, who married Zeb Havird; Patrick, who married Caroline Holley, and were the parents of Julius P. Langford. After the death of Patrick Langford, the widow married Anderson P. Derrick. Father John's monument was moved to Old Lexington Baptist Church from the lake area.

James Langford, Jr., (1810-1875), a son of the first James Langford, who married Ascenith Davis (1808-1897) had a son named William (commonly known as "Hib") Langford who died in 1900; who married Sibbie Crout, daughter of David Crout. Their home was near the home of his father, and he operated the once popular Langford flour and grist mill which had been established at the Langford shoals on Saluda River. Their children were James D., who married first Mary C. Goff, and then Lilla Lee Swygert; and Amanda (1873), who married James L. Shealy.

James Langford, Sr., had another son, John J. (1818-1892) who lived at his father's old homestead. He first married Rosannah Holley (1815-1842) as stated, and they had one son, George, who married first Vina Shealy, a daughter, of Michael Shealy, a sister of Mrs. Billie Derrick; he second married Fannie Powell. George moved to Blythewood, S. C., and was the father of Dr. Mike and Clark Langford, both of Blythewood. He was killed at 82 by an automobile. The second wife of John J. Langford was his cousin, Sarah Ann Langford (1839-1881), as already mentioned and by whom he had eight children, all of whom died young except Lewis J., Joan and Joshua.

Lewis James Langford (1848-1937) married first Sarah Stockman, by whom he had one son, George W. (1868) who married Minnie Harman, daughter of Luther Harman, and who was county supervisor of Saluda County. The second wife of Lewis J. Langford was Mary Louise aBnks (1843-1914), daughter of George Banks. The children of this marriage were: Lizzie (1870-1942) who married William L. Taylor; Estelle (1872-1935), who married Lindsey Boozer; John Lewis "Bub" (1876-1940), who married Viola Wallace of North Carolina; Susie (1877-) who married Dan J. Taylor; Daisy (1879-1898) died young; Harry Lee (born 1882), married Eula Derrick, great niece of Billie Derrick; Maude (born 1883) married Ed George; Frank (born 1888) who married Lucy Dominick, a niece of Rev. H. A. McCullough, of Columbia, S. C.; second marriage was to Eva Gantt; and Boyce (1887-1924) who married Rachael Yonce, daughter of Lewis Yonce, of Johnston, S. C. The dead of this family rest in the cemetery of Old Lexington Baptist Church. Frank is the only living Langford in this community any more.

Joshua Langford (born 1859) married first Mary Rivers. To them were born Henry and Ruth. After Mary's death he married Mittie Hill. We understand that Fred Kirby, the radio and minstrel singer whom many of us have heard perform, is a grandson of Josh Langford.

Joan Langford (born 1870) married Alec Calk.

The elder Langfords were buried in family plots along the river where their remains still lie except the "Hib" Langford family, which was removed out of the lake area to the Old Lexington Baptist Church, several of the monuments were moved to this church cemetery—the church of their faith.

Lewis Langford was an excellent politician and served as supervisor of Lexington County for a number of years. He was very poetic, writing several very pathetic poems.

> I have lived for eighty-one long years,
> I've had joys, sorrows, doubts and fears.
> My people all are loved most dear;
> For them I yet can shed a tear.
> My days on earth can not be long,
> And I must die live right or wrong.
> No one can tell how long or how short
> Nor when we all will have to part.
> The young, the old, the bond and free
> Must all cross o'er death's dark sea;

The rich, the poor, the young and brave
Must all lie in their silent graves.
I'll bid farewell to friend and foe
From this vile world I'll have to go,
The road is narrow and it's straight
That leads us all to the Pearly Gates.
—Written by Lewis J. Langford.

DR. J. R. LANGFORD

RECENTLY Dr. J. R. Langford, of Swansea, Lexington County, passed away in his 83rd year. Doctor Langford was born and reared near Prosperity, Newberry County, and his father was a physician before him, and a gentleman who played a conspicuous and dramatic part in the delivery of the state from radical rule. Doctor Langford and his forebears have always been amongst the state's most upright and exemplary citizens.

For more than 40 years Doctor Langford had practiced his profession in the vicinity of Swansea. He was an excellent physician and loved his profession with an intense devotion. When one was in pain and suffering Doctor Langford responded, and spared no effort to relieve the sufferer and compensation for his services was never a factor. He would respond to the call of a suffering Negro or person without worldly goods as quickly as he would to a call of the rich and influential. His great heart went out to all, whether their distress was of suffering or other misfortune. So in his passing we find that there has gone from us the perfect type of "the family physician," and many hearts will be sorely distressed by the losing of the help and advice of this kindly, knightly old gentleman of the old school.

I have known Doctor Langford for many years, and I have never seen a man who literally took the Word of God as his daily guide as did this gentleman. Whenever he was not busy in his office, he could be found reading his Bible. From many notations on the margin of his Bible it could be seen that he not only read the Bible many times, but he had studied it and lived from it.

In more recent years of his life he suffered a great deal of pain, but no one ever heard him complain. He was active in his profession up to the day of his death and took a keen interest in the affairs of the nation and his beloved state. Truly a "man after God's own heart" has passed from our midst into a very rich heritage.

E. O. DePASS, Columbia.

Dr. John R. Langford was born April 19, 1856 and died August 21, 1938. The above is a copy of a newspaper clipping in the possession of Herbert Langford. He says it was clipped from the "State" newspaper shortly after Dr. Langford's death. The copy was made by Maude Langford in November 1951.

The following appeared in "The State," dated December 14, 1926:

(147)

SAMPSON BRIDGES WON BY LANGFORD
Prosperity Doctor Induced Negro Legislator to Turn, Giving Democrats Control.

An interesting and critical incident of 1876 is related in the following letter, published in "The State" some years ago.

To the Editor of "The State":

The recent Red Shirt reunion in Columbia brings back to me memories of the past. Though then a mere lad of 18 years, I rode in the Red Shirt ranks and belonged to the Prosperity Rifle Company, which, 65 strong, was ordered out and went to Columbia by special train to report for duty in the trying and exciting times of '76 and in the days of Reconstruction. We were there when all the militia of the state was brought to Columbia, when Gen. Mart Gary made that famous speech at night on a dry goods box in front of the Grand Central Hotel and advocated a cleaning out of the Republicans from our state capital; when every patriotic citizen was wrought up to fighting heat; when Gen. Wade Hampton counselled peace and quiet, and advised that we do no rash act; when it was decided to organize a Democratic legislature and the "Wallace House" as it was then called, was formed and the record of which all are familiar with.

I know no more fitting times to record one more historic fact: When the opposing political factions were at fighting pitch and each clamoring for government control, when the Democrats decided to take charge of the government and to organize a general assembly and Governor Hampton, being declared chief executive of South Carolina, the general assembly was organized and after every effort had been brought to bear to get a working majority; but we were still lacking one member to give us that majority; then it was that the crowning act came. This is what actuates me to make this true statement which has never been recorded.

It was due to the many, courageous and patriotic effort of Dr. A. F. Langford, of Prosperity, that he and I went quietly to hunt up the Negro Republican, Sampson Bridges, who had worked under my supervision frequently on my father's farm near Prosperity. I remember well that after a diligent search we found Bridges, coming across him while in company with some other Republican members of the Legislature on the street. Doctor Langford attracted his attention and led him back through an alley way, and when away from the then crowded street and in private and in my presence, not by force or arms, nor threats nor intimidation, but by logical reasoning, Doctor Langford induced Sampson Bridges to turn over to the Democracy; and we marched him into the Democratic Assembly, and he was sworn in as a representative of that body. This was the climax and final turning point for the triumph of Democracy in South Carolina.

The Democracy of Newberry County nor of South Carolina never gave Doctor Langford just praise, credit or reward for what he did in those trying times. He was a man of superior mind and ability and an able physician. Having been a student of his, as required at that time, he served me as preceptor when I read medicine, and though he some years ago "passed over the river," I want his children, who are Mrs. J. F. Lyon, of Columbia, Dr. J. R. Langford, of Swansea, Dudley and Pickens Langford, of Prosperity, and his relatives and friends to know the important part he played in the days of Reconstruction. Let us give credit now to whom credit is due.

The Negro, Sampson Bridges, was above the average of his race in intelligence, and was of no mean character. Doctor Langford was Bridge's physician as long as he lived and had always a wonderful influence over the Negro.

Bridges afterward worked frequently on my father's farm under my supervision, and often told us that he thought it was his duty to stand by the people who raised him and cared for him.

D. M. CROSSON, Leesville.

JACOB DRAFTS' OLD HOME, BUILT BEFORE THE REVOLUTIONARY WAR

DRAFTS

A CCORDING to the census bureau at Washington, D. C., a young man, Jacob Drafts, at the age of 17, landed on the shores of Carolina in the year 1750. Jacob Drafts came from Germany. A few years after his arrival in this country, he married Christena Kelley and settled on Big Hollow Creek in what is now Lexington County. They erected a log house which had an attic ceiled with 20-inch boards. This house was erected before the Revolutionary War. Enormous lightwood logs were used for sills. This old building was torn down in 1947. These sills were still perfectly solid. They were sawed into sills and used again for the foundation of a house in the town of Leesville. The chimney was built of rock with a brick funnel. These bricks came from England.

We have no record of how many children were born to this union, but we do have a record of at least five who married and produced families.

Jacob Drafts lived to be a very old man, evidently in the high nineties when he lost his life. Being old and feeble, he fell from his porch and broke his neck. He is buried near his old home about 200 yards from Big Hollow Creek, now a part of Lake Murray. The cemetery contains nine grown graves unmarked. However, he died in 1835. The cemetery is covered with a bed of flint rock crossed by an REA electric line. This property is now owned by the writer, a great-great grandson of Jacob Drafts. He was the father of three sons, Daniel, Henry and Jesse.

Two of these, Daniel and Henry, settled in the same community not far distant from the paternal homestead. They became large land holders and owners of numerous slaves.

Daniel married Juliann Wingard, from the Dutch Fork, and she became the mother of eleven children, namely: Eliza, Maria, Irvin, Franklin, Jefferson, Henry, George, Samuel, John, Juliann, and Sarah.

Daniel married twice, his last wife was Anginetta Henrietta Hayes, who was the mother of three children, Moses, Ruth and Inez, who married Dr. D. R. Kneece and is still living at Pelion, S. C. Moses and Ruth died young with diptheria when that terrible epidemic swept through this area causing the death of more than fifty percent of the children born about 75 years ago.

Back to Daniel and Juliann Drafts' children. Daniel was born 1803 and lived 'till 1888, being 85 years old at death. He married Juliann Wingard on the second day of February 1829. The first child born was a girl, Eliza Bethany, 1832. She married Walter Hook, who lived near Columbia, S. C. Mr. Hook was keeper of the toll bridge across the Congaree River and owned hundreds of acres of land lying northwest of West Columbia, around and including Green Hill. They reared a large family and have a number of living descendants in and around West Columbia. They are buried in the Hook cemetery, near Hook's store. This section has become a thriving suburb of West Columbia.

The next child, Maria Almenia, was born 1834. She married George Caughman and settled near Ridge Road schoolhouse on Ridge Road. Their children were Edwin, Irvin, Henry, Ansel and Ann. Their write up comes under the Caughman sketch. The old home is owned and occupied by a great-grandson, Carl Swygert.

Maria Drafts Caughman was the writer's grandmother. She, with her husband and several sons, is buried in a family plot near the old homestead.

Jacob Franklin Drafts was born 1836. He died while he was a young man. unmarried. Daniel Drafts had a number of sons in the Civil War. They loved horseback riding and all belonged to the Calvary.

Jefferson Luther was born 1838. He married Polly Buff and settled near Barr's, later lived near Columbia. He has a number of living descendants living in Lexington County and other parts of the state. Quite a few are prominent citizens, among which are Rev. J. L. Drafts, a Lutheran minister, now located in Newberry County.

Daniel Irvin was born 1840. He married Carrie Craps. They settled near Cedar Grove Church. They were the foster parents of Ida and Pierce Leaphart, also Rev. C. I. Morgan. Franklin Drafts now owns and occupies their old home.

Henry Elias Drafts was born 1842. He lived near Saluda River, later he built near the old home, where he could look after his aged father and family. His father had lost one of his legs, thereby causing him to become an invalid during his last years.

Mrs. Andrew Addy is his only living child. His grandchildren are the sons and daughters of Mrs. Viola Hayes, Mrs. Ophelia Jumper, Otis Drafts and Mrs. Andrew Addy. A Mr. Suter, from West Virginia, occupies the old home.

George Michael was born 1844. He settled near Kingsville, below Columbia. He married Kate (?) and became very wealthy. He left a nice sum of money for the Lutheran Theological Seminary in Columbia, also a bequest to Cedar Grove Church.

Samuel Patrick was born 1846. He married Sedecia Lewie. He was once in business at Summit, later at Lewiedale, now Gilbert. He once was sheriff of Lexington County. He, with part of his family, is buried at Summit.

John Calhoun Drafts was born 1849. He married Dora Bodie and lived practically all his married life at Leesville. He was a good man and was loved by everybody. Among his descendants is James Drafts, of Leesville.

Julian Medora Drafts was born 1851. She married George A. Kaminer, of the St. John's section. They reared a prominent family, among them was W. A. Kaminer, who was for a long time governor of one of the Philippine Islands. Miss Belle Kaminer, a trained nurse, is her only living daughter. A son, Frank Kaminer, of Spartanburg, is still living.

Sarah Margaret Drafts (1854-1903) married her cousin, Thomas P. Drafts (1851-1898). They continued to live in the community where they were reared, not far from Beulah Methodist Church. They have a number of living grandchildren living in the home community. Dr. James Drafts was their son, also Poindexter, who lived near the old homestead.

Daniel Drafts was a very prominent man in his day. He was one of the founders of Cedar Grove Church and was often sent as a delegate to represent his church in the Tennessee Synod.

At one time he was wealthy, owning 2,500 acres of land and more than 40 slaves. He was post master of the Draft's Mill Post Office, located at the identical spot where the concrete bridge crosses Horse Creek on Highway 43.

This was the only post office in this territory during the Civil War. At this place he operated a flour mill, ground corn, sawed lumber, ran a shoe shop and carried on other business also. All machinery was operated by water power.

A large king snake stayed around his flour mill and he was careful to give it adequate protection, because it kept the rats away from his bolting cloths. He charged those who were operating the machinery never to injure that snake. His most important miller was a slave, whose name was Maize. One day while Maize was alone grinding wheat, this snake fell out of the loft on Maize. Maize said he killed it so quick he didn't have time to think what "Boss" said about protecting the millhouse snake.

After the Civil War, the post office was moved to his residence and the name changed to Lorena.

Henry Drafts (1809-1882), son of the first Jacob Drafts, married Maria Poindexter (1814-1883). They had two children, Thomas P., who married his cousin, Sarah Drafts, and Mary J. (1847-1898) who married Pickens Bodie, of Leesville, and to them were born Henry and Sallie, who were beloved citizens of Leesville all their lives.

Jacob Drafts and wife had a daughter named Celia, who married Jefferson Hook and settled near St. John's (white church). They reared a large and respectable family; among their children were Marshall, Edwin, Scott, Sydney, Amanda, Ellen and Arrie.

Another daughter of Jacob Drafts, named Sophian, married Uriah Crout, whose write up is under the Crout sketch.

VERONA (HOLLEY) SCHOOL (1897)

HOLLEY

WITH the best information available, concerning our Edgefield Holleys, we have been informed that there once was a character named James Holley, who had a son, John, that married Rosannah Waters. The presumption is that she was a daughter of Philemon Waters, who settled in the extreme northeastern corner of Edgefield District and established a ferry across Saluda River called Water's Ferry.

John Holley settled near the river on the south side. This identical settlement was later known as the Daniel D. Holley place. The old Water's Ferry had been moved farther up the river. It became the property of Dan Holley and was afterwards known as Holley's Ferry.

John Holley's children were John, Jr., who went to Kansas before the Civil War; Daniel D. (1822-1899), who with his descendants, became the central subject of this sketch; Wilkes, who settled further up the river in this same Edgefield District; there was one daughter in the John Holley family named Rosannah (1815-1842), who married John Langford. Rosannah Langford is buried in the family plot at the Dan Holley old homestead.

Daniel D. Holley (1822-1899) married Rosannah Leightsey (1824-1888), and occupied his father's old home. He was twice married, but his first wife was the mother of all his children. His first wife is buried in the old family plot at the old homestead. Dan Holley is buried in the then new cemetery of Rehoboth Methodist Church, which he was very instrumental in organizing about ten years prior to his death.

The children of Daniel and Rosannah Leightsey Holley are as follows: Caroline, Lucy, Jane, Belle, Elizabeth and Georgiana. These were the daughters. The sons were Samuel B., William B., James C., Daniel Pickens and John E.

Daniel D. Holley's last wife was Mary Martin, who was postmistress at Dupler, the post office in that community during the nineties and up until about 1905.

Caroline (1843-1930), the oldest daughter, first married Patrick Langford. They had one child, Julius (1861-1939), who married Etta Oxner (1859-1913). They became the parents of Fred Langford who married Katie Belle Harmon. Their children are James, Berley and Carrie. Julius Langford's second son was Middleton, who married Beulah Goff and had Duretha, Legrande and Jenelle. The third child of Julius Langford was Zula, who married Wade Price. They live in West Columbia and are the parents of Roxie, Lillie Belle, Julius, Leo and Mattie. The fourth child was Sallie. She married Jimmie Harmon and had Julian, Etta and Ozelia. The last and youngest son of Julius and Etta Langford was Dan, who married Sallie Shealy. One son, Ray, came from this union. Dan's second marriage was to Ruby Quattlebaum, who was the mother of Edwin and Julius.

Caroline Holley Langford's second marriage was to Anderson P. Derrick (1851-1936). Their oldest son's name was Daniel "Cap" (1868-1947), who married Caroline Rawl (1866-1932). They had Fannie, Tillman, Joe, Lottie, Broadus, Lula, Ryan, Mary Lee, Annie, Noah, Myrtle, Ernest, Sammie, Jessie and Roy.

The second son was J. H. L. "Pete" Derrick (1872-1942), who married Lillie Taylor and their children were Carrie, Bessie Lee, Blease, Satcher, Lillian, Simon, Silas, Trannye and Charley.

The third son, Hampton, married Corrie Epting. Their son's name is Clyde.

The fourth son, Jacob, married Eva Harmon, who was the mother of Bernice, William and Helen.

The fifth son, James P. Derrick, married Bessie Charles and had Ray, Guy, Gladys and Jimmie.

A daughter, Amelia, married Sam Price. They had no children.

The next daughter, Mary, married George Price. They were the parents of Eula, Gerstle, Jennie Lee, Boda, Mary Sue, Croney, George, Frank, Dial and Holley.

The next daughter, Trannye, died unmarried.

The youngest daughter, Lula, married William Rawl. Their children are J. D., Rosa Mae, Harold and O. C. Lula and William have just celebrated their golden wedding.

The second daughter of Dan Holley, whose name was Lucy, married Franklin Shealy. Their children were James L., who married Amanda Langford. (This couple was the parents of Sallie, Inez, Annie, Ray "Dutch," William "Bill," and Mary Lee); Rebecca married Mance Berry. No children were born to this union. Drayton Shealy (1881-1919) who married Nettie Rogers and had Eleanor J. T. and Drayton. Thomas Shealy, who married Nellie Berry, had no children. Mary Lou, who married Lenadra Gunter, had no children. Daniel and Rodella died of typhoid fever in their teen ages.

Jane Holley became the wife of Henry Dickert. Their children are G. K. Dickert, who was the father of H. K. Dickert, L. S. Dickert and Georgia Belle Dickert; C. W. Dickert, whose children are H. D. Dickert, Mrs. Ernest Kye, and Louise Dickert; Mrs. O. D. Osborne, whose children are E. W. Osborne, Manly Osborne, Mrs. Johny Love, Mrs. W. T. Smith and Killy Osborne; E. E. Dickert, whose children are E. E. Dickert, Jr., Mrs. G. E. Hyatt, Mrs. Max Bowens and Lewis H. Dickert; Mrs. A. C. Lott, whose children are Mrs. Mamie Crain, Mrs. Leo Kirfe, Mrs. Tom Swygert and Mrs. L. J. Furtick; Mrs. Bennie Crain, whose children are Gerald Crain, Mrs. Charles Jones and Mrs. Albert Lumus; Mrs. W. E. Aiken "Ella" Dickert, whose children's names I was unable to get correctly.

Isa Belle Holley (1856-1924) married Boston Price (1843-1927). We will now take up their descendants. D. Henry married Bertha

Lybrand. They had Myrtle, Aster, Vernon, Seth, Brady, Ralph and Guy; Alice married Noah Shealy. Their children are Cora Shealy Miller, Carlisle, Quinton, Leroy, Thelma Shealy Ballington; Addie married George Long and had Lila, Pearl, Esther, Zara Lee, Carrie Ruth, D. G., Rembert, Iva B. and Faye; Sallie married Butler Kaminer and had Felder, Verdie Mae, Sarah Belle, Harvey, James and Bill; Mae married Charley Caughman and had Leonelle and Verle; Lillian married a McCarty to whom no children were born; Carrie married Claude Hook. Their children are Marcesta, Aubrey, Rev. Ray Price, a Methodist minister; and Frances Rose; Rosalie married Maze Price and had Gary Lee, Hoyt, Earle, Ryland, June and Dial; Ethel married Ernest Lybrand and had Westray L. Fallaw, Billie E., Moran, Carl Edward, Rebecca and Roston; John married Mary Shealy and reared one son, A. Eschol; Sam married Viola Snelgrove. They had two daughters, Teura Price Koon and Laura Belle Boles; Virgil married Lillian Shealy. Their offspring are Rondelle, Festus, Trevor, Holley, Martel and Martha; Almaree (1895-1926), first grave at Beulah Methodist Church.

Elizabeth Holley (1860-1926) was the wife of H. Luther Shealy 1859-1933), and they were the parents of Nannie, who married Charley Corley and were the parents of Ennoree, Alma, R. C., Rhett, Ollie Mae, Verma and Herman; Leila, who married Paul Harmon and had Myrtle, Mae, Leroy, Annie Belle, Marzie, Roxie, Rose, Erline and Everette; Mamie married James Gillian and had Vernon, Leona, Emma and Jimmie Lee; Jessie married Reuben Taylor. Their children are: Mary, Lewie, Annie Lou, Lanier, Vernelle, Berley, Donnelle and Rachel. Annie married R. L. Bryant, and had Martha Ann, Robert and Butler; Rosa Belle married John Frazier and was the mother of Vera and Dwight; Minick, the only son of Luther Shealy and Elizabeth Holley Shealy, first married Frances K. Epps (1880-1919), who was the mother of William Luther. His second marriage was to Stella Oswald who gave birth to Idell, Emily, Christine and Opharell.

Georgiana (1863-1934), the youngest daughter of Daniel and Rosannah Holley, married Albert Price (1863-1934). Their children were as follows: Anna who married Jesse Swygert and had Alice, Albert, Sallie, Mamie Lee and J. A.; Nezzie, who married Mack Crout and bore Ethyl, Lucius, Grady, John, Norman, Ray, Seth, Alma, Permelle and Etah; Mary who married Abe Smith and had Alvin, Adelle, Lourine, Lois and Lathan; Nina, who married Lester Smith and had Cletus, Paul, James, Milford, Dorris, Luray and Eugene; Addie Lee who married Sam Schofield and bore him Catherine, Margaret, Nelson, Samuel and John William; Lillie Belle who married Willie Gunter and had Melba, Jack and Charley; Erastus (1897-1950), who married Alma Wingate. They are the parents of Leonard, Georgia Ella, and Wilma; Fletcher, who married Emily McCartha, had no children.

Samuel B. (1847-1917), the oldest son of the Daniel Holley family, married Drucilla Lindler (1845-1908), who was the mother of all his children. After the death of his first wife he married Mary L. Wingard Cromer.

Samuel and Drucilla's children are as follows: J. Bowman, the only son, who married Jenny Smith, had Ruth, James and Boyd; Bowman was a Baptist minister of the Gospel and spent his life in that work. Ellen married Dillard Oxner. Their children are Gula, Asa, Velma, Mildred, Willrose, J. D., and Imogene. Mary married Henry Oxner. They were the father and mother of Eugene, Rosa Ella, Jennie, Sammie, Prelto, Dannie Rae, Stetson and Henry B. Zula was the wife of Gary Caughman, and the mother of M. G., Jr., Lillie was the wife of George Goff and mother of Ethyl, Virgil, Homer, Varlee, Tura, Louise and Georgia. Minnie (1877-1899) married Albert Parrott and had Carrie.

William B. Holley (1851-1929) married Debbiean Nichols (1848-1937) daughter of Luke Nichols (1808-1882), one of the founders of Union E. L. Church. Their descendants are George, who married Willa Senn and had Sophia and Eunice; Hampton married Edith Harmon, who was the mother of Nezzie, Ollie, Rosa Lee, Willa, Eloise, Marjorie, Edgar, Gladys, Cleo and Leo, twins; Emmie married Tally Senn and had Enos, Lillie Belle, Corrie Lee and Fara Mae; Dr. Oliver C. married Lilla Shirey, one son, George Ray; Lillie (1874-1891) was unmarried.

D. Pickens Holley (1849-1914) married Margaret Price (1845-1911), sister of Roston and Albert Price. Their children are: Bass, who married Sallie Crout, and whose children were Ballenger, Mildred, Ray, Clyde, Verne, Hazel and Catherine; Hampton married Lula Shealy, who was the mother of Blanche, Herman and Lester; McCain, youngest son of D. Pickens and Margaret Holley, who married Marie Fulmer. Their children are Gordon, Brice, Bonnie, Louise, Robert and Dorris; Lizzie married George Rawl and had Essie, Henry, Lawrence, Izene, Jessie, Edress, Daniel and Gussie; Reina (1873-1930) married Sam Crout (1862-1934) and had Jason, Eugene, Irene, Herman, Evelyn and Margaret; Gertrude married Thomas Nichols and was the mother of Brady, Mae, Ruby, Norene and Roxie; Vennie married Lee Berry and had Clinton, Eula Mae, Jessie Lee and Holley; Lessie, the youngest daughter, married Willie Derrick and gave birth to J. P., Lucille and Jesse.

James C. Holley married Ella Derrick. James entered the ministry in young manhood, joined the Methodist Conference and continued active as long as he lived. His offspring are as follows: Ida, who married Joe Brown and had Ethylyn; Mattie, who married a Garvin and had no children; Eddie and first wife had Frances and Dorris. His second wife, Louise, had Robert; Herman married Osma Shull and to them was born William R.

John E. Holley, the youngest son of Daniel and Rosannah Holley, married Mary Rawl and was the father of Ellie, who married Jodie Derrick and was the mother of Haskell, Bennie, Ruby, Sara

Frances, Faye, Agnes, Leora and Hoyt Ray; Virgil, who married Eva Lou Asbill, who was the mother of J. M., Virgie, Lavoy, Jewell and Onetia; Ethel married Raymond Bedenbaugh and had Jeffie, Voigt, Odesso, Sarah, Ruth and Lorine; Minnie, who married Pace Asbill and was the mother of Brinton, Victoria, Izilla, Roberta, Virgieree, Jesse, Elma, Dorris and Uva; Fletcher, who married Lillian Hallman, who was the mother of Catherine, Jannie and Harold; Ruth who married Willie Sease and had Mary, Rose, Alice Ruth, J. A., Evelyn, John, Jimmie, Everette, Elliot, George, Clyde and Charles Ray; Floy, who married Heber Rogers and had Veola, Dannie, D. J. and Marylyn.

CROUT

JOHN Crout, with his wife and some children, including two sons, John and Jacob, came to this country from Germany. They first settled in the Dutch Fork or at least located there temporarily for one year, then came over and took a grant of land from Governor Charles Pinckney in 1790 on Big Hollow Creek, near where Salem Church was located, and settled thereon.

John Crout, his wife and one child lie buried in an unmarked plot near the home of Monroe Bedenbaugh. Tradition tells us that he went out to chop wood one day and did not return. His people found him dead, lying by the side of a log.

The second John Crout married a Caughman and settled some miles farther up, and on the opposite side of Big Hollow Creek. Among his childrn were David and Uriah. David Crout married first a Fikes, a sister of David Fikes, and among their children was a son named Azariah, who married an Austin, in all probability a relative of Davis Austin.

Azariah settled on what is known as the "Geiger" place and is buried near the writer's cow barn in the edge of the woods in an unmarked grave. He left the following children: Georgiana, who married Churchwell Rinehart; Juliana married Jake Martin; Missouri married Davis Austin, Jr.; Walter, the youngest, I don't know who he married.

Azariah had a sister named Juliana.

David Crout's second wife was Sallie Rice, and of this union the following childrn are named: Mittie, who married Zeddo Swygert, Levi, who died in the Civil War, Eliza who married John Shealy, son of Jacob Shealy, of Leesville; Ellen married Robert Addy; Sibbie married William Langford (better known as "Hib") and Patrick married a Shealy. David Crout's third wife was Lucinda Moore; two children came from this marriage, namely, Ann, who married J. Walter Keisler (1854-1949), and Jefferson M., who married Trannie Kinard, of Saluda County. David Crout was born in 1800 and died in 1875, is buried in a family plot on the old homestead, which is now known as the Tom Addy place. His last wife and two of his daughters, Ann (1854-1949) and Sibbie are buried in Cedar Grove Cemetery.

Uriah Crout (1806-1886) the other mentioned son of the second John Crout, married Sophia Drafts (1815-1877), a sister of Daniel Drafts and a daughter of Jacob Drafts and wife, Christena Kelley. The children of Uriah Crout and wife were as follows: Barbara, who married Henry Addy and moved to Mississippi; Caroline married Dr. William L. Addy; Lavinia married Fred S. Hendrix; Henry married Martha Black; Bettie married Grant Smith; Jimmie never married; Evelyn married Frank Smith; Alice married first Walter Drafts, then W. J. Assman; Belle married Newton Kyzer. Besides these there were two girls who died young. Uriah Crout, his wife, his son, Henry, and several others are buried in a family plot near the old homestead, which passed on to a grandson, D. U. Addy, now to a great-grandson, Nelson Addy. This place was the site of the ante-bellum post office of Hollow Creek, kept by Uriah Crout who also did extensive merchandising business, hauling all his goods from Columbia and Augusta with teams. He also ran a mill on the creek nearby, in addition to his extensive farming.

Uriah Crout evidently was an excellent man. He was secretary of Cedar Grove from the time it was organized in 1852 until he became an old man. We find a neat, accurate and well kept record revealing to later generations many facts of importance that we now appreciate. May God bless his memory.

Jacob, the other named son of the first John Crout, married first a Jackson and to this couple were born eleven children as follows: Dr. John (1799) marrid Christena Shealy, daughter of the first Adam Shealy; Isaac (1801); Nancy (1803), married a Kelley; Mary (1804) married David Fikes; Thomas (1806) married a Hallman; Ephraim (1809); Lewis (1811) married Rebecca Risinger, sister of Adam Risinger. They produced two sons who went west. They are buried near Red Star School House. Elizabeth (1813) married Henry Shealy; Epsie (1815) married a Wingard; Achsa (1817) married Jeremiah Rawl; Jemima (1819) married Jacob Clemmons. Jacob Crout's second wife was Polly (Mary) Shealy, a sister of his son, Dr. John's wife and to this union the following children were born: Polly (1826) never married; Catherine (1829) married Solomon Son; Susannah (1831) never married; Lorena (1836) never married; Julia (1838): and Lorenza (1843), who married Eliza Price.

Jacob Crout, both wives, several children, including Lorenza and wife and child, are buried in a family plot near the old homestead of the first John Crout on Big Hollow Creek.

Lorenza Crout lived on the original homestead of the first John Crout and reared his family of four children, namely: Almenia, who married Alonzo Gillian; Mary maried a Godwin of Nevada, and is now living in California; Ella married Killian Sease and Wade F. married Allie Warren.

Dr. John Crout, the eldest son of Jacob Crout and whose wife was Christena Shealy, had the following children: Samuel, Michael, and Isaiah, of which three we have no further record. Ephraim married Elizabeth Price and had Samuel W. who married Reina Holley; John C. married Effie Keisler and Mary C. married John Rogers.

Elias Crout, son of Dr. John Crout, married Jane Hillman and had Henry, who married Laura Shealy; Emma, who married Wm. C. Shealy; Luther, who married Leila Maffett; and Pinckney who married Dona Lybrand.

Jared Crout, son of Dr. John, married Martha Price and had John W., who married Susie Hendrix; Georgiana, who married Walter Derrick; and Laura, who married Frank Taylor.

Mary Crout (1835-1928) first married George Price, then Lewis Rawl (1840-1912).

Celia Crout married Abraham Hite and became the mother of Paul Hite, who married Mary Taylor; John Hite, who married Eliza Oxner Caughman; and a daughter who married Andrew Oswald, of Blythewood.

Lavinia Crout married Lemuel Nichols and moved to Mississippi.

Katie Crout married a Burnett. Lizzie Crout was the third wife of Jesse Shealy; Rosannah Crout married Chelsea Snelgrove. Their write-up will come under the Snelgroves. Artemissa Crout married Emanuel Taylor.

Dr. John Crout (1799-1884) was a unique character. In the pioneer days of our early settlers, there were few who were trained to practice medicine or preach the gospel. This John Crout did both in a very effective way, to the delight of his many friends who lived in his day.

Dr. John lived on Rocky Creek, which is now in Saluda County. He, with a number of his family, is buried near his old home. The cemetery is partly covered with waters of Lake Murray.

Thomas, another son of Jacob Crout, and who married a Hallman, settled down in the Black Creek Section of Lexington County and lived there a number of years. Several of his children remained in that neighborhood their entire lives, including William, Celia, who married Anderson Shealy, and Wesley Crout, who was the father of Rev. John Crout, a Methodist minister.

Thomas Crout later moved to Edgefield County where the family lived for a number of years. Finally he settled on Hollow Creek where was later the home of one of his sons-in-law, Carwile Shealy. Among the other children of Thomas Crout were Rosanna, who married Paul Craps, Achsa, who was the wife of L. Pinckney Hare; Sarah (1841-1911) married Addison Vansant (1848-1933); Nancy (1853-1918) married Carwile Shealy (1852-1933); Eliza married Wm. L. Gable; Henry married Harriet Gregory.

Thomas Crout and wife, his sisters, Polly and Lorena, also Achsa and Catherine are buried in Cedar Grove Cemetery.

This sketch of the Crout family is very incomplete, as are the sketches of other families, but in this edition you will find many references of these pioneer families who intermarried with other pioneer settlers and their descendants.

SHEALY

ACCORDING to the last Shealy tradions, all the Shealys of our territory sprang from one Johann "John" Wendell Shealy, who came from Heidelberg, Germany about 1763 with a colony of Leitziers, Setzlers, Cromers, etc., sponsored by John Adam Epting. It appears that this John Wendell Shealy, through the English law primogeniteire, inherited a great area of land between Crims Creek and the present town of Little Mountain in Newberry County from his father, John Shealy, to whom it had been granted in the year 1753. The father is presumed to have died before 1769.

John Wendell Shealy married Mary Anna, the daughter of the John Adam Epting, who brought over the colony, and settled on the southeastern part of his inheritance, at a site about one mile north of Little Mountain. The spring on the head waters of Coleman Creek, which this family used is still in use, and the burial place of the father and mother are pointed out to the visitor.

John Wendell Shealy and his wife had twelve sons and one daughter. Of these sons we have record of only eight: Hon. Wendell, William, Adam, John, Henry, Matthias, David and Andrew. The daughter married a Quattlebaum.

Our principal interest in this sketch centers in Adam who was the progenitor of the greater part of the Shealys of Saluda and upper Lexington County.

Adam Shealy, according to our best tradition, married a Swittenberg and settled near the old Edgefield-Lexington County line on the waters of Rocky Creek, about four miles south of Holley's Ferry. The traditional home site lies just a few hundred yards north of the present home of Purvis Bedenbaugh, known as the Ephraim, or George R. Shealy place. Of the children of this couple, we can list the following: Matthias, Martin, David, Michael, William, Wendell, Ephraim, Christiana, Kate and Mary "Polly".

Matthias Shealy married a Fulmer and they settled first in the rear of the present Delmar school house and had the following children: Richard (1828-1863) married Mary Ann Corley (1833-1915) and had Rozilla (1851) who married Milledge Snelgrove. Stanmore D. married Epsy Mary Ann Derrick (1859). Eugenia Angeline (1854) married Samuel S. Shealy (1840-1916). H. Arthur married Cornelia Derrick. William M. (1858) married Mrs. Mary McCartha Ballentine (1853). Elijah W. (1861) married Lula E. Fulmer (1868-1932) and Laura A. (1862) married Henry Crout (1857-1932). Littleton married his cousin, Nancy Shealy and had Carwile, who married

Nancy Crout; Levi married Corrie Rinehart; James E. married Missouri Rawl; Kiah (1862-1936) married   ; Louannie married Adam Rawl (1854-1925); and Dorothy married Asa McNure. Wm. "Tug" married Emma Crout.

Wilson Shealy married a Johnson and moved to Georgia. Amos Shealy married Jemima Corley and had Luther (1859-1933), who married Elizabeth Holley (1860-1926); and Malissa, who married John C. Snelgrove. Epsey Shealy (1819-1908) married Edward Hare and bore him John Wesley (1840-1910) who married Catherine Fulmer (1833-1918). They are the parents of W. H. Hare to whom we are indebted to this write-up.

Levi Pinckney, son of Epsy Shealy and Edward Hare, lived from 1842-1895, married Achsa Crout. D. Tillman Hare (1843-1925) married Mary Goff (1843-1923). Nancy Hare married Albert L. Eargle (1843-1918) and Julian married Luther Snelgrove. They moved to Georgia. Kesiah married her cousin, Abram Shealy, and bore him Ellen, Mary and Hiliary S., who married Nancy Bedenbaugh. Minnie married Samuel Sanford and bore him Tillman. Simeon, whose first wife was Lucy Snelgrove. Willie Sanford married Annie Taylor and Eda Sanford married Luther Hallman. Besides these, Rosa and Artemissa never married.

After the death of his first wife, Matthias Shealy married a Risinger.

Continuing with the children of the first Adam Shealy, son of the original John Wendell Shealy: Martin (1803-1878) married Roda Harris (1804-1867) and their children included Samuel S. (1840-1916) who married first Susannah Derrick (1845-1899) and had Tillman W. (1861-1936) a Lutheran Minister, then Samuel married his cousin, Eugenia A. Shealy.

This Susannah Derrick Shealy was my first Sunday School teacher at Union E. L. Church.

Martin Shealy's next son, W. Andrew, married Jane Inabin and had several children; Levi married Jane Inabin and had M. Pinckney; Ephraim married Polly Black and had Amanda, who married Walter Hite and was the mother of Dr. P. W. Hite.

Susannah Shealy, daughter of Martin, married Bennett Oxner who bore him Simeon L. J. L., Boyd, John L., Dr. W. A. Oxner, who lived in West Columbia, Killian, O. Cromwell, Dickson, Etta, Louise, Carrie and Isabella. Patsey Shealy married John T. Derrick and bore him Amanda; Nancy married her cousin, Littleton Shealy; Lizzie married A. G. Charles. Besides these were John, and Nora, who married Chesley Price.

Now we take up David, another son of the first Adam Shealy. David Shealy (1799-1880) of whose first wife we have no record Second marriage was to Polly Hare (1809-1863). Their home was on the upper waters of Rocky Creek in Saluda County and their children included Jemima (1826-1898) who never married; Lewis (1828-1909) married Elizabeth Risinger and had Jason, Henkel,

Elliot, Lura and Elmore; Eli married Lemanda Oxner (1838-1921) who had Sallie who married Leppard Derrick; Sarah Ann married Irvin P. Eargle; Wiley married Miley Hallman and was the father of the Rev. Jefferson Davis Shealy (1862-1926); a son, Lemuel, who died young; Henry married Louisa Addy. They were the parents of F. Pierce (1861-1951). David, his wife, Polly, and a number of their children sleep in the Cedar Grove cemetery.

Michael Shealy (1806-1892), son of the original Adam, married Sara Rawl (1815-1890). They had no children, but reared D. Tillman Hare as an adopted son.

Adam Shealy's next son was William, who married Barbara Hare. Their home was on Rocky Creek at the place later known as the Jeremiah Rawl place. Among their children were Noah, who married Frances Fallaw and had Sheppard, Caldwell, George, Laura, Catherine and Mary, who married Bluford Bisanar. Abram married his cousin, Kesiah Shealy. John Adam married Sarah Addy, daughter of Joel Addy and wife, Catherine Lybrand. Their children were H. Ed, who married Emma Nichols. Eliza married Henry Eargle. Alice married Emanuel Shealy. Grace (1858-1947) married Irvin Shealy (1862-1903). Betsey married Shade Steele, and Peter who was the father of John E. Shealy, who married Clayton Fulmer and lived near Blue Star or Climax school house.

Adam Shealy's son, Ephraim married Achsa Snelgrove (1824-1905). They had Paul, who married Eva Keisler; Pressley, who married Minerva Risinger; George, who married Rodella Lybrand; Rosa, who married Wesley Risinger and was the mother of Rev. P. D. Risinger, of the Lutheran Ministry. Ruth married Fred Eargle; Tyre and Bennet died young.

Adam Shealy's daughter, Christiana, married Dr. John Crout. Their large family has been noted under the Crout sketch.

Kate Shealy was the mother of Hasten, who married Julia Lindler, whose children were Reuben, Ruthy and Laura. These, with their families moved to Georgia.

Adam Shealy's Mary married Jacob Crout. Her children have been listed under the Crout sketch.

Now we take up Wendell Shealy's family. This Wendell was a son of the original Adam. The name of his wife is not in our records. Their children are Jesse, whose first wife was a Hare, who bore him Elias, Wesley, Caroline and Elizabeth. His second wife was Harriet West who bore him John A. (1865-1950) and three children who died young. His third wife was Lizzie Crout.

Hazel married Barbara Craps Derrick and had Simeon, Pierce, Mary, Fannie and Martha. Emanuel first married Rebecca Price and then Eva Ann Jackson. His children were Albert, Calhoun, Walter, Franklin, Irvin, Jane, Sarah Ann, Emanuel, Sedecia and Laura. The last three by his last wife. Wendell's Uriah married Eliza Miller. Their children were James, Earl, John, Eudocia and Cornelia. Isaiah married Sarah Miller. Mary Ann married Hiram Keisler.

Julia was the second wife of George Banks. Juriah was the second wife of Rev. George Kelley.

Adam Shealy and wife are supposed to be buried where Ephraim is buried at the old homestead; graves are unmarked.

Hon. Wendell Shealy, son of the original John Wendell, had a daughter, Katie, who was the wife of James Ballentine and the mother of John William Ballentine, whose family has many descendants in our territory.

Another son of the original John Wendell Shealy and who is extensively represented in our territory south of the Saluda River was William, whose wife was a Wertz. Among his children whom we wish to note further were George, Andrew, Daniel, Tom, Nancy and Catherine.

Daniel married Rosa Frick and had Malichi who married Elizabeth Shealy. They settled at Summit, S. C. and had Frank, Wade, Cyrus, Mittie and Cora; Andrew married Elmetta Fulmer and had Edwin, Rufus, Lester, Jacob, Victor, Lincoln, Laura and Ella; Henry C. married Elvira Sease. One of their daughters is Murray Wessinger, treasurer of Lexington County; Lydia married Daniel Harman; Edith married Frank Rawl; Ann married George Shealy; Almenia married S. B. Lybrand; Elizabeth never married.

LEESVILLE SHEALYS

AMONG the pioneer settlers of the territory now embraced in the town of Leesville was one Shealy whose name was John, a son of the first John Wendell Shealy in the Dutch Fork. We do not know who was the wife of this pioneer Shealy settler of Leesville, but we have records of the following children: Jacob J., David C., Andrew, George, Mary, Polly, and Elizabeth.

Jacob J. Shealy (1800-1874) married Mary Hallman, who was a daughter of Andrew Hallman and a sister of David Hallman, the father of the Rev. Samuel H. Hallman, of the Lutheran Ministry. Jacob Shealy's home was in the suburbs of Leesville on the northern side and he is buried in a marked grave, near the old home which is still standing. The children of this couple included W. Riley, Noah, Samuel, John, Ozier, Mittie, Deborah, Elizabeth and Polly.

Riley married Roselia Snelgrove and was the father of James Edward, who married Frances Lindler. He outlived all his sisters and brothers, was high in the nineties when he died. J. Walter married Ann Caughman; Davis married first Florence Koon then Ophelia Shealy; Elmore married a Price; Georgiana married Noah Steele and Mary Jane married Earl Shealy.

Jacob Shealy's daughter, Elizabeth, married her cousin, John T. Derrick, then Tillman Black. No children.

Polly, youngest daughter of Jacob Shealy, married Tyre Johns. No children.

His daughter, Deborah, married William Long, of Edgefield;

Mittie married a Smith and was the mother of "Big" Henry Smith; Noah Shealy married Louisa Hartley, and was the father of Corrie, who married Jacob Son, and Nolie, who married Felix Quattlebaum; Samuel and Ozier died in the Civil War and perhaps other sons; Jacob Shealy's son, John, married Eliza Crout. To this couple four children were born and reared—Aquilla married Anderson Sligh; Etta was the wife of Simeon Steele; Sallie married Lawrence Rawl and Samuel, the only son, married Ida Keisler, daughter of Lemuel Keisler.

David C. Shealy (1802-1884) married Nancy Wooley (1805- 1882), his home was in Leesville. The residence is still standing opposite the south end of Main Street and is now occupied by the family of Walter Rose. On the coming of the railroad in the late '60's, Mr. Shealy donated to the company considerable land including the site for the depot and much of the public square north of the railroad tracks.

We can name the following children of this couple: Wellington (1834-1860); Irene (1826-1892), who married D. D. D. Mitchell; a daughter who married B. Frank Banks; Frank, who never married; John J. (1845-1905) who married Anna, daughter of Rev. Henry Smith; Rufus W. who married Victoria Wise; a daughter who married Dr. John T. Dent; Irby and his twin brother, Yearly; Yearly married Rebecca Lowman and was the father of John D. and Ross Shealy.

Of the children of John J., the blacksmith, we remember only Wellie, who lives in Alabama. The children of Rufus M. are Jesse and Lawrence.

Andrew Shealy married a Lowman and George Shealy went to Georgia. We have no further record of these two sons of this pioneer, John Shealy.

Mary Shealy married Daniel Caughman. Her children are listed in the Caughman sketches.

Elizabeth married Lewis Derrick and their descendants live in the Mt. Calvary and Johnston sections of Aiken and Edgefield Counties.

Polly married Samuel Derrick. Her offspring has been written up under the Derrick sketches.

ROBERTS

THE earliest Roberts record we have at hand are those of three brothers: Absalom, Noah and Acel. We have been unable to find out where they came from or who the earliest ancestor was in this country. Absalom married Barbara Caughman and Acel married Elizabeth Caughman. They were sisters, and daughters of the first Andrew Caughman. Both of these families settled on Big Hollow Creek near where Cedar Grove Church is now located. A daughter of Absalom married Billy Geiger and settled what has always been known in this country as the "Geiger" place. They had one child, that died young. William Geiger (1784-1859), his wife and child, along with Absalom Roberts, who died in 1828, Elizabeth Roberts died in 1827 and others with unmarked graves are buried near Mrs. Blanche Long Shealy's, not far from the confluence of Joe's Creek and Big Hollow Creek.

Acel Roberts and Elizabeth Caughman were the parents of four children: Moses Summers, Isaiah, Sybil and Reba.

Moses Summers Roberts (1814-1883) married Emeline, daughter of Daniel Derrick, and had 13 children. In 1853 the family moved to Smith County, Mississippi, where Mr. Roberts died, leaving his wife and six of his children.

Isaiah Roberts (1816-1899) married Ellen S. Lindler (1835-1911), daughter of Jacob Lindler and sister of Rev. A. W. Lindler. They had the following children: Leppard B. (1852-1881) who married Ridona Craps and had two children: Roddy and Aquilla.

Mary or Mollie Roberts first married John C. Derrick and had three children: J. Willie, Mattie and Anna. Her second marriage was to her cousin, Wily Lindler.

Amanda Roberts married James Coats and was the mother of five children: Jessie, Minnie, Mena, John and James.

Leila Roberts married Simon B. Coats and had six children: Luther, Eugene, Charley, Floyd, Leon and Ella.

Isaiah Roberts and wife had an adopted son, Cleveland Leech.

Sybil Roberts, daughter of Acel and Elizabeth Roberts, married Jack Harman of Attalla County, Mississippi, but had no children.

Reba Roberts, the other daughter of Acel Roberts, married W. Thomas Derrick. They had four children as follows: Oliver A. (1847-1917), who married first Catherine Fulmer (1850-1887) by whom he had one child, William H. The second marriage was to Catherine Keisler, daughter of Fred Keisler.

The second son was George Marion (1850-1930), married Katie Kinard, of Saluda County, whose children were Bachman, Luda, Billy and Braddock.

Leppard Scott, the third son of Reba Roberts and Thomas Derrick, who was born in 1855, married Sallie Shealy who was the mother of Noah, Leo, Omar, Maxie, Rev. Victor and Maud.

The only daughter, Louannie, married Simeon Black.

Soon after the marriage of Isaiah Roberts 1851, he moved with his family to Mississippi, where he lived until after the close of the Civil War, in which he was a valiant soldier of the Confederacy. About 1867, at the request of his wife's people, he came back to South Carolina and took charge of his father-in-law's home and farm, which he managed for several years. Finally he settled on the lands of his grandfather near Cedar Grove Church, where he spent the remainder of his life. He, as well as other members of his family, was a member of Salem Church, where he was baptized by Rev. J. Yost Meetze in the first log building. He saw the second Salem Church building (the old gallery structure) erected near the first about 1825. Isaiah also assisted in building the last structure in 1890. He was a very popular singing master and taught many singing classes, was a master of vocal music. He and his wife and son, Leppard, and daughter, Leila, with other relatives are buried in St. Mark's cemetery, Saluda County.

SEASE

IN the Elias Sease Cemetery, located on Highway 43, is a monument erected to the memory of Frederick Sease, his wife and children, with no dates. Frederick Sease and wife were members of Salem Church and when Cedar Grove Congregation was organized in 1852, Frederick Sease was one of the Elders. The graves of the early Seases are under the waters of Lake Murray. Their old home was last owned by Sydney Nichols, formerly owned by his father, Wesley Nichols, before it went into the Lake Murray area.

Among Frederick Sease's children we know of Elias and Richard. Tradition tells us that there was another son whose name was Jacob, who was a carpenter and was killed by a scantling striking him.

Elias Sease (1823-1898) married Ella Jane Lewis (1833-1923) and first settled on Big Hollow Creek not far distant from the ancestral Sease home and later near Little Hollow Creek on Highway 43. They reared a large family of prominent people. In the cemetery with the graves of Elias Sease and wife is the grave of Oliver Lafayette (1867-1876), their son.

Their oldest son was Cephas, who married Amanda Shealy and were the parents of Pickens, James, Samuel, Crosson, Henry, Sallie, Lula, and Irene, also Noah Lester (1884-1885) who is buried in the Elias Sease cemetery.

Luther Sease married Ellen Hook and had Walton, Roy, Tallie, Cora and Vera.

Henry Sease, Sr., first married Arrie Hook who had Festus and Mrs. Bryan Keisler. His second marriage was to a Miss Shealy, who is the mother of Laban.

Simeon Sease married his cousin, a daughter of Rufus Lewie. His sons are Lewie and Milas. They lived at Gilbert, S. C. They had several daughters, also.

George Sease married Corrie Jumper. They had Alpha, Cora, Essie, Alice and Carrol.

Killan Sease married Ella Crout. They had Ethel and Janie.

Dent Sease first married a Rogers who was the mother of Willie.

Almenia Sease married Paul Amick. They had Claudius, Silas, Erastus, Leila, Maggie, Belle and Lessie.

Dora Sease married W. Toland Craps and reared Rufus, Fred, Horace, Dawson, Rafred, Refo, Betha, Grovie, Lala and Lever.

Elvira Sease married Henry Shealy and among their children

is Mrs. Murray Wessinger who has been Treasurer of Lexington County for the past ten years or more.

Lillie Sease married a Mr. Simms, of Georgia and had one daughter named Day.

The other son of Frederick Sease and wife was Richard (1830-1912) who married Frances Rawl (1832-1908). Among their children were Ella, wife of Prof. S. S. Lindler, who lived near the Sease home on Big Hollow Creek and was Post Master of Ella, the post office at his home. Prof. Lindler was a school man by profession, also a land surveyor.

Maury Sease married Marshall Hook and lived near St. John's Church. Among their chldren were Richard, Ambrose, Killian, Scott, Mrs. Quinton Keisler and Mrs. Jesse Price.

Fannie Sease married Pierce Taylor. Their children were Ruth, Lessie, Lou Ella, Cline and Schafer.

Lawrence Sease married Fanny Hunter from Prosperity. He was a Professor at Clemson College and was the first school teacher of the writer of this family sketch.

The children of Professor S. S. Lindler and Ella Sease Lindler were Essie, Lella, Frances, Sheppard, John, Harry, and Stephen. The majority were educated. Frances was a classmate of mine.

Richard Sease and wife are sleeping under the waters of Lake Murray where Mount Pleasant Church once was. It was necessary for this congregation to disband on account of the development of Lake Murray.

Later, I have found the old family record of Frederick Sease, born Sept. 18, 1791 and his wife, Elizabeth Bickley, born March 12, 1795.

Anna Sease, 1819; Samuel Sease, 1821; Elias Starling Sease, 1823; James Wily Sease, 1827; Josiah Richard Wesley Sease, 1830; Jacob Anderson Sease, 1832; David Isaiah Sease, 1834; Permelia Ann Luseda Sease, 1836; Frances Marion Sease, 1843.

ADAMS

WILLIAM Adams (1814-1889) came out of Newberry County and married Nancy Boyd (1818-1894) from Edgefield County. His first work in the Big Hollow Creek Valley was supervising a farm for a Mr. Hall on Saluda River near where Big Hollow Creek empties into the river. While working in that capacity, he bought a farm near the Frederick Sease place, later known as the Wesley Nichols place, later covered by waters of Lake Murray. Here William Adams established a home and reared the following children: Frances, who married Anderson Mayer of the upper Dutch Fork. They became the parents of Willie and Emma; Ira was killed in the Civil War; Cornelia married Enoch Swygert and was the mother of Ida, Louannie, Lena, Emanuel, Lilla, Minnie, Yoder, John, George and Mittie; Nannie married Jacob Bedenbaugh, of

Edgefield County. They were the parents of Andrew, Ernest, Nina, James, Calvin, Willie and John A; Lou married Henry Lowman, of Batesburg and had John and Wood.

James Adams first married Edy Swygert. To them were born Henry, the husband of Carrie Craps Drafts; Rufus who married Sallie Winningham, Jesse (1873) who married Lucy Adams (1876) of Newberry County; Mattie, Viola, Leila and Zora.

James Adams' second marriage was to Laura Lybrand Swygert who had Wofford and Gertrude. His third marriage was to Carrie Aldridge.

George Adams' first marriage was to Lula Lowman, of Batesburg and reared the following children: John William, Julius, Nila, Ruth, Webb, Pettus, Horace and Effie.

Jesse Adams and wife, Lucy, with part of their family are still living on Big Hollow Creek.

William and Nancy Adams are buried in Shiloh Cemetery.

ADDY

THE Addys are of German extraction, the first Addy we have any record of was John S. Addy, Sr., 1779-1841. His wife's name was Catherine, 1790-1857. They settled on Big Hollow Creek and are buried in the old family plot on what has been known to later generations as the Dr. William L. Addy farm.

According to the best information we can secure, they had the following children: David, Joel, Simeon, William, M. D.; George, Ada, Elizabeth, Henry and John S., Jr. These are not listed in order of their ages.

John S. Addy, Jr. (1807)

Celia Addy was the wife of John S. Addy.

John S. Addy, Jr., was one of the first elders of Cedar Grove Lutheran Church. John S. and Celia Addy's children's birth dates are listed as follows, from old church records: Henry E. Addy, 1829; Polly C. E. Addy, 1832; Robert I. Addy, 1833; Martha A. Addy, 1835; Daniel M. Addy, 1836; James D. Addy, 1837; Martin V. Addy, 1841; Mary Ann Addy, 1843; Simeon L. Addy, 1846; Elias I. Addy, 1847; Presley Addy, 1849; and Walter P. Addy, 1851.

Joel Addy

Joel Addy married Catherine Lybrand, 1807-1884. Their children were: John Simeon Addy, 1858; David Addy, 1833-1862. He married Lucy Wise. Sarah Addy, 1830, was married twice. She was first married to Adam Shealy. Their children were H. Edwin, Eliza, Gracie and Alice. Her second marriage was to O. D. Rawl. Their children were George, Caroline and Mary. Eliza Addy, 1831-1926, married James W. Craps, 1833-1918. Their children were Allie, Luther, William, Milledge and Dona. Louisa Addy, 1837, married Henry Shealy. They had one son, Franklin Pierce.

Henry Addy

Henry Addy married Barbara Crout, 1834. They moved to Mississippi. We have record of one daughter, Nancy, who married Isaiah Vansant. She died in Texas. They had a daughter, Katherine, who married John Seay and was the mother of Oscar and Mattie, wife of Abb. Hendrix.

Simeon Addy

We have no record of who Simeon Addy married, but we have been informed that he was the father of James "Jim" Addy who married Adeline Derrick. Their children are John, who married Lena Swygert; Rufus, who married Irodine Jumper; Derrick, who married Barbara Roof; Jesse married Essie Wyndham; Ida, who married W. S. Craps; Lula, who married Elvin Ricard; Camilla, who married Ed Porter; and Mattie who married Callie Caughman.

Ada Addy

Ada Addy, 1815-1883, married Henry Craps, 1810-1878. This Henry Craps gave the land where Cedar Grove Church is located.

Their children were Anne, that first married a Fellers, whose children were Luther, Kenneth and Hattie. Her second marriage was to Thomas Cason. Their son was John. Carrie Craps married Irvin Drafts; adopted children were Pierce and Ida Leaphart, and C. I. Morgan. Her second marriage was to Henry Z. Adams, no children. Barbara married Henry Derrick first. To this union was born Walter and Etta. Second marriage was to Hazeal Shealy. Their children were Simeon, Mary, Fanny (1872-1923); Martha and Pierce (1877-1948). Grace Craps (1845-1930) married J. Wynn Morgan (1843-1878). Their children were Henry, Jesse, Rev. C. I., Charles and Mary "Mollie." Ridona Craps married first Leopard Roberts. Their children are Roddie and Acquilla. Her second marriage was to Walter D. Long. Their children are Abner, Eugenia, Berley and Belton. Samuel P. Craps married Sibby Ann Taylor, no children. Simeon W. Craps married first Rosannah Wise. Their children were Hattie, Mary, Willie, John, James, Jason, Carrie, Lizzie, Lula and Nezzie. His second marriage was to Jane Taylor, no children.

David Addy

David Addy married Alice Perry. We have no record of but one child, Edward Addy, who died in the Civil War. I have no record of who his wife was; however, I know that her second marriage was to Sam Dean.

Edward Addy was the father of three sons, Thomas, Oliver B. and H. Edwin. These three sons established homes in the Cedar Grove community, lived and died there and are buried in Cedar Grove cemetery.

Thomas (1853-1922) first married Josephine Black. His second marriage was to Lizzie Ridgell (1874-1940). Their children are Curtis, Lena and Josephine.

Oliver B. Addy (1859-1926) married Lenora Long (1855-1940). Their children are Carrie, Andrew L., Clarence V., Evans O., Ruth, Ethel and Pearle.

H. Edwin (1864-1929) married Mary (1866-1947), a daughter of Dr. W. L. Addy. Their children are Frank L., Carrol, Clyde, Rev. Roy A., Henry E., Louise and Evelyn.

Elizabeth Addy

Elizabeth Addy first married a Hallman. Among her Hallman children were Patrick, of Orangeburg, Elizabeth and Amanda. Her second marriage was to a Davis. Her home was on Horse Creek.

Dr. William L. Addy

Dr. William L. Addy (1821-1883) married Caroline Crout (1836-1928). Their children were Simeon, Dixon (1855-1929) who married Corrie Crout (1858-1928). Their children are Jessie, Belle, Laura, Bertha, Estelle, Lloyd (1882-1941), Nelson, Mina and Nina, twins. William married a daughter of Henry and Susan Price. Among their children are Birdie, Reed, Kemel and a Mrs. Hallman. Laura Addy (1858-1940) married Reid Keisler (1850-1934). No children. Mary married H. Edwin Addy. Their write-up comes under the David Addy sketch.

Dr. William L. Addy lived in the Cedar Grove area his entire life. He was a very succesful practicing physician, and according to old church records was a leading member of Cedar Grove in his day. A number of his descendants are now members of Cedar Grove and are classed among its leading members. Some have made good in the political world and some as Christian leaders. As a whole they are good citizens and accommodating neighbors. Dr. Addy is buried at the old Addy homestead in the old family plot.

Quite a number of the early Addys moved to Mississippi, Texas and other states. This sketch is very incomplete but we endeavored to trace out those who remained in our home community.

AUSTIN

THE Austins settled on the north side of Big Hollow Creek, opposite the settlement of Christian Swygert and his family on the south side.

This old settlement was made by David Austin (1771-1824) and his wife (1781-1819) and is located about one-half mile south of Ridge Road Schoolhouse on lands now owned by Richard H. Roberts, conveyed to him by the writer of this sketch, J. Ansel Caughman. The remains of Davis Austin and his wife sleep there in marked graves in the Austin family plot.

We don't know much about their offspring, other than Rev. Jacob Austin and the descendants of Harriet Elizabeth Austin, who became the wife of John Rawl of the St. John's (white church) section of Lexington County, near Beaver Dam Creek.

Rev. Jacob Austin (1828-1920) taught school in the home community when a young man. After he became an ordained Lutheran minister he moved to Effingham County, Georgia, near Rinceton, Georgia, and rendered fruitful service, preaching to the Moravian and Salzburgers Lutherans for forty-two years.

As a retired pastor the Reverend Jacob Austin, familiarly known as "Uncle Austin," returned to Leesville, S. C., and continued interested and active in ministerial work, serving as supply pastor for several years in the surrounding communities. He served as supply pastor for Mt. Hebron, Union, Salem, Enon, Bethlehem (Black Creek) and others. He had a good, strong voice and could do excellent speaking yet at the age of 90. Everybody loved "Uncle Austin." He married lots of young people and took pride in giving them advice to make life a success.

I understand he lost his wife and children in Georgia. Later he married Laura Etheredge, daughter of Tyre Etheredge, of Leesville, S. C. He died at the age of 92 and is buried in the Leesville Cemetery.

Davis Austin's oldest daughter, Harriet Elizabeth (1805-1858), married John Rawl. She became the mother of 11 children, among them were Benjamin, Jacob, Elijah, Philip, Frances, who became the wife of Richard Sease; Harriet, who became the wife of Harley Seay, and others I do not recall.

Harriet Rawl Seay (1825-1901) was the mother of Dr. Seay (1857-1887) who was a very successful practicing physician, his practice at one time covered the whole Saluda Valley south of Holley's Ferry. Of course, in his day his mode of conveyance was on horseback. His numerous friends made provision for his comfort by providing rooms in their homes for him to take refuge in case of bad weather or in case of having patients in severe sickness.

Among Harriet Rawl Seay's other children was a daughter, Elizabeth (1862-1942), who married Vastine Wessinger (1852-1938). Their children were Chalmers Wessinger (1884-1948), who was an educator, having graduated from the South Carolina University and Columbia University; Hoy Wessinger (1887-1939), an Agriculturist, being a graduate of Clemson College.

The living remnants of this family are a son and daughter, Horry and Eunice Rose, respectively.

Prior to the death of Chalmers, the three, Chalmers, Eunice Rosa and Horry presented to St. John's Church a Hammond Electronic Organ as a gift in memory of their father, mother and brother, Hoy. Soon after the installation of this organ Chalmers died, so the first service in which this organ was used was for the funeral service of the oldest donor.

We have now reached the point in this family sketch where all the interested, progressive Christian leaders of the Evangelical Lutherans of the South Carolina Synod were made happy.

We understand that the aforesaid Chalmers Wessinger left an estate of $49,000 at his death; his sister, Eunice Rosa and brother Horry being the beneficiaries.

After his death these devoted beneficiaries expressed to the South Carolina Synod a desire to carry out the wish of their deceased brother in conveying this entire estate to the South Carolina Synod to be used as a revolving fund for Home Missions.

The good Lutherans of the South Carolina Synod will always be grateful to these generous and gracious characters who have proven themselves to be humble and devoted servants of the Most High.

In viewing and inspecting the beautiful monument erected to the family of Vastine and Elizabeth Wessinger in the church yard of St. John's we were impressed with the historical reference inscribed on the back of the monument which reads as follows: Direct descendants of Mathias Wessinger who with his family left Germany "on encouragement given to foreign Protestants", sailed from Fort Rotterdam landing in Charleston in 1752. Settled below St. Michael's church in the Dutch Fork on 250 acres granted by the King of England.

We cannot finish this sketch without referring to another outstanding character down this line who is a great-great-grandson of the original Davis Austin. This character is Walter Rawl, a great-grandson of Harriet Elizabeth Austin. Walter is a fine promoter. It seems as if he might be a genius in all his undertakings, knowing how to make a successful go of all projects. He began life as a poor boy, but by his grit and integrity has caused the whole country to look upon him with favor, because of his success in life. It is no uncommon thing for him and his wife to make large donations to Christian causes and charity. We understand that Walter and his good wife are supporting a missionary in Nigeria.

Walter is now a member of the Highway Commission of South Carolina.

DERRICK

IT appears that six Derrick brothers started over to this country from the German Fatherland. One died on the way over; one settled in Virginia; the other four came to South Carolina: Andrew, Jacob, George and Thomas. First we shall follow up the descendants of Andrew and Tom.

With the best information obtainable the first Andrew Derrick's children were Andrew, John, Tom, Barbara, who married a Corley; Bettie, who married a Wessinger and Julia who married a Caughman. We have no further record of these children except Andrew and Tom.

The second Andrew Derrick married Katie Hiller, daughter of Samuel Hiller, whose home was near Saluda River on the north side near the old Lexington road. From this couple we find there were 13 children; Mary Magdalene, Sallie, Nancy, Jemima, Emanuel, David, Jacob J. Levi, Solomon, Jeremiah, Josie and John S.

Mary Magdalene married John William Ballentine; Sallie married Wesley Lybrand and settled near Wagener in Aiken County; Nancy was the second wife of Rev. Emanuel Caughman; Jemima married a Solomon; Emanuel was the father of Laura A. who was the wife of John C. Caughman, son of Rev. Emanuel Caughman; Jacob J. Derrick married Martha Kessler and was the father of Dr. Sydney J. Derrick, a former president of Newberry College; John S. Derrick married Elizabeth Caughman, a sister of John C. Caughman. Their home was in Leesville and their children were Pickens, Charley, Noah, Anna and Mary.

George A. Derrick, a former auditor of Lexington County, born in 1854 and whose wife was Della Smith, was a son of Levi Derrick, likely a son of the second Andrew Derrick.

There was a Godfrey Derrick who had a son, John, who married Elizabeth Wise and was the father of Jesse Derrick, who married Ellen Caughman, sister of John C. Caughman. This John Derrick also had a daughter, Carolina, who married Rev. J. H. W. Wertz.

After the death of John Derrick of this paragraph, his widow became the third wife of Jacob Caughman, one of the brothers of Rev. Emanuel Caughman.

We will now take up the line of Tom Derrick, one of the original Derrick brothers, and who is said to have settled in Lexington County, presumably on Big Hollow Creek. We do not know who this Tom Derrick married, but he is the father of the following children: Rebecca (1803), Nancy (1805), Christena (1808), Polly (1814), Elizabeth (1820), W. Thomas, Samuel (1801), Daniel and Joseph.

Nancy Derrick married Martin Swygert; Christena and Polly never married, but their last years were spent in the home of their nephew, Oliver A. Derrick, where they died both in 1893.

Elizabeth (1820-1886) married Luke Nichols. W. Thomas Derrick married first Reba Roberts. Their children were Oliver A. (1847-1917), who married Laura Catherine, daughter of W. W. Fulmer; G. Marion (1850-1930) who married Kate, daughter of J. Adam Kinard; Leopard Scott (1855-194) married Sallie, daughter of Eli Shealy; and Lou Annie (1853) married Simeon Black.

W Thomas Derrick's second wife was Lucinda Moore Crout, widow of David Crout. His first home was on Big Hollow Creek where his grandson, Billy Derrick, now lives, and his latter home was in Leesville.

Samuel Derrick married Polly Shealy and their home was on upper Hollow Creek. Their children included Paul (1829-1877), who was a Lutheran Minister, married Amanda Hiller and reared the following children: Samuel J. who married Lillie Rawl. He taught in the public schools of Lexington, Edgefield and Saluda Counties all his active life. He and his wife are buried at Swansea; Henry David married Maggie Repass of Virginia. John E. married Mannie Rawl and died in Texas; Fred and Eusebuis died young; Pauline married Rosswell A. Barr and lives in Gilbert.

D. Wilson (1831-1863), second son of Samuel and Polly Derrick, married Christena Wise. He died in the Civil War and left two children, Frederick (1856-1880) and Mattie, who was the second wife of W. J. P. Kinard. They lived in Leesville and are buried there; Jasper (1839-1905) never married, was one of the pioneer merchants of Leesville. He was also at one time treasurer of Lexington County; A Edwin, fifth child of Samuel and Polly Derrick married Georgiana Wertz and had Samuel, Sydney and Jesse; Adeline married James D. Addy; David married a Wise and moved to Georgia. Mrs. D. I. Hite of West Columbia is a daughter of this couple; Henry married Barbara Craps and had Walter and Etta; Josephine mrried Joseph Wise and moved to Georgia; Sarah married Walter "Duck" Shealy and had Samuel, Maggie and Betty. Mary Ann never married.

Daniel Derrick married Mary, second daughter of John Black.

Joseph Derrick married Martha (1830-1918), daughter of Jacob Lindler and their home was on lower Rocky Creek in Lexington County. Their children were Anderson P., who married Caroline Holley Langford; Paul P. married Alice Dickert; Frank married Mary Caughman, of Lexington; Joseph married Dora Faulkner; and Epsy Mary Ann (1859-1944) married Stanmore Shealy (1853-1932).

John Derrick (1827-1896) married Patsy Shealy who became the mother of Amanda, who married her cousin, John Oxner. This John lived on Rocky Creek, also. His second wife was his cousin, Lizzie Shealy, from Leesville.

Back to Edwin Derrick's family who were members of Salem and continued to live in the Big Hollow Creek Valley. His son, Samuel, married Mamie Folk and moved to Newberry County. Sydney, a graduate of Newberry College, a school teacher by profession, also a representative once in our legislature, married Alice Jumper; Jesse first married Leila Warren, his second wife is Nina Goff.

CRAPS

OUR first reference is to one John Jacob Craps who owned a large estate in what is now known as the Sandy Run section of Lexington County, or perhaps partly in Calhoun County. He and his wife whose maiden name was Harriet Malone, were buried near the house on this estate, but nothing remains but a chimney base and a few catawba trees. A part of the estate is now or was recently owned by Willie Wolf.

The earliest reference to John Jacob Craps is found in Council Journals of May 7, 1755. His first son was named John. He married Catherine Lowman and moved to Georgia. There was another son, George, born about 1770 in the old Craps home at Sandy Run. He married Barbara Crim, daughter of Col. Lawrence Crim of the same community, and as he is the ancestor of the Lexington County branch, in which we are chiefly concerned at this time, we shall follow him up.

After his marriage, George Craps left Sandy Run and moved about 40 miles northwest; acquired an estate of about 1,500 acres in the little Hollow Creek section, near the present St. Paul's Lutheran Church and there set up his home. The old house is probably still standing and a row of cedars marks the driveway in from the spoolwheel road. He and his wife are buried about 150 yards south of the house in a clump of bushes—their graves marked only by stones without inscriptions.

The children of George Craps were as follows: Mary, who married Joel Keisler; Elizabeth (1798) married John Keisler; Katie (1850), married Isaac Vansant. Katie and her husband, who was once sheriff of Lexington County, left no children and are buried near the north limits of Summit, S. C.; Nancy (1816) married John Price and reared a large family of children. She died in 1837 and is buried in the John Price family cemetery; Jacob (1805) married Jemima Seay and moved to Georgia.

David (1805), twin to Jacob, married Polly Rucker, of Sandy Run. They settled on part of his father's estate, known as the Dave Craps place; John Lawrence Craps (1808) married Elizabeth Vick of Leesville; Henry (1810-1878) married Ada Addy (1815-1883), sister of Dr. W. L. Addy; William (1816), twin with Nancy, married Barbara Hildebrand, of Sandy Run and moved to Georgia, thence to Alabama.

David Craps and Polly Rucker reared several boys, all of whom, except Henry, was lost in the Civil War. Harrison was sent home sick, died and was buried in the family plot. Edwin and Patrick sleep in the dust of the unknown. His girls were Mariah, who married Emanuel Taylor; Julia Ann married Frank Leaphart, father of Pierce Leaphart and Ida Hyler; Rachael married Samuel Price, who was killed in the Civil War; Mary married William Jumper and Laura (1847-1917) married Daniel Jumper (1844-1929).

John L. Craps and wife, Elizabeth Vick, had the following children: James W., who married Eliza Addy, daughter of Joel Addy and wife, Catherine Lybrand; Georgian married Albert Leaphart; Eliza married Hiram Addy; Adrean married Jones Anderson; Davis, Jasper Black first and later Paul Corley; Mary Jane married Marshall Taylor first and then Allen Hallman; Paul R. married Rosannah Crout, daughter of Thomas Crout; George P. married Evylyn

Black, sister of Jasper Black; W. Toland married Dora Sease, daughter of Elias Sease and Mary Jane Lewie.

Since Henry Craps and wife, Ada Addy, gave the land where Cedar Grove Church was built, we wish to write up that family.

Their children were as follows: Simeon (1835-1909) married Rosanna Wise (1837-1901); Samuel married Sibby Taylor; Caroline (1840-1919) first married Irvin Drafts (1840-1885), later H. Z. Adams; Barbara (1838-1882) first married Henry Derrick, then Hazeal Shealy (1839-1906); Ann first married a Mr. Fellers in Newberry County then Thomas Cason; Grace (1845-1930) married J. Wynn Morgan (1843-1878); Ridona first married Leopard Roberts, then Walter D. Long. Samuel Craps left no children.

Simeon Craps and wife, Rosanna Wise, were the parents of Hattie who became the wife of Andrew Long; Mary married W. H. Hare a very prominent citizen and churchman in his day; Willie married Ida Addy; John married Julia Folk, of Newberry County; James "Jimmy" married Sallie Meetze; Carrie married Joe Reynolds; Lizzie married Luther Lybrand; Lula married Tyre Shealy; Nezzie married in Florida.

During the Eigteen Nineties there was a post office at Simeon Craps' called Brook; Mr. Craps was postmaster. At this time there was a telegraph line running from Delmar to Summit, a telegraph office was also there. The first Rural Free Delivery route from Leesville absorbed part of the territory served by Brook and the post office was discontinued.

Later another post office named Number was established there, helping to form a star route from Gilbert, going up by Priceville, Franklin Keisler, Postmaster; Lorena, Cephas Sease, Postmaster; to Dupler, Mrs. Dan Holley, Post Mistress; back by Monroe, E. F. Caughman, Postmaster; then to Number, S. W. Craps, Postmaster. Later all these post offices were discontinued, the entire community being served by R. F. D. Simeon W. Craps' last marriage was to Jane Taylor. He moved to Leesville and spent his last years merchandising.

SNELGROVE

THIS record begins with a Snelgrove family on the south side of Saluda River, below the mouth of Big Hollow Creek, living on what was known as the Mid Long Place, before 1800. We do not know the Christian name of this Snelgrove or who his wife was. It appears that he was married twice, a child of his first wife being Carey G. Snelgrove, and children of his second wife included Ezra and Epsy, the latter of whom married a Hallman and then a Rice. We are not able to trace the families of the latter two now, but still follow Carey, who was born in 1798, married Ruthy Richardson, who was born 1799; moved up in Edgefield District and settled where Lott Jennings once lived, and later known as the Julius Langford place.

The following children are named: Achsa, who married Ephraim Shealy; Lydia, who married William "Tice" Shealy; Rosannah, who married Simeon Harman; Rocelia, who married W. Riley Shealy and later Robert Faulkner (1841-1919); Chelsea, who married Rosannah Crout; George, who moved to Florida; Larkin W., who married Katie Rinehart.

Mr. Snelgrove's first wife died in 1838, in her 40th year and is buried in a family plot a few hundred yards south of the homestead mentioned above. His second wife was Annie Matthews, now Langford, and he moved from the old home to the old place near the present home of Noah Hare. His second wife brought a daughter, Elizabeth, into the family, who married Noah Caughman. She bore Mr. Snelgrove three other children as follows: Francis Marion, who was killed in the battle of Gettysburg in the Civil War; Luther, who served through the war and then married Julia Ann Hare; and Dollie, who married William Derrick.

Father Snelgrove died in 1858, and is buried by the side of his first wife in the old family plot.

Chelsea, one of the sons, of Carey Snelgrove, married Rosannah Crout, daughter of Dr. John Crout. Their home was just south of where Leon Corley lives between State Highway 391 and the new S-D Highway. They reared eleven children as follows: Milledge P., who married Rozilla Shealy; William, who married a daughter of John Price in the Priceville section of Lexington County; George T., who married the first Maria Oxner, second Laura Bailey, third Bessie   ; John C., who married Malissa Shealy; Eli, who married first Mary Miller; Willie married a Harris; Amanda married Nathaniel Oxner; Martha married Geo. W. Miles; Nancy married Calhoun Price; Kate married Samuel M. Myers; and Elizabeth who never married. Besides these children one son, Levi Tyre, died young.

Chelsea died in 1862 and with the little son who died in 1853, is buried in a family plot on the old homestead.

SWYGERT

CHRISTIAN Swygert came from the Dutch Fork and settled on Big Hollow Creek, six miles north of Leesville, near the residence of Leppard Derrick.

He was born in 1779 and died in 1841; he married Margaret Hallman who died in 1860. They are buried near where they lived.

This couple reared four sons and three daughters, namely, first John M. Swygert, who married Barbara Anna Derrick. They moved to Smith County, Mississippi, 1856. His wife died in 1862; he died in 1884. This couple were the parents of ten children.

Second child, John Zeno, who moved with his wife, Mittie Ann

Addy, to Marriwether County, Ga., died in 1889. His wife died in 1898. He left seven children.

Third child, George, died in 1848. Fourth child, or son, was Emanuel Zeddo, who settled on the old place where his youngest son, Job C. Swygert lived and reared his family. Zeddo married Mittie Ann Crout, daughter of Dave Crout.

Before the outbreak of the Civil War he was captain of a Military Company known as the Saluda Guards. At the beginning of the Civil War, he with Dr. F. S. Lewie, raised a company, which became C. 15, S. C. Reg. He served as First Lieutenant and was killed at Hilton Head Nov. 7, 1861. He was buried by the enemy, if buried at all. He was the father of seven children, namely, Enoch, Edy, Cephas, Sallie, Izilla, Job and Laura.

First daughter of Christian Swygert was Rachel, who married Simpson Corley. They moved to Smith County, Miss. She died in 1875.

Second daughter, Eliza, married Henry Brison. They moved first to Mississippi and then to Arkansas.

Third daughter, Elizabeth (1825-1891) married William P. Caughman (1823-1863). They lived in the home community, died childless and are buried in Union Cemetery.

Enoch Swygert (1846-1821), oldest son of Zeddo and Mittie Ann Swygert, married Cornelia Adams, daughter of William and Nancy Adams. They had ten children, six girls and four boys, namely, Ida, who married W. H. Derrick; Louannie, who married E. E. Haigood; Lena, who married John S. Addy; Emanuel "Bud" (1875-1950) married Vertie Risinger (1875-1950); Lilla Lee, who married James D. Langford; Minnie, who married Otis Drafts; Yoder married Lula Oxner; John married Inez Ricard; George W. married Cattie Caughman.

Enoch Swygert's last wife was Clara Moore. He lived in the home community all his life, died and is buried by his first wife (who was the mother of all his children) in Cedar Grove Cemetery.

Job C. Swygert married Sophrenia Rinehart, who was the mother of Cohen and Cora, twins; Dantzler, Charles, James, Georgia, Olin, Mamie, Jobie and Pickens.

Edy Swygert married James Adams.

Sallie Swygert married James Caughman and Laura Swygert married Wade Jumper.

Cephas Swygert married Laura Lybrand and she became the mother of Hattie, who married Oscar Eargle; Mary, who married Harry Rawl; Cromwell, who married Carmie Summers; Jessie, who married Willie Rinehart and Arnie, who married a Gibson, from Hickory, N. C.

Enoch Swygert left four sons, all of whom are now living in the Hollow Creek community, and are members of Cedar Grove Church, whom we will now write up in order.

Emanuel "Bud's" children are Etha, the wife of George Metts;

Essie, who married a Bush, living in Georgia; Jacob, who married a Price; Nephle, who married a daughter of Bunyan Shealy; Lila Belle married Joe Metts; Rean married Collie Monts; Elma married Charley Price; Mittie married Bruce Price; Wilson, who married a daughter of Butler Kaminer; Lula married McCoy Kyzer, and Ezelle.

Yoder and wife, Lula Oxner, were the parents of five children, the oldest being Rev. Legare Swygert, a prominent Lutheran Minister of the South Carolina Synod, who married Louise Addy, daughter of Mr. and Mrs. E. H. Addy; Annie, who married Andrew Jacob Bedenbaugh, son of A. L. Bedenbaugh; Viera, who married Lovelle Price and is a Contractor by trade. He was the contractor in building the new modern parsonage at Cedar Grove Church, built in 1948-1949, occupied first by Rev. J. Russell Boggs; Lilla, who married A. J. Black of Saluda County; Enoch died young.

John, who married Inez Ricard, have Gurney, who married Wakefield Risinger; Anglo, who married Lois Whittle and Rama Jane who is the wife of T. M. Kinard.

George, the youngest son of Enoch Swygert and the husband of Cattie Caughman is the father of 14 children, namely, Irvin, Edy, two others died young; Verley married a Lybrand; Carl married Sadie Craps; Nell Sue became the wife of Hoy Hyler; Robert married Delores Wiley from Minnesota; Hennis married a Warren; Alma married Leroy Oxner; Jane, Melvin, Deward and Martha not married.

HALLMAN

CHRISTENA Hallman, a sister of Christian Swygert's wife, bore two daughters, Harriet and Levisa. They settled on the place where J. Ansel Caughman now lives, about 1800. The tract of land contained 200 acres; at that time the purchase price was sixty dollars. It was the northeast corner of a 1,000 acre tract owned by a Mr. Hamiter of the Orangeburg District, that he had bought from the Government at ten cents an acre.

Harriet (1809-1854) was the oldest child; she died at the age of 45. Henry Eargle and family were among their nearest neighbors. He was at their home the night she died. He said her last and dying words were, "Oh death, where is thy sting; oh grave, where is thy victory."

Christena Hallman had only one eye. She was crossing Big Hollow Creek once on a foot log; an eagle flew in her face and picked out one of her eyes.

Christena and Harriet are buried here on the old homestead. Levisa reared Burrel Miles and gave her property to Geo. W., his son, to take care of her. He moved her with him and family to West Columbia, where she died. She is buried in the Eliza Hook family plot near West Columbia. Levisa planted an apple tree on this farm more than 100 years ago that is still bearing fruit. Levisa was the last person to see a wild deer in this community.

HUFF

NOT far distant from Cedar Grove Church, something like 300 yards, is the Huff family burying ground. There are only two marked graves in this cemetery, a mark to the grave of Sarah Jackson and a monument to Leah Banks, wife of George Banks.

The inscription on the first named tombstone reads thus: "Sarah Jackson died Oct. or Nov. 1825 so says her son J. D. Huff." I have not been able to find out who this J. D. or James D. Huff married, but among his children were Leah (1819-1879) who married George Banks. Their children were Louisa, the second wife of Lewis J. Langford; Butler Banks, married Fanny Dickert. They are buried at Colony Lutheran Church, Newberry County; Catherine Banks married Calvin Price of the Priceville section. They had five children. When the terrible Diptheria Epidemic passed through South Carolina about 70 years ago, all five died within eight days; Georgiana Banks (1850-1932) married Lemuel Oswald (1846-1926). They are buried at Beulah Methodist Church with their two sons, Frank (1871-1951) and Melton "Bub" (1879-1950).

James D. Huff had another daughter, who was the first wife of Rev. George Kelley; they had two sons Frank and John. Frank Kelley was a familiar character in the Pleasant Hill Community of Lexington County and is buried there. John went to Alabama.

The next daughter of James D. Huff was Isabell who became the wife of David Drayton Long, who was born and reared in the Macedonia section of Lexington Countyl near the Newberry County line. Drayton Long was a son of John Long and wife, who were charter members of Macedonia Lutheran Church when it was organized in 1847. Among the brothers of Drayton Long were Middleton, Wesley and Hilliard. He also had a sister, Caroline, who married Mark Shealy. They settled near Batesburg and became prominent church leaders at Wittenberg Lutheran Church at Leesville.

Drayton and Isabell Huff Long's children are Walter, Lenorah, Alice, John, William D., Lula, Edward, Thomas and Alma.

Drayton Long and wife Isabell got in possession of the Huff plantation and settled there in 1877. There was a skirmish between the Revolutionists and the Tories, on this plantation, during the Revolutionary War. All Tories captured were hanged and buried on this property. James D. Huff made the statement to Lewis J. Langford, the husband of his granddaughter, that he saw the ropes with his own eyes by which the Tories were hanged.

Isabell Huff Long had a half sister, Mary Jane Leaphart, who married Andrew Long of Newberry County. They lived near Murray in their declining years and are buried at Pleasant Hill Baptist Church.

The majority of the children of Drayton and Isabell Huff Long became members of Cedar Grove Lutheran Church, among them being Walter, whose first wife was Ridona Roberts Craps, and his second wife was Laura Eargle; Lenorah (1855-1940) married O. B. Addy (1859-1926); Alice (1858-1938) married Pierce Leaphart (1860-1923); John (1863-1942) married Blanche Sligh; William (1871-1932) married Josephine Nichols; Edward married Ollie Steele; Thomas married Mattie Shealy; Lula married John Summers and Alma married Geo. C. Steele.

William is buried at Union Lutheran Church; Edward and his parents are buried in the Salem Cemetery; Walter, Lenorah, Alice and John are buried at Cedar Grove.

Thomas, Lula and Alma are still living.

OXNER

THE family tradition is that three Oxner brothers emigrated to this country from their native Germany sometime before 1800. One of them, whose name is said to be Simeon, went to Mississippi; one settled in the territory of Laurens County; and the other settled in Lexington County or District as it was then.

We have records of three of the Oxner descendants: Alfred Jackson Oxner, Daniel Oxner and Henry Oxner. Alfred Jackson Oxner came from the Laurens branch and became the forefather of the majority of the original Saluda County Oxners.

We have record of several Oxners who were members of Salem Church between 1800 and 1825, among them were Henry and Susannah, who was likely Henry's wife. They lived on Horse Creek near the Sawyer place. Daniel and Celia, his wife, were members of Salem at that time also. Daniel was born about 1812 and married Celia Risinger of upper Hollow Creek.

Daniel settled first on Big Hollow Creek and afterwards on Rocky Creek in Lexington County. Mr. Oxner died in 1866 and his wife in 1898. Both are buried in a family plot near the old homestead about one-half mile from Old Lexington Baptist Church. The list of their children is as follows: William Bennet (1835-1887); Louisa Catherine (1837) died young; Mary Lemanda was the wife of Eli Shealy; Martha Ann Oxner married Joseph Hite. Their children were Davis, Henry, Allen, Enoch, who became a Lutheran Minister, Irvin, Emma, Dona, Minnie, Lillie and George; Nathaniel Oxner married Amanda Snelgrove (1850-1940), daughter of Chelsea Snelgrove and of their children we name George D., who married first Mary Corley, second Claudia Edwards, and third Olive Haltiwanger; J. Bennie married Aminee Asbill; M. Luther married Laura Shealy; Rufus L. married Blanche Eargle; Lula married Yoder J. Swygert; Nettie married J. Rufus Shealy; Willie died when a young man.

Nathaniel was killed by a runaway team, overthrowing the wagon body on him, and is buried at the old homestead.

Maria Oxner (1845-1918) was the first wife of George T. Snelgrove (1855-1945). Their children are Mary, Edna, Sallie and Maggie.

Mary married first Billy Keisler and second a Mr. Riley; Edna married Perry Harman; Sallie married Hamp Keisler and Maggie married Ephraim Norris.

Eliza Oxner married first Henry Caughman (1855-1875) and second John Hite.

Annis Oxner never married.

At one time the Nathaniel Oxner family operated a roller flour mill, one of the first operated in South Carolina.

RISINGER

DAVID Risinger (1762-1848) came directly from Germany and settled on the head waters of Big Hollow Creek. He married Catherine Swartz, daughter of John Adam Swartz. Catherine Risinger was born in 1791 and died 1878.

David and Catherine Risinger were the parents of 13 children, namely: Adam (1810); Celia (1812); Elizabeth (1814-1845); Rebecca (1815-1879); Anna (1816); Mary (1820-1916); Thomas (1822-1879); Ridona (1824-1875); John (1826-1845); Martha (1827-1831); Noah (1832-1864); Wesley (1832-1915) (Noah and Wesley were twins); David (1834-1863). Of these 13 children one, Martha, died when a child; three others died in the prime of life with typhoid fever; Noah was killed in the battle of the Wilderness in the Civil War; David died in a hospital in Virginia during the Civil War.

Adam, the oldest son of David and Catherine Swartz Risinger married Miley Hallman, born 1815. This couple married in 1832, and had Mary Mittyan (1833); Elizabeth (1836), who married Lewis Shealy, a school teacher and Clerk of Cedar Grove a long time; George Daniel (1838) who moved to Mississippi; Gency Ann (1839) who married Butler Hallman and had one daughter, Sedecia; Thursey (1842) who married Willie Oswalt and had no children; Tera (1845) who married Levi Caughman. Their latter days were spent in Saluda County and are buried at Good Hope Church. Their descendants are living in that community. Jacob Dederick (1847-1897) married Debbie Taylor. Their children were Ella (1871), Vertie (1875-1950), Ira (1874-1894), Pierce, Alice, Perry (1894-1904), Jacob, Lillie and Lottie (1894-1921). Ira was killed by a train in Montgomery, Ala. His father was also killed by a train at Leesville, S. C. Minerva Risinger was born 1850 and married Pressley Shealy, whose descendants are written up in the Shealy sketch; Edy (1852) was the mother of one son, Cleveland. She was twice married, first to James Addy, second to Bud Smith; Ady (1854) married Shuford Davis. Among her children is Alva who lives near the original Risinger homestead; Ervin Risinger, the youngest son of Adam and Miley Risinger, was born 1857. He was twice married; first to Savilla Davis and second to her sister, Eufala Davis. His first wife was the mother of all his children, which were Daisy, Erastus, Festus, Gairy, Eril, Genus, Charley and Jimmie.

Adam Risinger's last wife was Lavinia Hallman (1823), who he married in 1869.

Celia Risinger, the first daughter of the first David Risinger, was born in 1812. She married Daniel Oxner. Their write-up is under the Oxner sketch. Rebecca Risinger (1815-1879) married Lewis Crout. They lived and died near the present Red Star School House and are buried there. They had two sons who went West.

Mary Risinger (1820-1916) never married. She lived her long life of 96 years on the original Risinger homestead or plantation where she was born. Her life's story is very interesting. In the terrible conflict between the states, her brothers being in the war, the responsibility of holding the home together was on her shoulders. With the help of a hired boy she was able to produce a living and keep the stock together until about the close of the war when thieves and vagabonds stole them. Losing two of her brothers, Noah and David, in the war, Wesley, the only single brother to return home, found Miss Mary still with the same perseverance and unselfishness, ready to help regain their wasted fortunes, thus this sister and brother lived happily together for almost 83 years. In Sherman's Raid down Big Hollow Creek she related to her nieces with whom she lived in her declining years, the following account of what happened. Expecting a raid at any time, she with some help dug a large hole in the ground. There they buried a bale of cotton, their flour and their meat, camoflaged the place and saved that. She hid the money and a gold watch in a rock pile and saved that. The molesting enemy went in the kitchen and took all they wanted, stole or drove off the livestock.

Miss Mary was blessed with good health. She didn't even know what medicine tasted like until in her last sickness. She with her parents, sisters and brother, Wesley and wife are buried in a family plot at the old homestead. Their graves are marked with magnificent monuments.

Thomas Risinger (1822-1879) settled near the original homestead but nearer where the town of Leesville is. Among his children were Lawson, John, Henry, Jane and Etta.

Ridona Risinger married a Rish. They lived near the town of Summit.

Wesley Risinger (1832-1915) married Rosannah Shealy (1848-1915), daughter of Ephraim and Achsa Snelgrove Shealy. Their children were Paul David (1870-1950), who became a very prominent Lutheran Minister. Annie (1873) married a Mr. Williamson of Pomaria, S. C. Jessie Catherine (1879) married Perry Taylor. Cora Edna (1881) married Bunyan Asbill. Alberdie (1888) married Moses Taylor.

Alberdie, the youngest daughter of Wesley and Rosannah, lived with, and cared for, her parents and Aunt Mary during their de-

(185

clining days. She lost her husband, Moses Taylor, in 1950. She is now living at the old original Risinger Homestead. Her family is all married except one daughter, Mary Ruth, a graduate of Winthrop College and a teacher in the Batesburg-Leesville High School. Her oldest daughter, Rose, married Franklin Drafts. She is a graduate of Newberry College and is teaching in the Gilbert High School. Another daughter, Fay, a graduate of Newberry College, married James Cato. She taught for a long period in the Monetta Schools. Her son, J. W., is a high officer in the U. S. Army. Her other daughters are college graduates and rank high in church and civic life also.

This Risinger family has always been devout Lutherans and loyal members of Cedar Grove Congregation.

Thomas Risinger, son of the first David Risinger, married Caroline Florence Seay in 1845. His family were once members of Cedar Grove. I have been able to secure some church records of this family. Their descendants were Jane Levina (1846); Lora Antinet (1847); Mary Louisa (1851); Henrietta (1850); Silas Edwin (1852); John Roston (1854); Henry Arthur (1860).

LYBRAND

THE Lybrands first located in the Dutch Fork and settled on Bear Creek. Sometime in the late 1700's a Lutheran Church was built in the Lybrand settlement and was called Lybrand's Church St. James'. For some reason unknown to the writer, this congregation disbanded in the early 1800's. Nothing remains there today except a number of unmarked graves. This old church site is about five miles southeast of Macedonia Lutheran Church. When Macedonia Church, or congregation, was organized this old Lybrand Church was used for a few years until a new building could be erected, or until a school house was used at Macedonia.

We find several Lybrands mentioned among our pioneer settlers on Big Hollow Creek. Catherine Lybrand (1807-1884), who was the wife of Joel Addy. Rev. Eli Lott Lybrand, who was pastor of Cedar Grove for 13 successive years from 1883 until 1896 was directly related to Louis Lybrand, around whom we wish to center this sketch. Wesley Lybrand came from the Dutch Fork and settled at Wagener, S. C. He was a first cousin to Louis Lybrand.

Louis Lybrand (1811-1878) married Emily Baker (1811-1898), daughter of Billy and Catherine Baker and was reared near St. John's Lutheran Church, her ancestors came from England. She had two sisters and a brother who reared families. One brother, "Billy," died at the age of 22 with measles. One sister, Charlotte, married Bill Hallman. They lived on Highway No. 1 then known as the Augusta Road. Their home was the identical spot where Godfrey Taylor now lives. The beautiful magnolia tree in the yard came from a seed one of her sons brought home with him out of the Civil War.

This was then a prominent place, a stopping place for the Stage Coach to change horses. Horses were changed every six miles.

The other sister, Gadsey (1808-1883) first married Isaac Vansant. Her second marriage was to John Rawl (1800-1892). This was John Rawl's third wife. They lived near St. John's Church. Gadsey was killed by lightning in August while picking cotton. Also a colored man was killed who was some distance from her. The bolt killing the two was supposed to have been a forked bolt.

Her brother, John Baker, lived in Newberry County. One of his descendants was John A. M. Baker of the Bethel section.

Two sons were born to Louis Lybrand and his wife, Samuel Wesley (1832-1888) and William, who lost his life in the Cival War, and is buried near Greensboro, N. C.

Samuel married Beulah Fikes (1836-1888). They settled near Union Lutheran Church and had twelve children, namely: Ellen (1854-1929), Laura, Rodella (1856-1896), Cebastian, Frances, Cornelia, Barbara (1865-1893), Ridona, Joseph (1871-1932), Willie, Hampton, and Bertha. Ellen was twice married, first to Henry Taylor and secondly to Edwin Caughman (1853-1938). Her Taylor children were William and Lillie. Her Caughman children were Carrie, Ansel, Calvin, Mattie, Noah, Sallie and Birdie.

Laura was married twice, first to Cephas Swygert, second to James Adams. Her Swygert children were Hattie, Mary, Cromwell, Jessie and Ornie. Her Adams children were Wofford and Gertrude.

Rodella married Geo. R. Shealy (1852-1928) and became the mother of Luther, Sydney, Lula, Lessie, George, Samuel and Carrol.

Cebastian married Almenia Shealy and had Samuel, Henry, Eddie, George, Viola, John, Collins, Noah, Ernest, Chester, Maxcy, and Quincy.

Viola was the only daughter in the family. She married Hampton Kyzer and became the mother of sixteen children. They live in Georgia.

Frances married Reuben Shealy and moved to southwest Georgia. She was the mother of Drayton, Wesley, Lawrence, Ethan, Loderick and Roscoe.

Cornelia married Samuel Waites, of Newberry County. To this couple were born Osborne (1884-1922), Ollie, Ornie and Abner.

Barbara married John Bedenbaugh (1859-1935) of Edgefield and bore Sallie, Samuel and Jesse.

Ridona became the wife of Pinckney Crout and was the mother of Wightman, Ryan, Voigt, Bachman, Quilla, Brinton and Daisy.

Joseph Lybrand married Ella Risinger and they were the parents of Willie, Ollie, Minnie, Annie, Zula, Elot, Azilea and Jacob.

Dr. Willie Ezra Lybrand married Agnes Fulmer. He died childless. He was a graduate of Baltimore Medical College. He lived only six months after he received his diploma. He is buried in the Macedonia Lutheran Church Yard.

Hampton Lybrand married Amanda Taylor. They had Eula, Broadus, Jefferson, Brady, Leo, Fay and Kenneth.

Bertha, the youngest daughter of Samuel and Beulah Lybrand and the only one now living, married D. Henry Price and is the mother of Myrtle, Aster, Vernon, Seth, Brady, Ralph and Guy.

Samuel and Beulah Lybrand died the same day and were buried in a double grave at the old homestead with his parents, Louis and Emily Lybrand. Emily Lybrand, my great-grandmother, lived with us while I was growing up. She was old and like the majority of aged people, was living her life over again. She handed down to me a lot of tradition that is being recorded in these family sketches. She would often relate to me how they would grow indigo and other early money crops; how she would spin thread and weave cloth. She was very economical and conservative. I have in my possession today a beautiful pair of variegated socks which she spun and knit for her son who lost his life in the Civil War, also one of his beautiful silk handkerchiefs. She gave me a beautiful home woven counterpane with fringes that she made more than 100 years ago.

EARGLE

THE Eargles of the Dutch Fork of Lexington District are the first of that line of which we have any records at hand. From this settlement came Henry Eargle, who married Nancy Rawl, a sister of Sarah Rawl, wife of Michael Shealy and a sister of Christian and Jeremiah Rawl. This couple first settled on Big Hollow Creek, on what was then known as the "Dickert" place, near Frederick Sease. Some of their children were born there. Among them were Fred P., Albert, Eliza, Rebecca, Irvin, Henry and Pressley.

Rebecca was kicked by a mule and killed.

Eliza later became the wife of George C. Shirey, a striking co-incident is that this couple was born in the same house. This couple was the parents of Dora Shirey, the wife of the writer of this sketch.

Later Henry Eargle and his family settled near the Lexington-Edgefield line on Whetstone Creek about 1800. This family reared six children, five sons and one daughter.

Fred P. married Ruth Shealy and was called to the service of his country in the Civil War. He died soon afterward, so did his wife and child. They are buried in Cedar Grove Cemetery.

Albert E. (1843-1918) also was a soldier of the Civil War, returned safe and sound, married Nancy Hare (1845-1927) and settled near the old home, now known as the Delmar section. They reared ten children: L. Sedecia (1867) who married J. L. B. Oxner; Rodella Jane (1869-1914), who was always a cripple and never married; John Oscar, who married Hattie Swygert (1875-1898); Anna Victoria

(1872-1941), who married Dr. P. W. Hite; Jason Ira (1874) who married Lizzie Rinehart; Quilla (1876-1907) who married Rev. W. L. Darr, a Lutheran Minister; Jesse Lloyd (1878), who married Bessie Moore (1880-1941); Florence Ruth (1880-1928), who married James E. Wertz, she was the mother of Rev. Lester Wertz, a Lutheran Minister; Minic Luther (1883) a graduate of North Carolina State University, married Blanche Shealy, a childhood sweetheart; and Agnes V. (1887), who married James H. Eargle.

Leroy B. Eargle, Editor of the "Saluda Standard," is a grandson of A. L. Eargle.

Irvin P. Eargle (1847-1923) married Sarah Ann Shealy (1844-1887), settled in the Delmar section and reared a large family of sons and daughters, namely Henry P., who marired Ada Ballentine; Andrew, who married Fannie Foster; Wesley who first married Bessie Derrick and second Maggie Oswald; Charley married Fanny Addy; Laura, who married Walter D. Long; Eliza became the wife of Shelton Taylor and Bertha married Julian Shealy.

Henry E. Eargle married Eliza Shealy and became the parents of Bessie, who married F. Lester Shealy; Blanche who is the wife of R. L. Oxner; Ralph, who married Annie Shealy; Ezelle, who married Imo Hare; Edgar, who married Jessie Metts; Gordon, who married Daisy Bedenbaugh and Henry Adam, who married Satcher Derrick. W. Pressley Eargle (1858-1930) married Leila E. Shealy (1882-1931). They became the parents of W. P., Jr., who married Fannie Bedenbaugh; Bertie, who married Nevins Whiteside and Van, who married Myrtle Risinger.

It is quite co-incidental that all these Eargle sons married descendants of Adam Shealy who was a son of the original John Wendell Shealy of Little Mountain.

The daughter of the family, Eliza, married George C. Shirey, a once prominent citizen of upper Lexington County. They were the parents of Henry, who died when a child; Prof. A. P. Shirey, a graduate of Peabody College, Knoxville, Tenn., who died in 1898 at the age of 26 years; Nannie, first wife of Frank W. Shealy, who was treasurer, Clerk of Court in Lexington County and also Railroad Commissioner; Dora, who married J. Ansel Caughman, and taught in the schools of Lexington and Saluda Counties for 40 years; Rebecca, who married Charley T. Koon; Scott P., who married Lucy Dennis, of Newberry County; Lilla, who married Dr. O. C. Holley, who has been a successful practicing physician in this section for more than forty years; G. Clarence, who married Alice Hartley of Batesburg.

The first Henry Eargle in this section was a soldier in the Confederate War. He lost his life in this great struggle. He was a sick man, had been captured by the enemy and was being transported from one point to another. Being extremely sick, he fell off the vehicle. Dying, the enemy kicked him a few times and saw that he was dead. The enemy made the statement, "If he has any friends we will wait long enough for you to bury him." His friend Mordecai Shirey began immediately to dig a grave and buried him somewhere in North Carolina. His widow, Nancy, and several sons are buried in Cedar Grove Cemetery.

HITE HISTORY (By D. I. Hite)

HITES came from Germany to Hyde Park, England, then to the United States.

The first Yost Hyde or Hite came to Virginia, having obtained a grant of land from the King of England for 10,000 acres. After this was settled, he then returned to England, received another grant for 100,000 acres which was to be settled by 100 families. He furnished his own ships and brought people over and settled them as promised, but he and the King of England had some difference, which ended in a law suit, that stayed in court for 50 years after his death, before a verdict was rendered in his favor.

History shows one of his descendants settled in the Shenandoah Valley of Virginia, but his family was massacred by the Indians except one little girl. She was years later found in Florida. She never could be induced to go back to Virginia, but continued with the Indians. Others of his descendants went west; two came to South Carolina; one settled on Saluda River out from St. John's Lutheran Church and is buried in a family cemetery which is now under waters of Lake Murray. His name is on a marker in St. John's Cemetery as Michael Hyde, whose wife was named Charity. His son, Abram is buried in St. John's Cemetery as Abram Hite. When and how the name was changed we do not know. This same Abram Hite, later known as Abraham Hite, is the father of Joseph, Walter, John, Simeon, Paul and on down the line.

The second Hite or Hyde settled at Batesburg about where Uriah Collum now lives on Highway One, from thence comes the Batesburg Hites.

Abraham Hite once lived between Union Church and Holley's Ferry. He once lived where Jesse Derrick now lives, also on the Jim Addy place, from there to near Emanuels Church near West Columbia, died there about 59 years ago.

In our records we find that the first John Black married Susannah Catherine Hite, born in 1771. She could have been a sister or near relative of Abraham Hite, or perhaps his father, Michael Hyde or Hite.

D. I. Hite was formerly a member of Cedar Grove Church, but now a resident of West Columbia, S. C. Cedar Grove is his first love. He has made provision for his and his wife's last resting place to be in Cedar Grove's Cemetery, by having erected a substantial mausoleum for that purpose. Cedar Grove Congregation is indebted to him for the historical monument in front of the church, also for the permanent sign "Cedar Grove Lutheran Church" made in large aluminum letters.

(By the Author).

FULMER

THE Fulmers came from Germany and settled in the Dutch Fork of what is now Lexington County; thence they scattered to different parts of the state; but a majority of their descendants still remain in proximity to the original home nest.

One of these, Eberhart Fulmer, who was a grandson of the original immigrants and who was born in 1778 came over to the border line of Lexington and Edgefield, married Mary Ann Long (1783) and settled on the headwaters of Hollow Creek in Lexington County. This couple were married by the Rev. Frederick Joseph Wallern, one of the pioneer Lutheran ministers of Lexington District, and whose remains now lie in the church yard of St. Paul's near Pomaria, having been moved there in 1917 from his old homestead nearby. He had been buried there about one hundred years before in a walnut casket. A large tree had grown up near the grave and roots from this tree had grown around the casket, holding it in perfect shape, so that it could be easily handled without any part giving away.

Eberhart Fulmer and his wife had the following children, Elizabeth (1809), Mary (1811), Joseph William (1816), James Wilson (1818), Julia Ann (1823) and Nancy (1826).

Elizabeth Fulmer bore three children: William Wilson 1836-1861) who married Martha Jennings and died in the Civil War; Henry Edwin, who also was lost in the Civil War; and Catherine (1833-1918) who married John Wesley Hare (1840-1910) who was the mother of W. H. Hare, to whom we are indebted for this sketch.

Mary, familiarly called Polly (1811-1884) married Bert Goff and her children included Shady Ann (1840-1880), who married Owen Cannon (1830-1916); Mary, who married D. Tillman Hare, and James Goff, who married Martha Fikes. James Wilson (1819-1888) never married.

Julia Ann married John Hodges Moore, and their children were James, who was wounded to death in the Civil War; William, who was a Confederate soldier; Nancy, who married J. Ed. Price; Clara, who was the second wife of Enoch Swygert; Thomas C., who married Catherine Derrick; J. Andrew; R. Calvin who married Ellen Bedenbaugh; Ann, who married Tom Rhoden, of Johnston, S. C.; Ellen, who married W. G. Powell, of Graniteville, S. C., Lucinda and Alice, three girls, died young.

Nancy Fulmer married a Dudley who went off to the North whence he had come and never came back. They had one daughter, Josephine (1862-1901) who married N. R. Bartley.

Joseph William Fulmer married Jane Sawyer and they had six children; Laura Catherine (1850-1887), who married Oliver A. Derrick; James Michael (1852-1859); George Aberhart (1851-1887);

who married Mattie Matthews; William Franklin (1837-1859); John Wesley (1859-1899); Mary Liza (1861-1933).

Other Fulmers came over to Edgefield later, including Noah Fulmer, who married Carrie McNary and settled near the old McNary Ferry on Saluda River. They reared the following children: John N. C., who married Lillie Goff, daughter of Noah Goff; Patrick L., who married Emma Crouch; Tyre W., who married Ione Mitchell, daughter of Andrew Mitchell. Tyre and Ione's youngest daughter, Virginia, married Robert Hoy Caughman.

George W. Fulmer married and lives in Columbia, S. C.; Lula E. married Elijah W. Shealy; Nannie married James L. Fulmer; Mattie married John Wise; Sallie, who married Thomppson L. Shealy, and is the mother of Rev. James Lee Shealy, a Lutheran Minister who was once pastor of St. Paul's (Hollow Creek) Church; Mary, who married Mike Derrick; and Fannie, who married Ernest W. Riser.

Aberhart Fulmer and others organized a Lutheran Church named Mt. Zion, located near the old Fulmer homestead, on the identical spot where the residence of Cornelius Derrick now stands. On account of the great destruction coming about by the Civil War, the remnant disbanded and became members of Salem, a history of same is written in this edition.

NICHOLS

WE begin this sketch with Luke Nichols, who was born in 1808. and whom we find settled down on Whetstone Creek, near the Lexington-Edgefield line, and near the present location of Union Lutheran Church which he helped to found about the year 1855 and in whose church yard he and his wife lie buried. It is presumed that Luke Nichols was related to the Nicholses of Newberry County, many of whom were settled in the St. Luke's section. Luke Nichol's wife (1820-1886) was Elizabeth Derrick, who was a sister of W. Thomas Derrick of the upper Hollow Creek section of Lexington County.

The children of Luke Nichols and wife were: Lemuel, who married Lavina Crout, daughter of Dr. John Crout. He moved to Newberry County, thence to Mississippi where he died; Sarah Ann (1840-1883); Levi (1842-1902) married Margaret Harman (1844-1911). They had only two children, Jacob (1871-1896) and Minnie (1870-1901) who married Brooks Lindler. They first settled on Rocky Creek, but later settled on Beaver Dam Creek where they lived and died. They with their children are buried in Union Cemetery.

Wesley Nichols married Mary Jane Bedenbaugh (1847-1923), daughter of John A. Bedenbaugh in 1866 and after living near the old homestead a few years, settled on the Frederick Sease place on Big Hollow Creek where he reared his family. They had four children: Carrie Lucinda (1867-1876); Frederick (1869-1914), who married Mary Derrick, daughter of Jesse Derrick; Jasper (1873-   )

who married Mamie West; Sydney (1877) who married Nettie, daughter of P. Wash Shealy, and lived on the old homestead, after his father moved to Leesville, until the place went into Lake Murray development; then he moved to Ninety-Six, where he now lives. Wesley, wife and daughter are buried in Union Cemetery.

Debian Nichols married Willam B. Holley and reared five children: George, Hampton, Lillie, Emmie and Dr. O. C. She was the last of Luke Nichol's children to die.

Thomas Luther (1851-1880) never married and died while attending the Atlanta, Ga., Medical College. He is buried in Union Cemetery.

Stanmore Nichols (1854-1928) married Barbara Taylor (1851-1934), daughter of Joel Taylor, and settled near the old homestead. Their children were Nezzie, who married Luther Shealy; Josephine, married Willie Long (1871-1932); Thomas married Gertrude Holley; Napoleon married Annie Belle Shealy; Nettie married Emanuel Price; Mary married Leo Davis; Josephus married Vestus Crout and is now Post Master at Leesville, and Noah married Inez Shealy.

Leppard Nichols' first wife was Sarah C. Addy (1872-1892), by whom he had one daughter, Anna Blanche, who married Clarence Wertz of Orangeburg. His second wife was Hassie Wertz (1861-1914) and his last wife was Mrs. Catherine Keisler Derrick, widow of Oliver A. Derrick. He is buried at Leesville with his last two wives.

Martha Emma Nichols (1864-1914) married H. Ed Shealy (1861-1937) and we have record of seven children from this couple; L. Julian, who married Bertha Eargle; Ernest married Lula Craps; Minnie became the second wife of Alva Davis; Jesse, who married Georgia Swygert; Fred married Mamie Swygert; Lillian became the wife of Virgil Price and Silas married Birdie Caughman.

EARLY SETTLERS IN THE VICINITY OF THE HAYES BRIDGE ON HOLLOW CREEK

TRADITION brings to our attention the fact that quite a number of early settlers established homes near the mouth of Big Hollow Creek on Saluda River, among them were Halls, Monts, Hendrix, Hayes, Kelleys, Lewies, etc.

Dave Holman settled the place where Mrs. Gladys Shealy and family now live. About 1860 Mr. Holman sold out and moved West. His farm was purchased and occupied later by Mr. James Koon and family from the Dutch Fork. Near this place one of our first settlers carved a small farm out of the forest in this fertile valley and built a log hut for a dwelling with one door and a small window. He owned a pet deer on which he kept a bell. He would feed the deer regularly in order to get it to come up. In coming up for food, wild deer would follow it, so when he would hear the bell coming, he would conceal himself in the house and would shoot a wild deer through the little window. By this method he kept his family well supplied with venison.

This community was thickly settled and in this area was Mt. Pleasant Lutheran Church which had to be discontinued on account of the development of Lake Murray.

This entire section is now included in the lake area, except the Dave Holman settlement, which was the property of Frank W. Shealy, when the Lexington Water Power Company established this artificial body of water.

BLACK

IN the latter half of the 1700's we find one John Black settled in what is now Lexington County on the upper waters of Joe's Creek, tributary to Big Hollow Creek, at the place later owned by Samuel Black, and now in possession of the descendants of the said Samuel Black, the McCarthas.

The records we have at hand do not say whence this John Black came, nor what the original nationality of the family. He was born in 1777, and his wife was Susannah Catherine Hite, born in 1771. They both lie buried in the soil of the old homestead, together with a young son, Jacob, a couple of infants of Samuel Black, in a heavily cemented family plot.

This first John Black and his wife reared eight children as listed below, with their birth dates: Catherine Elizabeth (1798), John (1800), Mary Magdaline (1802), J. Adam (1804), Susannah (1805), Rebecca (1807), David (1809) and Samuel (1811).

Catherine or Katie Black married George Vansant. They had one son, Hiram, who died young, and one daughter, Deborah (1834-1890) who married D. Isaiah Derrick, and they had one daughter, Louannie, who married Giles Willing, and one, Hiram, who married a Cullum. Mr. and Mrs. Vansant are buried in St. Mark's Cemetery, Saluda County.

John Black, the second, (1800-1870) married Jemima Caughman (1805-1877), daughter of the first Andrew Caughman. They settled in Edgefield County and had the following children: Daniel (1823), Polly (1824), Jacob Wilson (1830), David (1833), Henry (1835), Jesse Wilson 1838), George Washington (1841), Mark Pope (1843), and Nancy Elizabeth (1846).

David Black went to Tuscaloosa County, Alabama, in 1846. There he met Margaret Kyzer at a revival meeting and they were married in 1848. They settled in Coaling, Ala. There were born unto them fourteen children.

Daniel Black had a big family but none are South Carolinians. Polly Black (1824-1912) married Ephraim Shealy. They had two children, Laura and Amanda. Amanda married David Walter Hite (1847-1908) and bore him Pope W. (1867-1903) who married Victoria Eargle. Pope W. became a practicing physician. Sedecia (1873-1888); Estelle (1883-1921). Estelle was organist at Cedar Grove Church for a number of years. Wightman Hite (1886) married Mae Stranger; and Ethel (1891) married John Moore, of the Delmar section. Polly Black, D. Walter Hite and his children, Dr. Pope W. and wife, Sedecia, and Estelle are buried in the cemetery of Cedar Grove Lutheran Church in Lexington County.

Jacob Wilson Black (1830) was killed in the Civil War. Before the war began he married Elizabeth Clark. They had one son, Jacob Wilson, Jr., who married Georgia Webb and had Adah, Kellah, Ella and John Benjamin. These descendants live in Barnwell County, S. C., except the latter who is a practicing physician in Jacksonville, Fla.

David Black (1833-1908) married Ada Elizabeth Kinard (1838-1909) and had no children.

Henry Black (1835-1915) married Georgiana Rutherford in 1858. They had Joseph William (1859), who married Matilda Matthews (1861).

George Washington Black married Rebecca Josephine Fillers.

Nancy Elizabeth Black (1846-1929), the youngest of the children of the second John Black and Jemima Caughman married James Hare (1838-1929) and bore him the following nine sons: John Allen, who married Mellie Bedenbaugh, and had James Wright, Anna Ruth, Imo Elizabeth and Carl Allen; Samuel Jacob married Maggie Stone and had one child which died in infancy; Noah Ephraim, who married Laura Medorothy Derrick and had Agnes Laura and William Bryan; Butler Black (1875), who married Katie Etheredge and had Robert Hayne (1910) and James Butler (1918); Joseph William (1877), who married Laura Shealy and had Lucy Grace, Ernest Henry, Vanessa Eloise, Henry Benjamin (1880) married Catherine Sarratt of Gaffney (1926); James Lee (1882) married Lucy Bedenbaugh and had Julian M., J. Roston, Troy Lee, Georgia Elizabeth, Mildred Annette, Lucy Corine and Remo Black; George Tillman (1885), who married Mrs. Ona Padgett Black, widow of George T. Black and had Henry Byrnes and Winona Nannie; Sydney Bowles (1888-1933) who married Jamie Iva Crout and had Dorothy Elnora, Mary Ruth, Geraldine Elizabeth and Sydney Bowles, Jr.

Quite a number of this family of Blacks in Saluda County are college graduates, one Rev. H. J. Black, a Lutheran Minister, was once president of the South Carolina Synod. Butler Black Hare has been a representative at Washington. His son, Robert Hayne, has been a representative in Congress.

Mary Magdaline Black (1802), a daughter of the first John Black, married Daniel Derrick, son of the first Tom Derrick, and settled on Big Hollow Creek. Their children were Emeline, who married Moses Summers Roberts, brother of Isaiah Roberts, and moved to Mississippi; Noah married Cattie Roberts; Forest married first

Fowler Brocton, then Martha Caughman; Frances married R. M. Currie; Ellen married Jacob Crout; Elmore was killed.

Adam Black, the fourth child of the first John Black (1804) married Catherine Chapman and settled in Edgefield County. Their children were William W., Tillman L., Noah Lott, Wesley A., Henry S., Emanuel M., John D., Samuel D., Matilda, Mattie S., Emma M., Catherine E. and Sallie M.

We will now follow up Noah Black's family. Noah Black married married Bessie Rauch and had one child, Sarah Edna (1901); Louisa Derrick. Their children were Wesley Edward (1870-1935), Frances Janie (1872) married Rev. O. B. Shearous, a Lutheran Minister, and bore him four children, Bernard, Floyd Noah, Louise and Eleanor; Cornelius Haskell (1875-1899); Luther Alonzo (1878) married Lillie Buck and had Virginia Carolina (1908) and Ralph Buck (1911); Walter Pickens (1881) married Maud Moose and lives in Georgia; Arthur Lloyd (1885) who married first Corrie Knight, second Lottie Belue and is a physician in Orangeburg County; Javas Monroe (1889), who married Maggie Fairey and lives at the old homestead. They have one child, Fairey Louisa, (1919). Maggie was a classmate of mine in Leesville College. Essie Valula (1895) married Jacob Singley and bore him Eloise (1919) and Marion Allette (1925).

Of the sons of Noah Black, Wesley Edward, Luther Alonzo and Javas Monroe were graduates of Newberry College 1894, 1903 and 1913, respectively.

David Black (1809-1895) son of the first John Black, married Hana Serena Hendrix (1816-1901) and settled on Joe's Creek in Lexington County near the parental homestead. We list the following children of this couple: Paul, William, Simeon, James, John, Martha, Charlotte, Amanda, Jasper, Ridona and Evylyn.

Paul Black married Susan Morgan and settled on Lower Hollow Creek. Their children were David, Welles, Villie, Lula, Trannie, Wilbur, Luther and Lawrence.

William Black (1836-1918) married Cal Donia Eubanks (1856-1922). Their children were David, John, Josie, Nezzie, Katie and Rosalie. They lived on lower Hollow Creek.

Simeon L. Black maried Louannie Derrick and lived in Leesville. Their children were Minnie and Thomas of Atlanta, Ga., and Bessie and Ruth in the Lowman Home at White Rock.

John Black married Louisa Taylor and had William, Jessie, and two children that died in infancy.

James Black married Rebecca Taylor and lived near the parental homestead. Their children were Nezzie and Tallie, who died young; Augustus, Chester, who married Lula Shealy and Nettie who married Jason Craps and bore him Curl, who married Philis Johnson; Lenoree who married D. B. Shealy, Drover, Venus and Christine.

Martha Black married Henry Crout. Their daughter was Corrie (1858-1928), wife of Dixon U. Addy (1855-1929). Martha married a Koon the second time. Evylyn married George Craps. They settled near the Black homestead. Their children were Girlie, wife of Roddy Roberts; Lonnie, who married Cora Swygert; Belle married Luther Hite; John married Maud Keisler; Truman married Mamie Leaphart; Celeste married Noah Lybrand; Butler married Eloise Ricard; Elon married Beatrice Ricard; Voigt married Lessie Taylor; Lillie and Newton died young.

Amanda Black married Samuel Stockman and they lived in the neighborhood of the Black homestead. Their children were Blanche, who married Hampton Hartley; Floy married Julius Taylor; Gairy married Annie Lynch; Eugene married Lora Leguin; Lamar married Mae Shirey; Olin married Bessie Westbrook; Dewey married Agnes Craps. Edgar never married. Two children died young.

Rewben Jasper Black married Lydia Craps. Their write-up is under the Craps sketch. However, in case of some ommissions perhaps I will rewrite this large family.

Jasper and wife had George Pierce who married Eliza Harman and had Lilla; Washington Elmore (1864) who married Etta Goff and had Unus Erstin (1883); Lillian Lee (1885); Lester Rewben (1887); Minnie V. (1888); Lottie Blanche (1890); Harden Curtis (1892); Kema Winford (1894); Dallie Mae (1897); Oza E. (1900); Armour Cornelius 1902) and Celee Efu (1904).

Alice Josephine (1866-1888) married Thomas Addy and had one child who died in infancy.

Lottie Corine (1868) married Bouregard Harman.

Ridona Black married a Smith and lived at Cross Hill. They had no children.

Charlotte Black married Benjamin Earhart. She was the mother of Tallie, who married Essie Wright; Arthur, who married Josie Seay; James who married Maggie Watson; Fred married Jane Miles and Virgie who became the wife of Jeter Rhodes.

Samuel Black (1811), the youngest son of the first John Black, married Priscilla Williams and settled on the paternal homestead. They reared only one child, Ritta, who became the wife of J. E. B. McCartha. They settled on the old homestead of the original John Black, where they lived until about 45 years ago, when the family moved to Leesville, where a part of the family is still living.

J. Elliot B. McCartha was one of the pioneer rural letter carriers of Leesville, serving from 1902 until 1930.

The McCarthas had eight children, as follows: Jonas (1879), Nettie (1882), Randolph (1883), Reuben (1885), Chicola (1893-1898), Eugene (1899), Carl (1901), and Gussie Lee (1903).

Jonas McCartha married Ola, daughter of Pickens Derrick, of Batesburg. They have one daughter, Lois Margaret 1911.

Nettie McCartha married Horace D. Crosson, who was one of the first rural letter carriers in the state, having begun his service April 3, 1899.

Randoph McCartha married Bessie Agnew. They lived in Rome, Georgia.

Reuben McCartha married Ina Coliff. They live in Denmark, South Carolina.

Eugene McCartha married Lois Rudisill.

Carl McCartha married Effie Meacham.

Gussie Lee McCartha married Minnie Williams.

Eugene, Carl and Gussie Lee are graduates of Newberry College.

SECTION IV

SHERMAN'S RAID DOWN HOLLOW CREEK

WILLIAM Tecumseh Sherman and his army made a raid through South Carolina in February 1865. They left Savannah, Georgia about the first of February and travelled north toward Columbia destroying everything in their pathway. All the able-bodied men were in the Confederate Army. No one was left to protect the women and children except the aged men and a few dependable slaves.

Most of you have read of the burning and destruction of Columbia about the 17th of February, 1865, by Sherman's outlawed army, but very few living people know anything about what happened in the Big Hollow Creek section of Lexington County.

This destructive force travelled in squads covering a pretty wide strip of territory. One group came down on one side of this valley and another group came down the other side, laying waste to everything in their path. The inhabitants in this valley heard of the approaching army a few hours in advance. Every person able to travel began to assemble their most valuable possessions together in bundles and hurried to the woods, concealing them from the enemy.

These rebellious soldiers had no mercy on anyone. They would go into the kitchens and smoke houses and bring out barrels of molasses, sauer kraut, flour and other provisions and pour it all out together in the yards, and then throw shovels of dirt into it to ruin it. They would carry with them everything that they could in the line of provisions, even great herds of cattle, sheep and horses. The herds of sheep and cattle were so great they couldn't keep them together. Some would drop out by the wayside and later would be taken up by our people as refugee cattle.

My great-grandmother, Emily Lybrand, was born 1811 and died 1899. She lived with us the last ten years of her life. Often she would tell me about those tragic days of the Civil War. She said that when Sherman's forces raided their place, there was no one at the house but herself and a neighbor, Dempsey Caughman. She related that a bunch of men rode up to the front gate, all on horseback. One demanded the shot gun. She gave it to them. One took it and broke it to pieces over the gate post. Then they told her to bring them all the gold and silver money. They threatened to burn the house down if she didn't bring it to them. She was slow about moving so they began building a fire under the house. The neighbor ran in the house shouting, "Lord, God Almighty, Emmy, give it to 'em." She gave them the two sacks of money. They left immediately without further destruction, except for taking part of the livestock.

By this time, several groups had gotten together, moving on toward the Saluda River. They stopped next at the plantation of my great-grandfather, Daniel Drafts, who at that time possessed quite a bit of property. He ran about 20 plows. He and his slaves had been able to hide most of the horses in a creek swamp. However, a search began immediately. They went to the big barn, bridled two nice horses, hitched them to the carriage, drove it up to the smoke house and loaded it with meat, getting everything else they wanted that could be found. They set out, crossing Big Hollow Creek, going north on the old Charleston Road toward Holley's Ferry. In traveling up a rough hill the carriage broke down. They loaded the meat on a wagon, rolled the carriage out of the road, bade farewell to the Hollow Creek section.

Practically every settlement from the source of Hollow Creek, near where Leesville now is to Saluda River was molested. Food and livestock were stolen or destroyed, money stolen, clothes and bedding carried away and, in some cases, homes destroyed. Yet, through all this trying ordeal, the faithful slaves were devoted to their "Masters and Misses," all suffering together. The majority of these faithful and devoted slaves continued to live and labor with these same "Masters" 'til death. No promise by any carpetbagger could ever have the least influence over these devout slaves.

When we look back and see what our ancestors had to endure and overcome in establishing homes among savage Indians, then later passing through the terrible Civil War, losing the cream of our manhood, losing nearly all their earthly possessions, nothing left but the wounded and aged men, widows and orphans to overcome these ravages and repopulate this section and, too, the country was so poor it couldn't provide any kind of pension for the helpless, these things should cause our present generation to begin to take stock and think.

Realizing what our ancestors went through with, endured and overcame, proves to us that they were superior to us. They had no doles or pensions from the government, for the government was too weak for anything like that. The boys and girls of 85 years ago made good on their own. Gentlemen, we of the present day, will have to do better than we are doing to compare with our forefathers.

SECTION V.

J. RUSSELL BOGGS

J. RUSSELL BOGGS (Pastor 1949—)

FOLLOWING the division of the Parish and the resignation of Pastor J. C. Derrick, it became our duty to secure a minister to serve Cedar Grove. This was to be the first time in our long history that we were to have one man to serve the one Church. Doubts and fears filled the hearts of many as to whether this new program could be inaugurated or not. Others reached forth in faith believing that with "the help of God" Cedar Grove could well carry on its own program.

No one knew better than our former pastor, the Rev. Mr. Derrick, that this could be accomplished and he worked unceasingly and laid the groundwork for all that was to follow when the church became entirely self-supporting.

A call was extended to the Rev. J. Russell Boggs, serving the Liberty Parish, Liberty, North Carolina, and he moved to Cedar Grove February, 1949.

Born of Fitzhugh and Verdie Lee Loftin Boggs, November 18, 1923, he was reared in the rural section of Catawba County, N. C., He is a graduate of Claremont High School, Claremont, N. C., and of Lenoir Rhyne College, Hickory, N. C., in 1944, and the Southern Lutheran Seminary, Columbia, S. C., in 1946.

Sixty-seven adult members have been received and seventy-five children have been baptized within the last three years.

Soon after his arrival on the field, a program enlisting as many as possible into the work of the church was inaugurated. A Brotherhood was organized to give more men an opportunity to serve the church. The Luther League was re-activiated and along with the hard work of the League counselors the young people of the parish have become very energetic in the work of the church. Through their hard work many worthy gifts have been given to the church, which include a private communion set, a mimeograph machine, a lectern Bible, and an annual grant of a $100 scholarship to a student from the congregation studying for full time Christian work. The Youth Evangelism Program has exemplified the keen interest the young people have in the greater work of the church, that of bringing youth into a closer fellowship with God.

Realizing the importance of the Youth of the Church, the Brotherhood purchased the old Cedar Grove School House and converted it into a Youth Center.

We believe it can truly be said that Pastor Boggs has become one of us, feeling our infirmities, realizing our conditions, knowing our strength. He feels the pulse beat of the congregation and wherein it is weak, seeks to strengthen that part; wherein it is wrong, endeavors to guide to the right; wherein there is need, trys to help. His philosophy "All of Life is to be Christian" guides him as he serves our parish.

Under his leadership improvements in the physical plant have been made. Among them are: the gifts of a Hammond Organ, a public address system, brass altar desk, the liquidation of the parsonage debt, and the renovation program of the interior of the church in preparation for the celebration of the 100th anniversary of the organization of the congregation.

The Evangelism program of the church has been one of his chief concerns. Under his direction the Evangelism Committee planned a preaching mission during 1951. Securing the service of the Associate-Director of Evangelism of the U. L. C. A., the Rev. Peter J. Dexnis of Philadelphia, the committee with the cooperation of the congregation under the guidance of the Holy Spirit had one of the most successful missions ever to be conducted at Cedar Grove.

As leader, pastor, coordinator, Pastor Boggs works, plans and studies how he and the congregation can be more effective witnesses for the Christ we serve.

ABOUT THE AUTHOR

JOSEPH Ansel Caughman was born August 3, 1885, son of Edwin Franklin and Ellen Elizabeth Lybrand Caughman. He received his elementary education in the common schools of Lexington County. He received his high school education at Summit High School, Summit, S. C. He took his sub-freshman and freshman years at Leesville College. His sophomore work was done at Lenoir College, Hickory, N. C. His junior and senior years were spent at Leesville College, a co-educational institution, located at Leesville, S. C. His class consisted of nine young ladies and himself, receiving their diplomas in June 1905. He was 19 years old. The class roll was Joseph Ansel Caughman, Maude Fay Crosson, Carrie Wightman Shuler, Margaret Ella Fairey, Mazie Bell Bannister, Ottolee Gunter, Frances Longenia Lindler, Clara Elizabeth Riser, Eugenia Tomlinson Bateman and Evie Olilian Smithe.

Since he was the only young man in the class, he had to be the Class Orator. The following is the oration he delivered at the Commencement Exercises. It was a requirement from the faculty that this oration be written entirely by the orator without any help or assistance from anyone. The subject assigned to him was:

FACE TO FACE WITH THE HERE AND NOW

The surrounding conditions of the Here and Now have concerned every nation since the beginning of the world. It is not necessary to deal with the centuries in their succession, but let us at least scan the annals of those past centuries. Their history is made up of the deeds of great men and the movements of grand events.

However, we are not concerned so much with the history of one thousand or even five hundred years ago as we are with the Twentieth Century.

Of all the centuries past the, nineteenth has been the greatest and more glorious. We can rightly claim it as our century, and we are at liberty to enjoy the many blessings which it brings to us. Its claims are many and mighty; they cover every field of human effort; they have to do with practical development, the relations of capital and labor, invention, science, art, literature, production, commerce, and all other of the activities of life's interest.

One hundred years ago the political aspect of the world was quite different from that of the present. Many of the kings wer tyrants, people, as a rule, were slaves—in fact, if not in name—comforts were confined entirely to the rich, the law was merciless, punishment was of a cruel nature, the broad sentiment of human fellowship had hardly begun to develop.

But one hundred years later, what do we see? The republic of the United States has grown from a feeble infant to a powerful giant, and its free system of government has spread over the entire continent of

America. Today we see that not only every independent nation has become a republic, but the love of liberty has crossed the water, and we see France is also governed by the people.

Throughout the American Continent every male citizen has the right of voting, and the human slavery, which held captive millions upon millions of men and women one hundred years ago, has now vanished from the realms of civilization, and a vigorous effort is being made to-day to banish it from every region of the earth. The sentiment of human compassion has become strong and compelling; it is felt in the courts as well as among the people; public opinion has grown powerful, and a punishment today too severe for the crime would be visited with universal condemnation. So we see that we are face to face with an age when justice rules instead of cruelty.

The nineteenth century saw the modern world in its making. The grand political revolution with which the century began was followed by a notable and industrial revolution. The invention of the steam engine had brought to an end the mediaeval system of industry; the old individual household era of labor, where every man could be his own master and supply his own capital ceased to exist; costly labor-saving machines which needed large accumulations of capital, came into use; great buildings and centralization of labor became necessary; and the factory system, which has had such an immense development in the nineteenth century, began its career.

With the opening and progress of the nineteenth century came other conditions of very great importance. Invention, which first began near the end of the preceding century, now flourished until its results seemed rather the work of magic than of plain human thought and work. Science, which had already made some notable triumphs, gained undreamed of activity, and hundreds of the deep secrets of the universe were unfolded. Literature and art, while they can claim no works of acknowledged superiority as compared with the masterpieces of the past centuries, have displayed a remarkable activity, and the number of meritorious books now annually issued is one of the most extraordinary events of our time.

What part is education playing in this age of progress? Immense progress has been made in the last twenty-five years. Today schools and colleges form a great mile post on the highway of progress. It is everywhere in evidence; remarkable advancement has been made in the methods of education. Man is going back to nature, observation is supplanting book knowledge, and experiment is taking the place of authority. In fact, education is making its way in the humblest homes by means of books and newspapers, and man is now everywhere beginning to see the necessity of an education for the fitting of himself for an intelligent discharge of his social, industrial and political duties.

Another great stage of advancement has been made which is of high and significant importance, namely the great progress made in the educational, industrial and political position of woman. Today the distinction between boys and girls in education has nearly ceased to exist in this country, and is in a fair way of vanishing in Europe.

In industrial occupation the advance of woman has been as great. A century ago few positions were open to them outside the household. At present there is not an industry which they desire, or are fitted to follow, from which they are debarred, and the last census enumerated four thousand branches of employment in which women are employed or are engaged in. Women physicians are numerous; women lawyers and preachers are coming to the field; women professors teach in schools and colleges, and women authors have given us some of the best books of the past century. Yea, woman is now acknowledged the equal of man socially and financially, and the day seems fast approaching when she will be regarded everyhere as being on a political equalization with man. With uncovered head and with the glad hand of welcome extended, we greet our sisters in their onward march and assure them that men are manlier and the world better for their struggling with and conquering the world, and we join Joaquin Miller in his tribute to "Woman, the Kingliest Warrior born."

We are living in an age when brain power is mightier than the sword, and when most difficult questions should be settled mentally. Therefore the world is calling out for men and women who are equipped for the battle which confronts us.

One of the most significant and promising movements of the time is that taken with the object of bringing to an end war, which has raged upon the earth since the primitive day of man.

Today international discussion is the most effectual means of insuring all the people's benefits, and a real durable peace, and above all, putting an end to the progressive development of the present armies, and regard the preservation of peace an object of international policy.

No other age was ever so bright, so glorious, so grand, nor so noble as the one with which we are face to face. We have grand institutions towering heavenward to bless the children of men with liberty, both civil and religious, and with progress, and countless other blessings, the conditions favorable for successful careers are most excellent.

And now while we are in the morning of the twentieth century we behold a clear sky and breathe a purer and sweeter atmosphere. The sun shines brighter than ever before, hope and confidence still exist and inspire American hearts. And now we must cross the great deep and help the poor, down-trodden heathen. You ask why? Because it is our duty; we are living in prosperity; they are dying in adversity. Yea, we must bring the dull-minded nations of the world under our subjection and help them to raise their standards of morality. All the sons and daughters of America should enlist and equip themselves for battle. They should be disciplined in the schools and colleges of our country. The battlegrounds in this campaign will be fortified with walls and bulwarks of Education.

In the beginning of this grand and glorious century, let us realize that it requires us to put forth our very best efforts, "let it cost what it may."

Young men and young women, the world is calling out for you. Then come forth and be marshalled in the battle line for life. "During the military drills this army will be supplied with arms for service: the sword of truth, the bayonet of integrity, the musket of justice; instead of the rapid fire guns, the helmet of hope; instead of the cannon, the law of right as broad as eternity; for the torpedo, energy; for the navy, the gospel of peace; and with the infantry of determination and the calvary of benevolence this mighty army will be sent forth to battle and to conquer."

He won two oratorical medals in 1904. Being reared on the farm he continued to assist in the farm work. His first work in serving the public was teaching. He taught in the following schools: Summit School (1905-1906), Cedar Grove School (1906-1907), Sharpe Hill in summer of 1906; Hollow Creek School (1907-1909), Centerville School (1909-1910), Cedar Grove School (1910-1913), Blue Star School (1913-1914), Ridge Road School (1914-1919), Holley School (1919-1920), Red Star School ((1920-1925), Cedar Grove School (1925-1928), and Holley School (1928-1931).

He married Dora E. Shirey, daughter of George C. and Eliza Eargle Shirey, on September 8, 1910, Rev. J. C. Wessinger officiating. This couple with one son, Robert Hoy, made up the family. Robert Hoy was born on April 25, 1918. He went to school with his parents, for both were teaching, until he completed the elementary grades. He took his high school course at Batesburg-Leesville High School. He completed his college course at Clemson College in 1940, receiving a B. S. diploma specializing in Animal Husbandry.

While teaching, Mr. Caughman continued to operate his farm, with the help of hired labor. He would teach from 8:00 a.m. to 4:00 p.m., then when weather was at all favorable, he would do a day's work at home on the farm. He often said that changing work rested him. He would plow, dig stumps, open ditches, and many other farm jobs at night time, but at about 45, overwork brought him to a halt. Due to a severe heart ailment, he was forced to give up teaching. For several years he was not able to do much physical labor, but was able to supervise his farm. Finding that he was successful in this vocation, he forgot about teaching.

Mr. Caughman now devotes his entire time to Agriculture and cattle raising. He and his son are operating their farms on a partnership basis.

J. Ansel Caughman was given a Certificate of Service, which reads: "This is to Certify that J. Ansel Caughman has honorably served as a member, Advisory Board for Registrants in the Selective Service System of the United States from November 30, 1940, to March 31, 1947."

J. Strom Thurmond, Governor.
Holmes B. Springs, State Director.

Joseph Ansel Caughman has been chairman of the P. M. A. formerly A. A. A. Committee for a number of years and at present is serving in that capacity. He is also Chairman of Lexington County Agricultural Mobilization Committee. He was Chairman of Lexington County's Farm Home Administration Committee for seven successive years.

He has served his church in practically every office. He was a member of the Council for more than 30 years, was treasurer of Cedar Grove Congregation a number of years; was secretary of Joint Council for more than ten years; was secretary when Cedar Grove-St. James Pastorate dissolved, therefore the duty and responsibility became his to straighten out all joint matters between the two churches composing the parish.

He was Sunday School Superintendent for 35 years.

Mr. Caughman has been trustee in charge of the cemetery for 21 years.

He is now chairman of Publicity Committee in Cedar Grove Brotherhood.

He was baptized by Rev. E. L. Lybrand and was confirmed by Rev. W. H. Roof at the age of 14.

J. Ansel Caughman's life is characterized by his profound interest in community betterment. He has sacrificed unselfishly and wholehearted that his community, his state and his nation might be a better place in which to live. He has always been very much devoted to his church and community. He taught school for 17 years within less than two miles from where he was born and reared. He often makes the statement that "one reason why he has such good a community to live in is that he taught his pupils forty years ago to be good Christian Citizens." He loves his former pupils and they respect him, too. Those who have become professional men and are making good in life, get much praise from him. He boasts of the fact that he "got them started right."

We can never judge unfinished work. So, in this write-up we will conclude by saying that the final appraisal of a man cannot be made while he is alive.

WALTER DANIEL WISE

WALTER DANIEL WISE

WALTER Daniel Wise, the third child of the late C. L. Wise and his wife, Sarah Ann, first saw the light of this world May 12, 1880. His father being a farmer and living in a rural community, this boy grew up on his father's farm and did all kinds of farm labor. He would by no means place himself on a par with Abe Lincoln as a rail splitter but in his younger years rail splitting had not become entirely a lost art on his father's farm and he did help split some rails.

At the age of six he entered public school and when fourteen, had finished the public school curriculum and the next four years of his school life were spent in a boarding school or an academy as it was called.

At the age of eighteen he began teaching in the public schools of his county and taught for four years when he entered Lenoir College, now Lenoir Rhyne, and graduated from this institution in 1905 with the degree of A. B.

In the fall of 1905 he entered the Lutheran Theological Southern Seminary, then located at Mt. Pleasant, Charleston, S. C., and graduated from this institution May 1908. Before leaving the Seminary he had received and accepted a call to the St. James' pastorate, near Newton, N. C., and began work there the fourth Sunday in May, 1908. This pastorate was in what was then known as the Old Tennessee Synod. While in this first pastorate he saw finished and dedicated a beautiful and modern church building which at the time was considered one of the best rural churches anywhere to be found.

He was ordained by this Synod at New Market, Va., September 26, 1908, the ordination services being in charge of Doctors C. K. Bell and the late R. A. Yoder, and J. C. Moser. When he had been in this pastorate for four years, the pastorate divided and formed a new pastorate known as the Claremont Pastorate. Both pastorates wished him to be the pastor, but as this could not be under the new set-up, he accepted the call to the newly formed pastorate and moved to Claremont in May 1912, and labored here for six years, still serving what had been a part of the St. James Pastorate with the addition of a new congregation.

During his stay in Claremont he remodeled one of the churches, adding several rooms to it and repainting inside and outside, also putting down new carpet and adding additional furniture and other improvements.

In 1918 he accepted a call to the Maiden Pastorate, Maiden, N. C. While here he built a modern parsonage.

In September 1921 he received a call to the Cedar Grove Pastorate near Leesville, S. C., which call he accepted and began work there in October of the same year. Here he labored for a period of a little over seven years and had the happy experience of seeing built in the Cedar Grove Congregation one of the most beautiful and best churches to be found anywhere in the State. This church is not only beautiful but is well furnished with modern pews and other furniture. He also repainted and installed art windows in St. James Church, Summit, S. C., a part of the Cedar Grove Pastorate at that time.

On the first Sunday in November 1928 he began work in the Silverstreet Pastorate having received and accepted a call to this parish. Some of the things accomplished in this pastorate was the finishing and dedicating the new Corinth Church which had been begun under the ministry of the late Rev. Enoch Hite, the recovering and repainting and planting shrubbery at the Silverstreet Church.

On March the first, 1936, he began work in the Blountville Parish, Blountville, Tenn., and labored there until Oct. 1, 1944, when he removed to Rural Retreat, Virginia, having accepted a call to the Kimberlin Parish, Rural Retreat. Ill health forced him to resign and relinquish all labors in this parish during the fall of 1947.

On the fifth of October, 1909, he was married to Miss Fannie Lavinia Frick, of Chapin, S. C., who, until the time of her death, took a deep interest in the work of the church and was of invaluable aid to her husband in the various pastorates he served.

They had three children. Bernard Frick Wise was born at Claremont, N. C., Jan. 10, 1916, finished Newberry College with the class of 1937, finished Mt. Airy Seminary with the class of 1942. He is now located at Charleston, S. C. Evelyn Ruth Wise, now Mrs. William Clarence Horr, born at Maiden, N. C., Dec. 12, 1918, finished King College, Bristol, Tenn., with the class of 1939, now located at Blountville, Tenn. Worth David Wise, born at Leesville, S. C., Feb. 23, 1924, finished Lenoir Rhyne College with the class of 1945, finished Lutheran Theological Southern Seminary, Columbia, S. C., with class of 1948, now located at 39 Franklin Ave., Concord, N. C.

NOTE—Material on W. D. Wise came in too late to be incorporated in its proper place in the book.—*Editor*

www.ingramcontent.com/pod-product-compliance
Lightning Source LLC
Chambersburg PA
CBHW031123020426
42333CB00012B/201